ON A NOTE OF TRIUMPH
Norman Corwin
and the Golden Years
of Radio

by R. LeRoy Bannerman

Foreword by Erik Barnouw

W9-AHH-919

A Lyle Stuart Book
Published by Carol Publishing Group

Copyright © 1986 by
The University of Alabama Press

A Lyle Stuart Book
Published by Carol Publishing Group

Editorial Offices
600 Madison Avenue
New York, NY 10022

Sales & Distribution Offices
120 Enterprise Avenue
Secaucus, NJ 07094

In Canada: Musson Book Company
A division of General Publishing Co. Limited
Don Mills, Ontario

Originally published under the title
Norman Corwin and Radio: The Golden Years

Manufactured in the United States of America

Library of Congress Cataloging-in-Publication Data

Bannerman, R. LeRoy, 1921-
    On a note of triumph: Norman Corwin and the golden age
of radio.

    Bibliography: p.
    Includes index.
    1. Corwin, Norman Lewis, 1910-   2. Radio producers
and directors--United States--Biography. 3. Radio broadcasting--
United States--History. I. Title.
PN1991.4.C64B36   1986
791.44'0232'0924 [B]
ISBN 0-8184-0512-0   85-1028
                                              CIP

To my wife, Rita

Contents

Photographs / vi

Foreword / vii

Acknowledgments / xi

1. The Era: The Man and the Golden Age / 1

2. The Beginning: An Old-World Heritage / 13

3. The City: Publicity to Poetry / 25

4. The Network: A Liberal Mountain / 39

5. The Series: Deadline Times Twenty-Six / 55

6. The Anniversary: Bill of Rights Show / 73

7. The War: Radio to Arms / 93

8. The Challenge: Dedication and Dreams / 111

9. The Assignment: Pursuit of Peace / 125

10. The Victory: On a Note of Triumph / 144

11. The World: Flight of Unity / 169

12. The Art: Beginning of the End / 187

13. The Blacklist: Cast of Concern / 202

14. The Future: Of Film, Footlights, and Philosophy / 218

Appendix: A Chronology of
Norman Corwin's Radio Programs / 233

Notes / 249

Bibliography / 264

Index / 268

Photographs

The Corwin Brothers / 89

Sam and Rose, Corwin's Parents / 89

Corwin and Cpl. Jimmy Stewart, Rehearsing / 90

The Cast for *We Hold These Truths* / 91

Corwin Directing / 91

Corwin Answering Control Room Telephone / 92

Martin Gabel Narrating VE Day Broadcast / 163

Orson Welles and Corwin / 164

Lee Bland and Corwin / 165

Corwin in the Rubble of the Warsaw Ghetto / 166

Norman and Kate Corwin / 167

Corwin and the Author at Indiana University / 168

Corwin Conducting a Class in Creative Writing / 168

Foreword

Turning these pages has meant for me reliving a fascinating period of media history and experiencing again one of its most wondrous phenomena, the work of Norman Corwin. I know him as a friend but think of him also as the brightest light of a surprising period, the final climactic decade of pre-television network radio. It was a time when radio emerged rather suddenly from a period of tawdriness and began to redeem itself. It is a period almost forgotten, but worth recalling.

An industry crisis had set the stage. Early in the New Deal years, broadcasting leaders had a scare. A coordinated movement representing the arts, education, labor, agriculture, religion, and the non-profit world in general launched an unprecedented attack on the radio status quo, which they described as "pollution of the air," a "cultural disaster," a "huckstering orgy," a "pawnshop," a "sickness in the national culture." As remedy they proposed a radio measure far more drastic than any being proposed by the Roosevelt administration. Their bill, presented in the Senate under distinguished sponsorship, provided that all existing station licenses be "declared null and void 90 days following the effective date of this act" and that during that time an entirely new allotment of frequencies should be made, with one fourth going to "educational, religious, agricultural, labor, cooperative, and similar non-profit associations." These channels were to be "as desirable as those assigned to profit-making persons, firms, or corporations." This "new deal" in channel allotments seemed headed for Senate passage.

An intense lobbying upheaval began, along with hard bargaining. The radio industry had been making large profits in the midst of the Depression, mainly by concentrating on time sales and worrying about little else. The networks found it convenient to let advertising agencies make the programming decisions for time periods they bought. A dozen advertising agencies were the main programmers of network radio. All this had brought prosperity to the networks, and their prosperity was clearly only beginning, for more than half of available network time was still unsold. This fact became the key to a compromise.

The networks began to talk enthusiastically about "cooperative broadcasting." Why should educational, religious, and social-service organizations go to the expense of maintaining their own stations? Commercial stations and networks could *give* them all the airtime they needed or could possibly want. Many hours were available that could be dedicated to their interests. Such assurances and arguments averted the threatening amendment. It lost in the Senate by 42–23—a margin that still indicated the depth of dissatisfaction and the need for follow-up action.

As the threat subsided, commercial broadcasters undertook license-protection measures. Networks and stations appointed officials with such titles as Public Service Director. Their task, to make use of unsold time in ways that would prevent similar crises in the future. Unsold time had generally been filled via music from small "house orchestras." These low-budget "sustaining programs" were considered time fillers. Now the unsold time acquired new functions.

It was in May 1935 that CBS advertised:

Wanted—

A BIG MAN

*for an important
creative and executive post in*

RADIO BROADCASTING

Soon afterwards the network hired William B. Lewis, with the task of piloting CBS into the age of public service. CBS became the network that tackled most imaginatively the upgrading of "sustaining programs" into a positive asset, reaching out to new constituencies. One of the first results was *The Columbia Workshop,* a weekly series dedicated to media experiments and inviting contributions from novelists, poets, composers, and others. Then came literary and political round tables, adaptations of classics, Americana, folklore, special programs of many kinds, often produced in cooperation with others. Some of these riches are detailed in the following pages. Amid the renaissance emerged, as writer-director-producer, the figure of Norman Corwin, one of Lewis's most perceptive talent choices. How Corwin became, within a few years, America's unofficial poet laureate is splendidly recounted by Professor LeRoy Bannerman. Corwin's *We Hold These Truths*, a brilliant special program on the Bill of Rights, was prepared during the fall of 1941 and scheduled for December 15. By the time the broadcast day arrived, the United States was at war, and the broadcast became a national manifesto of its war aims, carried by all four networks, performed by a galaxy of stars, and climaxed by a statement by President Franklin D. Roosevelt. In similarly eloquent fashion *On a Note of Triumph* in 1945 celebrated the end of the war on a powerful "lest we forget" note. Another Corwin special, *Word from the People*, marked the dedication of the United Nations. Interspersed with these were galaxies of other Corwin programs—comedies, fantasies, satires, and excursions into opera, poetry, and documentary. Many of these remain classics of the era. We owe a debt to Professor Bannerman for reminding us of them and detailing the stories behind them.

This book on the rise of Norman Corwin is also an account of American broadcasting during a turbulent period. It is often an inspiring story, but in the end the venality of earlier years made a strong return. Professor Bannerman has not shirked this aspect of the story. He tells it as it was.

Since the 1930s, when I worked with Corwin briefly on one of his CBS projects, I have cherished his friendship. In 1940, when my wife and I had our first child—our son Jeffrey—a gift from Corwin arrived at our house. It was a massive anthology of child classics inscribed: "For Jeff, to adapt for radio some fine day." Little could anyone guess that before long, no one would be privileged to adapt children's classics for American radio—or for television. It would have astonished us that such a change could take place.

But perhaps it was equally astonishing that an American radio renaissance began suddenly in the late 1930s and lasted a decade, as Professor Bannerman has chronicled. So renaissances do happen, and perhaps another will come—"some fine day."

ERIK BARNOUW

Acknowledgments

Of the many people who helped make this book a reality, none was more important than Corwin himself. He opened personal files and revealed invaluable, hitherto undocumented materials. Corwin also provided diaries and his unpublished memoirs.

I am indebted to his wife, Katherine Corwin, and to his brothers Emil and Alfred and their wives, Freda and Sarita; also his sister Beulah and her husband, Irving Belkowitz. An aunt in New Hampshire, Mildred Cohen, and an uncle from Boston, Harry Ober (now deceased), also contributed exceptional insight and detail. Most impressive of all were the vivid memories of Norman's venerable father, Samuel Corwin, who at this writing approaches his 110th birthday.

Interviews with involved people completed the portrait of Norman Corwin. Eighty-eight-year-old Lucy Drew Stuetzel remembered her days as his high school teacher. Countless friends and professionals traced his career of innovation and artistry in radio, but I wish in particular to thank William N. Robson, Martin Gabel, Elliott M. Sanger, and (before his death of cancer in 1975) William B. Lewis.

I am most appreciative of cooperation from the Columbia Broadcasting System, the Broadcast Pioneers' Library, Syracuse University, Boston University, the Library of Congress, the Lilly Library at Indiana University, and the British Broadcasting Corporation in London.

For criticism and encouragement, I must thank William A. Nail, Peggy Bakken, and of course my colleagues at Indiana University, especially Professors Fredric Brewer, Herbert Terry, and Robert M. Petranoff. I wish also to express my gratitude to my family, who helped enormously to nourish this special project.

R.L.B.

1. The Era: The Man and the Golden Age

The microphone is not an ordinary instrument.
For it looks out on vistas wide indeed

—Seems Radio Is Here to Stay

America, having emerged from the doldrums and despair of the Great Depression, now focused on international tensions that accompanied the encroachment of Nazism abroad. A national debate ensued between isolationists and anti-Fascists, and life took on a paradoxical demeanor of concern and carefree optimism. The Yankees were the perennial powerhouse in baseball, fashion edged skirts a little higher, business picked up, and dancers jitterbugged to the rhythm of the Big Band era. And radio, the centerpiece of almost every home, offered a cosmopolitan view of national life as the medium reached the zenith of its Golden Age.

Listeners of the late thirties and early forties found in radio a respite from the difficulties of their day, an imbuement of hope, a vicarious encounter. It proved a panacea to provincialism, it put people in touch with the world, and it provided a diversion by its many varied programs.

For most, it was a nightly ritual. Families would hurry through dinner to hear the news by Boake Carter or Lowell Thomas, tune to *Amos 'n' Andy*, and on particular evenings enjoy the music of the *Firestone Hour* or sense the Broadway ambience of "the little theatre off Times Square," before the curtain ascended on another drama of *First Nighter*. Homemakers, during the day, seemed addicted to the agonizing episodes of endless soap operas. And the kids, rushing home from school, sprawled before the living room Atwater Kent or the huge Stromberg-Carlson console to relive "those thrilling days of yester-

1

year" with *The Lone Ranger,* endure the dangerous confrontations of *Terry and the Pirates,* or follow the suspenseful adventures of *Little Orphan Annie.*

Radio of the era was a multifaceted medium, unlike the specialized form of contemporary broadcasting. And though many of its programs were as vapid as latter-day television's worst, there seemed a sense of striving, of experimentation, of timeliness. Its potpourri of programming appealed to a diversified audience, and its impetus was emotion. It made people laugh or cry, thrill or cringe in terror; it was an elixir of make-believe which often obscured the reality of uncertain times. Drama, of course, served best the imaginative dimensions of the medium, and as a theatre of the mind it engaged a small (by media standards) but appreciative following. Aside from music, drama was the most popular form throughout the thirties and into the forties, exceeding even news.

Not all drama was good. Some efforts seemed slickly commercial, trite, one dimensional—deficiencies normally blamed on poor scripts and, correspondingly, narrow, unchallenging format themes. But occasionally—indeed, with surprising frequency—radio reached remarkable heights in literary and dramaturgical expression. Leading writers and poets of the day willingly explored the aesthetic sphere of a medium which at last had achieved the technology to conceive sensitivity in sound. Established authors and performers discovered an appealing intimacy and involvement, and they were attracted to the broad scope of radio's proscenium arch.

Radio also developed its own artisans, writers, and directors who explored the medium to attain new goals, new techniques. As the Golden Age advanced, these talented practitioners examined more and more the ethereal reach of their microphone and extended the boundaries of audio and emotion. Among those who were successful, no doubt the most significant and influential—yet today relatively little known—was Norman Corwin. He was an innovator, a poet, an artist. He brought to broadcasting an intelligence and a language rare to the radio medium. "It was he who defined and shaped strict radio style, and through his influence the classic form was developed," wrote Charles Beaumont, and added, "If anyone deserves the title of Mr. Radio, it is surely he."[1]

When Corwin entered network radio in 1938, an aesthetic evolution was already under way, but only recently in evidence. The medium had struggled through an undefined infancy—first a novelty, a hobby, then a monitoring device (to listen for S.O.S. signals at sea following the *Titanic* disaster), eventually evolving into its conventional role as informer and entertainer. By the early thirties, the objective of broadcasting was clear, but programming for the most part was a mosaic of awkward moments. Beyond its fare of burlesque comedy, tinny music, stiff and blatant drama, there was in radio a frantic search for unusual and appealing programs—often the coverage of strange events, like the antics of a flagpole sitter and, once, a singing mouse contest.

In 1935, Corwin himself, at the time a radio critic for the *Springfield* (Mass.) *Republican,* candidly complained, "There is about as much creative genius in radio today as there is in a convention of plasterers and plumbers."[2]

The very next year, the Columbia Broadcasting System began a new, experimental series which would revolutionize radio drama and open new, creative frontiers for the expanding medium. It was the brainstorm of engineer-artist Irving Reis, who combined technical talent, ambition, and artistic curiosity in introducing what was to be called the *Columbia Workshop.* The effort, in time, would foster new themes, new techniques, new modes of production; and by its free form it served to showcase the originality of many directors, musicians, writers, and performers. Its programs were widely acclaimed. Yet its budget was only $400 a week. This prompted Robert Landry, for eleven years the radio editor of *Variety,* to suggest that "never has a network bought so much prestige for so little."[3]

By the time Corwin joined CBS, therefore, bold efforts had already been made to measure the medium's artistic potential. A list of prominent practitioners included William N. Robson, Earle McGill, Max Wylie, Wyllis Cooper, and a prolific writer-producer by the name of Arch Oboler, who enthralled listeners with strange horror stories on the NBC series *Lights Out.* The year Corwin came to network radio was the year the boy wizard of Broadway,[4] Orson Welles, terrified the nation with his dramatization of an invasion from Mars.

Albert N. Williams, in the *Saturday Review of Literature,* theorized that "to Norman Corwin, then, [is due] not the credit for first seeing what radio could do as an art form, but rather for so patiently nourishing it that other people would want to see the same thing."[5] Corwin, who came to radio with few credentials, profited by the experience of his predecessors and soon forged new expectations of artistic purpose. Max Wylie noted that Corwin "understood radio the first time he tried it."[6] So it was that, only eight months after his career began in network radio, Corwin gained nationwide attention for his defiant, anti-Fascist play *They Fly through the Air with the Greatest of Ease*. It was then that *Time* magazine acknowledged "his bid for a front row seat among radio poets."[7]

The remarkable radio career of Norman Corwin paralleled the peak ascension and ultimate decline of network radio. The Golden Age actually began with a creative movement that characterized the latter years of the 1930s, but not until the war years of the '40s did it fully materialize into radio's great aggrandizement of show business acumen and commercial opportunity. NBC, which reigned supreme as the oldest, richest, most prestigious of networks, remained equal to CBS in number of affiliates, even after divesting itself of the Blue Network in 1944 (which became the American Broadcasting Company). But CBS held faith and future promise in a philosophy that placed emphasis on *program* rather than *commercial* prowess.

It was almost providential that Corwin joined CBS, the network most responsible for the creative stirrings which, in the opinion of broadcast historian Erik Barnouw, "awakened much of the industry."[8] Timely, too, was the tenor of the period. Corwin was a liberal, very much a part of the idealistic, romantic era which, with World War II, affected his outlook and inspired many of his works. Either by design or happenstance, he would find himself at the center of various crises, charged with a mission to voice the feelings of the people. And he did it always with a rare eloquence for radio, touching with phenomenal success the temper of the times. He sang the song of America, it was said, in Whitmanesque cadences; he helped fire a nation with patriotic fervor; and he pioneered new purposes for radio. He made the medium a more durable art form.

Uniquely, too, he did it with enviable independence. At CBS, no Corwin work initially was ever sponsored. He enjoyed the munificence of a medium which could then afford the time and the ideals.

Flourishing in a freedom of "sustaining" programming, the hallmark of the Golden Age, Corwin gained a stature that permitted autonomy in decisions affecting his activity. He refused to forsake this liberty for commercial earnings, although corporations clamored for his talent and advertising agencies lauded him.[9] He did not object to sponsorship, but he insisted on firm principles: no sponsor was allowed to edit his scripts, no agency representative would be permitted in his control room. Clients found this difficult to accept.

World War II, with its overwhelming aura of common purpose, proved a catalyst for Corwin's career. Fate cast him as a principal spokesman for America's cause when he coincidentally produced, just eight days after the attack on Pearl Harbor, a moving, nationalistic drama-document, *We Hold These Truths*. He had been commissioned to commemorate the 150th anniversary of the American Bill of Rights. The program was to feature a star-studded Hollywood cast and would be broadcast over all four major radio networks. It reached the largest audience ever accorded a dramatic performance. It galvanized the nation.

Within months, Corwin was called upon to direct radio's first all-out effort at wartime domestic propaganda. The series of thirteen dramas, half of which he wrote, was titled *This Is War!* It was sponsored by the government, with stated goals "to inspire, to frighten, to inform."[10] It, too, was broadcast on all four national networks.

CBS then sent him to England to produce for American listeners dramatized impressions of bomb-shattered Britain, programs which were shortwaved to the States. After a year he returned, to continue programs for the cause: some serious and sensitive, some frivolous and funny, or filled with fantasy. His shows energized the people, marshaled morale, and two of his works significantly bracketed the war. *We Hold These Truths* was, in effect, a call to arms, while his hour-long VE Day special, *On a Note of Triumph*, celebrated an end to the European conflict. Both are considered American radio classics.

Corwin created milestones for a medium well into its acmatic era. Norman Rosten, radio poet of the period, observed that "something new has been added to the airwaves—a spirit of intelligence, integrity, and experimentation—and Corwin is its leading man."[11] Intellectuals of the day quickly embraced Corwin as the patron saint of quality programming. He was applauded by prominent literary figures, including Stephen Vincent Benét and Maxwell Anderson. Clifton Fadiman was so impressed by Corwin's versatility that he maintained the radio artist wrote as if he were several men.[12] And poet Carl Sandburg, in a rare fan letter, wrote:

> You assemble, orchestrate, time and chime. To have the technique and then have something of history, past and present, to shape and utter it so it haunts listeners with big meaning for the hour, that is being alive. I am proud to have known you.[13]

Critics saw in Corwin a fresh, new influence: an independent whose concept of broadcasting dared to be different. They saw in his work a literacy uncommon in the communicative arts. Radio's output, reasoned José Rodriguez, was "such a half baked, bumptious, whining, banal and meretricious compost of drivel, that the first man to top the clamor with ideas and words of sense and honesty was bound to shine like Apollo in a crowd of spastics." Corwin's consistency of quality, he maintained, was enough "to make us the more deplore the bad."[14]

Despite the accolades, Corwin's place in literature seemed to some critics an unsettled issue. And while Corwin himself agreed with comedian Fred Allen that "everything in radio is as fleeting as a butterfly's cough," his endeavors clearly evidenced an intrinsic merit which defied the transitory nature of the radio medium. In 1942 he received a grant from the American Academy of Arts and Letters, awarded on occasion to nonmembers whose creative work in art, literature, and music was considered meritorious. In 1944 the New York Newspaper Guild presented Corwin with a Page One Award for creative literature on the air. He was an accepted poet in prestigious and knowledgeable circles, including Sandburg, MacLeish, Benét. But William Matthews, an associate professor of English at the University of California, Los Angeles, was not impressed. In 1945 he wrote:

> I cannot subscribe to the widespread opinion that Corwin is a literary genius. He has an alert, ranging, fertile mind, and restless energy. But it is a mind that usually finds its place in the first of the bandwagons. He has endless ideas and excitements, but he rushes on breathlessly from one to the next without adequately digging into any of them. He is, as it were, a frontier spirit.[15]

Nevertheless, Corwin made a notable impact, and by a brisk, documentary mode of expression plumbed the dimensions of the medium as perhaps no one else had. His imagery spanned time and space. In *Daybreak*, a geographic mood piece, the listener was whisked around the world "a half degree ahead of sunup." In *On a Note of Triumph*, the listener overtook a bomber in flight, then plummeted to a convoy destroyer below, was lowered through a ventilator shaft to the engine room, and finally up and overboard to dive five fathoms beneath the sea. Corwin's aesthetic mastery of technology at times produced startling effects. And always, he wrote and produced with an acute awareness of his audience and endeavored to make each listener *see*, even *feel*, what had been heard.

Beginning writers were greatly influenced by Corwin—so much so that Max Wylie, in his text on radio writing, warned them not to attempt Corwin's approach. He noted that Corwin, by the inclination of his style, wrote not of people but of Platonic individuals, disembodied, remote, symbolic. Wylie acknowledged that Corwin gave his audiences a glimpse of human interaction, but maintained that "these rubrics and vignettes never serve to illuminate a character, nor to explore the emotional interior of a protagonist. Instead, they illuminate a mood."[16]

Wylie was not alone in his opinion. Gilbert Seldes, writer–critic– broadcast educator, also suggested that Corwin presented subjects through symbols and characters that were "more voices than people."[17] Corwin, on the other hand, insisted that he *did* create full-dimensional characters for many of his plays—Mary Pooter, for instance, in *Mary and the Fairy,* or young Runyon in *The Odyssey of Runyon Jones,* or even Hank Peters in *Untitled.* He admitted that he was often called upon to write what he described as "murals and polemics," a kaleidoscopic concept which dipped only briefly into lives and situations.

Corwin loved the medium of radio. "It is both my workshop and my playroom," he once said. He tried all forms—whimsy, fantasy, historical drama, poetic narrative, propaganda, satire, scientific essay, burlesque, parody—and with an uncommon Midas touch created for radio a continuing sense of excitement. He piqued listeners with aural pranks, unashamedly showed a penchant for punning, poked fun at institutions and foibles—even at the medium itself. And always, he did it with a pride that held the medium in high esteem. "I have a sense of dignity of a half-hour of God's time," he said.[18]

It was remarkable that Corwin's prolific output of quality was created against the seemingly impossible pressures of live radio. Because network policy of the day forbade the airing of recordings other than sound effects, all programs—even repeats—had to be produced live. He therefore had to produce his shows twice: once for the East and later for the West Coast. Not only did he rehearse and direct each show, a herculean task in itself, but he wrote and personally cast the programs on a week-to-week basis. "I often found myself trying to think of what next week's show might be while driving home after a Sunday night's broadcast. If it didn't come by Tuesday, I was in deep trouble."[19] Somehow—usually by writing through the night, by casting scripts before they were finished, by having music composed from a page-by-page development of the play—the live broadcast went on as scheduled.

Albert N. Williams suggested that Corwin's works might have lacked maturity, that faltering dramaturgy may have been in evidence here or there, but he pointed out that it was the fault of the medium rather than the man, that "the playwriting in his half-year series *Twenty-Six* was equal in volume to six full-length plays, a record of fertility that has rarely been matched."[20] Clifton Fadiman agreed. "What is notable," wrote the famed literary critic, "is that he is successful seven times out of ten."[21]

Corwin's successes—some, historical achievements—came only because he worked hard to probe radio's potential. He devoted long hours and worried incessantly that his next effort might not meet the level of his last. So total was his concentration that the business office at CBS once notified him that he had neglected to pick up several paychecks. He refused to be sidetracked by external influences, money included. And although tempted many times by huge salary offers, he resisted the lure of Hollywood. He remained loyal to the medium he had mastered.

Corwin's homage to radio during his reign at CBS so affected his lifestyle that he seldom took time for personal pleasures; he carried a clipboard everywhere, in search of ideas, and often seemed lost in a trance of thought. He neglected to get haircuts, often ignored his attire. It was no surprise to his CBS colleagues the morning he reported for work in mismatched socks.

Corwin was an avid revisionist. His scripts were so cluttered with penciled corrections that Cameron Shipp, in a *Coronet* portrait, claimed that each Corwin manuscript looked "as if it had been written by hand and corrected on the typewriter."[22] And of course his interest in language engaged him in a perpetual fascination with etymology. His scripts, his articles, his books were so spiced with esoteric facts that one assumed Corwin was an omnivorous reader. His reading, he suggested, was "catholic, widespread, buckshot."[23]

Music proved to be an integral part of Corwin's accomplishments. He learned early that music could be misused, especially in radio, and, as he explored broadcasting, he sought to avoid the musical cliché. He used music differently, as "more than mortar between the bricks."[24] He created interesting aural experiences, especially in the utilization of music as a story-telling device. In *Appointment,* a prewar radio play, music was employed by Corwin to portray a prisoner escaping, dashing across a prison yard, scaling a wall, being picked out by searchlights, then shot to death. Corwin, who never had a music lesson in his life, knew its emotional power, sensed its structure, and fused it into his rhythm of words and sound. He used music lavishly and, despite his obvious partiality to the power of the spoken word, incorporated striking motifs in support of his dramaturgical style.

His writing itself was musical. It soared. Moreover, he possessed an unusual ability to mix lofty, Olympian prose with everyday vernacular to provide an intimate, personal touch, yet affect an abstract, artistic approach that exceeded the commonplace convention of radio literature. He gave radio a language and a style which elevated the medium to new heights of artistic endeavor.

In the waning days of radio, as Corwin knew it, it became clear that the struggle and pressure imposed by competition, by a restive society, by the compelling appearance of television, would soon make radio dramatic art and artists like Corwin impracticable items. In 1947, CBS president William S. Paley happened to meet Corwin on a transcontinental train and, over dinner, confronted the writer-producer with the issue—if somewhat obliquely. "Well, you know you've done epic things that are appreciated by us and by a special audience, but couldn't you write for a broader audience?"[25]

The end seemed at hand. The future of network radio was an enigma, with the contest for higher ratings a pursuit of panic concern. The industry, uneasy on the eve of inevitable change, saw the buck passed from the FCC to the stations to the networks to the advertising agencies to the sponsors. Radio became hypersensitive, less venturesome. Sustaining drama disappeared. And to make matters worse, the infamous scourge of blacklisting enshrouded the nobility of broadcasting.

For Corwin, as for radio, an era had ended.

> The Golden Age of Radio need not have ended when it did. It did not die of natural causes. It was not buried under the detritus of censorship in this country, unlike the experience of radio in many other countries. It was manipulated to a halt. It was sedated, and it was sent into exile.[26]

With regret, with resignation, Norman Corwin spoke of radio's remembered past at a Broadcast Pioneers' luncheon in Los Angeles in November 1975. At the time he was being honored with the coveted Carbon Mike Award. It was yet another recognition for his contribution to radio's revolutionary age of creativity.

But Corwin never rested on his laurels of long ago; instead, he remained active: writing, directing, teaching. For fifteen years he chaired the documentary awards committee for the Academy of Motion Picture Arts and Sciences, and in 1980 was elected to its Board of Governors. He served the Writers' Guild of America, was named to several literary organizations, and even as he approached his mid-seventies he continued to add to his achievements in film, in television, in theatre, in print, and even radio. He entertained no notion of retirement. In 1983 his seventeenth book, *Trivializing America,* was published.

Although he was widely acclaimed as a paragon of radio's past, Corwin's devotees of that day existed always as a minority audience. He was not a household name—as, say, Jack Benny or Charlie McCarthy or Ma Perkins. And many potential listeners were away from their radios, doing battle in a war that Corwin prosecuted via the airwaves. But he left a legacy, a dream, and thereby occupies a prominent place in the history of broadcasting. He gave the Golden Age of Radio a greatness, a grasp of aesthetic principles, a promise of intellectual substance. He became a living legend, a symbol—so much a symbol of radio, suggested Erik Barnouw, "that he was bound to suffer a partial eclipse with the rise of television; his very prominence made this inevitable."[27]

Corwin brought not only talent to radio and the arts, he also brought pride, a personification of gentlemanly altruism. He was, Gilbert Seldes observed, "an admirable carrier of the liberal-patriotic ideals of the time, an admirer of the New Deal, a mature anti-fascist, with a poetic sense of dignity and worth of the individual life."[28]

Central to Corwin's character has been a concern for others. As a youth, he befriended unfortunate and lonely people, and later, at the height of his career, Corwin had time always for beginning writers or interested admirers. Many practitioners of the media credit their careers to Corwin's assistance and advice.[29] And because his life spanned a time of depression and war, he was sensitive to the plight of ordinary people. He popularized the Common Man.

Such solicitude often embraced the conflicts and problems of the world. He constantly attacked the existence of war, of tyranny and injustice, always in sharp, literate, often lyrical prose. His finest hours celebrated the dignity of mankind. "This is a very special gentleman," concluded the late Rod Serling, noted writer and impresario of television's former years. "Not only does his writing reflect his deep concern for his fellow man, but there is a sense of legitimacy and honor in the man you rarely find. But the key to Corwin—and this must be the key to all sensitive creators—is his awareness of human need."[30]

Corwin's life and career provide an interesting study of contrasts, of ambition and talent and mission in a world torn by conflict and cause. It began in the Bay region of Boston, where, born and reared in an immigrant community, he conceived a basis of social conscience. He only completed high school, yet in time he received honorary degrees and taught at leading universities throughout the country. He endured the depravity of the Depression era, the agony and involvement of a world war, the disgrace of unfounded accusations in the wave of terror that was the Communist witchhunt. He led an influential fight for the art and integrity of broadcasting. And by his dedication to the medium of radio, high moments were realized: important programs which often celebrated historic occasions and were, in themselves, eventful achievements.

It is quite a story. And its telling is long overdue.

2. The Beginning: An Old-World Heritage

Ah, but it was not a simple birth;
The seed of his father being out of cross-fertilizations of restless
  migratory peoples,
And the silt and backwash of a thousand continental waters . . .

—Untitled

It was May 3, 1910. It had been raining since midnight and the streets
of Boston glistened in the cold light of a new day. Behind the brick
facade of the McLean Lying-In Hospital, a hushed, antiseptic air of
efficiency filled the high-ceilinged corridor. A nurse confronted the
small man who stood waiting, nervously stroking his mustache; he was
the father of a boy, he was told. Samuel Corwin nodded, forced a
smile that failed to hide his disappointment. He had wanted a girl. He
had been certain that this time it would have been a girl.[1]

Norman Lewis Corwin came into a world already settled by hard
work and heartache, but his lineage began in uncertain times far
across the sea, in a European mix of poverty and pride. His genealogy
made his family roots most tentative—as, indeed his family name. It
often happened that in the course of transmigration noble names,
foreign and unpronounceable, were perverted at ports of entry by
uncaring, sometimes overworked immigration officials, or by the in-
comprehensible innocents themselves, who were quick to accept anything in the name of hope. Thus the name Corwin was a derivation of
countless conversions which, in the span of time and geography, dis-
torted the root origins that were distinctly Slavic. Norman's paternal
grandfather was Russian. His mother was born in Hungary.

13

Norman, the third of four children by Rose and Sam Corwin, was reared in the polyglot poverty of East Boston. His family occupied an apartment in a three-story tenement on Bremen Street, a frame building which fronted upon the sprawling tracks and roundhouse terminal of a railway yard.

He was, as a child, feisty. "If he was losing in a game, he'd either quit or start a fight," said Emil, the eldest. Alfred, Norman's other brother, agreed. "He had a short fuse."

Their father was a plate printer by profession; their mother was a quiet, enduring woman who, despite frequent illness from hereditary thyroid problems, exuded good humor, patience, and religious conviction. They were surrounded by relatives (the Obers, Rose's parents and family, lived in the apartment above) who reinforced parental affection with lavish attention.

As a child of four, Norman learned poetry by listening to Emil's arduous recitation of rhymes assigned in school. Norman enjoyed reciting for an audience and frequently climbed the stairs to the Ober flat to perform, with gestures, Felicia Hemans' "Casabianca": "The boy stood on the burning deck . . ." The family, greatly amused, would encourage him to act out other verses. At the climactic line of Robert Browning's "Incident of the French Camp"—"Smiling the boy fell dead"—he would fling himself upon the floor. The Obers would applaud wildly and even pitch pennies.

At this time, a fourth child was born into the Corwin family—to Sam's joy, a girl. She was named Beulah. Together, brothers and sister grew up in a family bond made more relevant by a constant struggle for dignity in their meager environment. On bitter evenings of a Boston winter, they would gather at the dining room table to read, write letters, do homework, or discuss family problems, in the greenish-white glow of a gas mantle lamp. On Friday of each week, all participated in a general housecleaning: polishing brass pipes that led to the boiler, scrubbing the bleached boards of the apartment floor with hot water and a sulpha-naphthol solution which left a lingering sanitary smell.

Norman, as his brothers had done before him, attended the James Otis Primary School and the U. S. Grant Elementary School in East Boston. Teachers early discovered his talent for writing, and encouraged him. At seven, he wrote his first full-length story, "The Adventures of John Ransford," described as a tale "about a super Sergeant York who won the World War single-handed."[2] It was Corwin's imagined escapades of a real-life hero, after whom an island in Boston Harbor had been named. With a pencil, he had written and illustrated the story in an old ledger, which the family surreptitiously read with much amusement.

To Corwin, his childhood in East Boston was an abstract of many impressions—of telling tall tales to spellbind his playmates at the early age of four; of being a perpetual prankster, to the chagrin of family and friends; of playing ball on hot summer days or chasing the ice wagon down dusty streets; and of course the day-by-day dominance of the railway yard, with the forbidden adventure of roaming among freight cars, the winter scene of poor people foraging for coal, the sight of World War I soldiers behind the dusty windows of shunting troop trains, workers with lunch pails at dawn, and being awakened at night by the sudden clang of couplings.

In 1923 the Corwins moved to a house in Winthrop—only a few miles, but a world away from the soot and grime of Bremen Street. It was a block from the ocean and afforded both space and privacy (Norman now had his own room in the gabled attic), as well as conveniences (electric lights!). Located on Perkins Street, the house also had a basement, in which Norman, enthralled by high school chemistry, set up a makeshift laboratory. He spent many hours conducting experiments, and from Mason-jar test tubes and battered broilers emerged foul odors and fearful concoctions (nitroglycerin once) which threatened the very existence of the building.

Of days in Winthrop, Corwin recalled:

> Now and then I would get up before the rest of the house—even before my father, who arose daily at 5 A.M.—and I would walk along the beach. The work of night waters had smoothed the strand's only stretch of sand and erased every print of man, dog, gull and crab. In those lambent moments I felt deliciously alone . . .[3]

At Winthrop High, Norman was gregarious, given to practical jokes. His school work was uneven, reflecting primary interests. "I flunked Latin, was weak in French and barely managed to stay afloat in math. Long suits were English and chemistry."[4] Although his brothers had ranked in the upper fifth of their class, Norman was positioned at the top of the middle third.

Young Corwin was undoubtedly influenced most by Lucy Drew, his English teacher at Winthrop High, who exposed her class to fine poetry by reading aloud the works of Keats and Browning and Shelley. Inspired, he wrote a poem about the sea, depicting the schizoid antics of the ocean as movements of music. Titled "Ocean Symphony," one section was called *andante*.

> And vesper time and all the winds have
>   gone off with the day,
> And darkness rises from the depths and
>   spreads out on the bay.
> The water is dispirited and hungry sea gulls
>   cry;
> The hills are prostrate in the west,
> The east is only sky.

The work envisioned an ocean of life: "For far beneath your moving prominences lives a world apart," and a philosophy: "Your tides enact a play of life: the charge, the triumph, the retreat," and, at times, a ghostly mood: "And now the bells of sunken ships, whose riding lights still glow / Are ringing requiescat, dull and somberly and slow." In a latter section, labeled *scherzo*, he described the wind as

> The giant plowman of the skies
> He toils an endless night,
> The iris of his sightless eyes
> Agleam with lunar light.
> In foam-filled furrows now he lays
> Typhoons to rise on sultry days
> And now he whets his share with rain
> And plants a madcap hurricane.[5]

Corwin considered Lucy Drew a firm disciplinarian in the art of writing. Her advice was crisp and to the point, her patience edged with persistence, her principles clear and forthright. He related to her enthusiasm, for she seemed to respect his ability. But given his prankish personality, he was not beyond testing her.

For the culminating assignment of the year, the senior essay, Corwin decided to write a treatise on words. It was to be a thousand-word theme on any subject. "My object," Corwin recalled, "was to write something so deep that even my teacher would have difficulty getting through it." He therefore constructed a carefully contrived pattern of polysyllabic wordplay and appropriately titled the piece "Words."

Just as he had hoped, Corwin was summoned by Miss Drew for an explanation of his essay. "I considered this a triumph, a reversal of roles. She often had to explain certain passages of Milton to the class; now, here she was, having to have certain passages of Corwin explained to her." His triumph was short lived, however; he received a grade lower than the A-plus he expected. Her approach was gentle. She quietly explained that although the paper was unique and creative, a simpler way of saying something was infinitely better.

Emil was already two years out of Massachusetts Agricultural College in Amherst and Al was completing his degree at Harvard when Norman was graduated from high school. It was expected, of course, that he would attend college, as his brothers had done; but young Corwin would have to retake Latin (for college entrance), and time was important to him. He was impatient to explore a talent for writing.

Five years before, his parents had presented him with a standard Oliver typewriter for his twelfth birthday. Now he sat down to type a letter which, with his father's help, was multigraphed and mailed to eighty newspapers within a hundred-mile radius of Winthrop. "The letter was full of eager humility and the burn to learn," Corwin remembered. He received fifty-five replies, most of them offering friendly, fatherly advice, but little else. Two answers, however, hinted of possible openings in the not-too-distant future, and one of them specified three months. The most hopeful, it was from the *Greenfield* (Mass.) *Recorder,* a small-town daily with a circulation of almost 25,000.

During the ensuing months, Corwin kept the hope alive by mail. Having indicated that he was pushing twenty, he grew a mustache to give an impression that he was older than his seventeen years. The editor apparently believed him, for in a subsequent interview he was hired, at $15 a week.

It was his first occasion away from home on his own. He arrived in Greenfield one colorful fall day to see a prospering town, nestled in the valley of the Connecticut River, within sight of the Berkshire Hills to the west. The portal to the Mohawk Trail, it possessed the idyllic charm of many New England communities, with a Main Street that bisected the principal route, leading south to Springfield. In a Main Street apartment called the Mohawk Chambers, Corwin shared a two-room setup with his second cousin, a glazier. Corwin missed his family, but journalism quickly became his life.

> The *Recorder* was my new home, and I loved the setback position on the street, its intent look, its business office entrance, its smells of ink and hot metal, the chattering telegraph bar which brought in the news of the world, and the big, placid telegraph operator with the gentle face of a scholarly beagle. He was a preacher on his days off. On the job, he sat before a bumpy Underwood typewriter with an air of benign expressionlessness, decoding dots and dashes, and setting down words with no apparent feeling one way or other about the sinning continents, the ceaselessly revolving squirrel cage of mayhem, disaster, rape and revolution, or the regular respiratory movements of law and commerce and sports.[6]

In his two years on the paper, Corwin served as a utility reporter and covered all things of general interest in Greenfield. His beat included the police station, the courthouse, the Kiwanis and Rotary meetings, high school events, and, occasionally, sports. Once, he surprised his editor with an account of a football game written in verse.

Corwin soon was awarded a $2 raise and assigned to serve as the *Recorder*'s motion picture critic. His reviews, published in a column called "Seeing Things in the Dark," were so critical that the proprietor threatened to bar the young reporter from his theatre. According to Corwin, "I was 19, opinionated, and felt secure in the power of the press."[7]

Emil, also a journalist, worked only 30 miles away. After college and an unsuccessful try at learning the paper mill business, he had joined the staff of the *Springfield Republican,* one of New England's leading newspapers. With the opportunity to become an editor for the Newspaper Enterprise Association in Cleveland, Emil informed the *Republican* of his brother Norman as a possible replacement. Norman, upon accepting the job, suggested Al as his replacement on the staff of the *Recorder.* This would not be the only time they would exemplify a brotherly bond by furthering each other's career.

The *Springfield Republican* was a paper of long tradition, over the years fostering prominent journalists such as Brooks Atkinson. It was the newspaper which Calvin Coolidge religiously read during his residency at the White House. Its austere front-page layout, not unlike the *New York Times,* proffered an air of sophistication unique to a city of such moderate size. It was fiercely independent, and even staffed specialists in fields like transportation, music, art, and drama.

Corwin joined the staff at $35 a week (cut to $32.50 with the advent of a five-day work week). The city editor, William H. Walsh, had him cover the regular run of news—courts, city government, police—but soon asked him to write human-interest stories.

At this time, Corwin published his first book, inspired by a brief affair with one of Springfield's prettiest young ladies. Called Hazel, she was the object of many attentive, mature suitors. To have an opportunity to be near her, Corwin decided to exploit her interest in the epigram and suggested that they collaborate on a compendium of quotations, which would update Bartlett by concentrating on current personalities. It was unthinkable that they should meet at his place, so he visited her house almost every day to organize an elaborate filing system.

It was all rather "antiseptic," Corwin recalled; not once did he muster courage to make a pass. One day, however, he impetuously proposed marriage, an offer tendered with great restraint, "like asking President Hoover if I could replace his Secretary of State." She seemed suitably touched, but resorted to one of the oldest clichés among marriage rejections: "I shall always love you as a friend." She granted him a kiss for his pains, and they returned to discussing a title for their book,[8] which they agreed to call *So Say the Wise,* subtitled *A Community of Modern Mind.* The volume contained a collection of quotes from a thousand sources on ninety-eight subjects. Quoted most often was columnist Heywood Broun, whom Corwin idolized, followed by H. L. Mencken and Will Durant.

Corwin took the manuscript to New York, where, at random, he selected a publisher from the Yellow Pages, located the address, and walked in. A short time later he emerged from the George Sully Company with a contract in hand. Publishing his first book had been deceptively easy.

It was in Springfield, too, that Norman Corwin was exposed to actual broadcasting. He had been introduced to the "miracle of radio" by his brother Al in East Boston, who had constructed a receiver from a Quaker Oats box, a galena (crystal), and a coil of wire. The family marveled at this reception of faraway sounds, but Norman never dreamed that one day he would be a part of broadcasting.

An opportunity to appear before the microphone came by way of a bizarre incident, when Carlo Tranghese, a muscular Italian, appeared at the *Republican* office and boasted that, as an experienced sanitation worker for the city, he could roll a can of ashes or garbage faster than anyone. After Corwin wrote of his claim in a humorous, two-column feature, a worker in another part of the city took issue and laid down the gauntlet. Corwin, finding himself involved as an involuntary promoter, arranged a contest. The challenger showed up, with a red, white, and blue can, but Tranghese won.

Not content with his Springfield title, Tranghese insisted on new challenges, and when Corwin offhandedly suggested that he might demonstrate his art in Times Square, the Italian urged him to write a letter to the New York Athletic Commission in his behalf. The Associated Press picked up the story and Tranghese suddenly became a local hero. The manager of Springfield's radio station, WBZA, asked Corwin to interview Tranghese on the air.

This was the beginning. Later, when the radio station requested that the newspaper provide a news reader, Corwin was considered the logical choice. This experience led to his selection as the radio editor of the *Republican*, a job he pursued with candor and concern. One particular peeve of his was the syrupy rendition of poetry, a radio staple of the day, which too often was backed by dreary organ music. To counter the trend, he proposed a poetry program of his own for broadcast over WBZA, on which Corwin recited a variety of verse while a friend, Benjamin Kalman, performed piano music *between* the readings. Titled *Rhymes and Cadences,* the program became quite popular in Springfield, and the pair was frequently asked to give concert performances in town.

About this time, young Corwin made two attempts to write a book. He completed an unpublished novella, "Epic of a Shadow," while recuperating at the Rutland State Sanitarium from a suspected case of tuberculosis. (Tests proved negative, although he was confined several months.) After his release, he began a full-length novel, with the intention of entering a publisher's contest. He labored hard to meet the deadline, writing while en route to his newspaper assignments— in cars, on trains—and he worked long into the night, writing and rewriting. He worked at it during his lunch hour, on his days off, after the paper went to press. At length he finished it, and when he read it, he disliked it and decided not to submit it; ultimately, he destroyed it.

Corwin, twenty-one, was restless. His world seemed bounded by the Connecticut River. He often stood by the Teletype to read of distant places and events, and wondered about people and locales he had never seen. He wanted to go abroad.

In that year of 1931, Emil Corwin's physician recommended, after an unusually severe Ohio winter, that he take more than a two-week vacation to recuperate from a persistent illness. Emil therefore agreed to accompany Norman on a trip to Europe, since Depression fares were exceedingly low. So, with Barney Zieff (a high school buddy), the Corwin boys boarded the *Albert Ballin,* a ship of the Hamburg-American Line, and eight days later landed in Le Havre. They journeyed directly to Paris, walked the Champs Elysées, visited the Louvre, climbed the Sacré-Coeur, and observed art and life in Montmartre. They made excursions to Versailles and Fontainebleau. They bicycled in the rain among the poplars and willows of the French countryside and made pilgrimages to the home of Jean François Millet and to an inn once frequented by Robert Louis Stevenson.

Then, for Emil, it was over; he had to return to his editorial post in Cleveland. Barney had already departed for Belgium, and Norman, now alone, left for a leisurely trip through Switzerland, Italy, and Germany.

In Venice, his luck turned sour. He encountered a series of mishaps "so consecutive and persistent" that even he began to wonder. In his diary he recorded, and later wrote in his unpublished memoirs:

> I smashed a portable typewriter by dropping it, dislocated a shoulder in diving from a raft at the Lido, was poisoned by ice cream bought from a vendor on the beach and came down with violent symptoms and fever so severe that I had to be taken to the British-American hospital; I shattered my eyeglasses reaching for them in the dark, and sprayed my only suit with ink while filling a fountain pen. There are times when one

is tempted to believe in a baleful alignment of the planets. No doubt there was, in my case, some zodiacal antagonism between Venus and Venice.

But it was in Germany that young Corwin would face sobering realities which, in time, were to form important references for the future. In Munich, he was deeply moved by the list of names inscribed on the Krieger Denkmal, a memorial to the city's dead of World War I. He wondered at the senselessness of war. Later, in Heidelberg, he chanced to meet and know a Nazi, the young son of a kindly couple at whose *pension* Corwin stayed. The parents shared an intimate understanding of their ancient city of learning and music; however, they seemed only vaguely aware of the political stirrings within their Weimar Republic. The destiny of their nation, nevertheless, was personified in their son, a bright, blond, seventeen-year-old who was committed to the National Socialist German Workers' Party and Adolf Hitler.

The boy took a fancy to the American newspaperman and followed him everywhere—as Corwin described it, "like a faithful dog." They wandered through the city, discussing issues, debating doctrine and politics. And although he listened attentively to Corwin's concept of life in the United States, the boy was adamant about his own country's course. He exulted over the party's progress, relished the banners, uniforms, and trappings of a well-organized *politiche Kraft*. To him, Nazism was important; it would restore German respectability and it would purge "the pollution of the race."

On the final day, after they had climbed the ramparts of Heidelberg Castle, Corwin revealed that he was a Jew. When Norman told him, the boy said nothing. They walked down together in silence.

To Corwin, the European trip was, in effect, a vision through a prism. There were refractions of beauty, revelations of natural splendor and history, but there were also distortions of vast uneasiness. He saw and sensed a people at the edge of crisis. And yet, he would not abandon his idealism.

While traveling by train through northern France, he even tried to cope with a young woman's unyielding pessimism about hope for peace along the borders of Alsace-Lorraine. He assured her, "We are beyond thinking of war as an instrument of political expediency."[9] He could not fathom war as inevitable.

His concept of a rational world would soon crumble and memories of a blond youth in Heidelberg, a stone monument to the dead in Munich, a Frenchwoman's dread would return to haunt him. These thoughts would be indelible when, years later, he was called upon to interpret a war which, in retrospect, he remembered was festering during a serene summer in 1931, when he was an innocent abroad.

Back home in Springfield, Norman Corwin resumed his routine of reporting civic events, freaks of man and nature, and the fumblings of radio. He took up news reporting on the air and commenced once more his program of poetry readings in the afternoon.

In the spring of 1935, Corwin heard of auditions being conducted in New York by WLW, Cincinnati, for announcers and news readers. WLW, then experimentally broadcasting on 500,000 watts, was the most powerful station in the country and was called "the Nation's Station." Being on vacation, Corwin tried out and was accepted for a two-week probationary period.

By the end of the first week, Corwin was hired, and he immediately wired Walsh from Cincinnati that he would return and work a reasonable time, as "notice" for the newspaper. The editor felt that was unnecessary, in view of the expense of traveling, and wished him well.

After two weeks on the staff, Corwin noted a managerial memo which decreed that no reference to strikes should be made on bulletins broadcast by the station. Days later, the order was extended to include even news programs—a directive that puzzled Corwin. Although new, he took to heart an administrative edict which requested suggestions from the staff and boldly pointed out to the WLW management that, should a spectacular strike be headlined by a newspaper, it would be embarrassing for the station to ignore it.

Two days later, he was summoned to the front office and informed that although he had performed yeoman service, the station had regretfully decided to abolish his job. No other explanation was given. Chagrined, Corwin returned to Springfield, where, with hat in hand, he approached Bill Walsh for his old job.

One evening, over dinner with a friend, Corwin recounted the WLW incident. In view of what his friend suggested was censorship, Corwin was urged to turn over the incriminating memos to the American Civil Liberties Union, which confronted WLW with the following charge:

> Such an order, secretly given, seems to us unjustified censorship. It indicates an effort to present a biased picture of current events to your listeners. It is unfair to the organized labor movement and its sympathizers. We feel that such censorship, of which the public knows nothing, is a breach of trust in a station licensed to serve the public interest, convenience, and necessity.[10]

The general manager of WLW, John L. Clark, denied the charge;[11] then remained silent after he was faced with the evidence: two orders, dated May 29 and 31. The issue was eventually dropped, but it undoubtedly affected future practices regarding fairness and full disclosures by WLW.[12]

Emil Corwin left his NEA post in Cleveland for New York, to join the publicity department of the National Broadcasting Company. After settling in Manhattan, he married his Ohio girlfriend, Freda Feder, a former schoolteacher. Emil was impressed by the city's energy and opportunity and, as a staunch believer in his brother's talent, imagined Norman's triumph in the big metropolis.

As the promotion writer for Arturo Toscanini and the NBC Symphony Orchestra, Emil came in contact with many public relations professionals. One was Leonard Gaynor, of 20th Century–Fox in New York, who mentioned an opening in the film company's publicity department. Emil immediately thought of Norman and made an appointment for his brother, then telephoned him to come by train the following Wednesday for a job interview on Thursday. Norman seemed doubtful; besides, he had a date for that Wednesday evening. It was one of the few times, Corwin recalled, that Emil showed annoyance.

"Norm," he said, "be there."

3. The City: Publicity to Poetry

I cannot bring
Myself to be
Just anything
That's asked of me.

I cannot chide
My inner soul:
I must confide
I've set a goal

—*The Undecided Molecule*

Then, as now, one was greeted by New York City's great, immovable grace, its stone buildings, straight and tall, and its avenues filled with purpose. Its air, frequently fouled by smoke and the smell of ceaseless energy, had the electrified essence of expectancy and excitement. New York, to Corwin, was the ultimate destination. He sensed the charge of competition within its boroughs, the struggle for success, the consummation of careers which demanded heroic dimensions of character and outlook.

Emil and his bride welcomed Norman to their two-room apartment at 306 West 75th Street. A short time later, they were joined by Al, who had been transferred to New York from Akron by the Goodyear Tire and Rubber Company. The two boys occupied the living room, sleeping on a rollaway couch and a collapsible cot and keeping their clothes in boxes. The only route to the bathroom was through Emil and Freda's bedroom. Ten months later, in October of 1936, the four would move to roomier, more comfortable quarters at 112 Riverside Drive.

At 20th Century–Fox, Norman adapted print-copy movie publicity to radio copy. He wrote interviews and commentary based on film news and gossipy bits out of the Hollywood studios, which were used by small-town reviewers and critics. It was part of radio's role of vicariousness which made the medium a significant influence during the days of the Depression. Through such features as Corwin created, listeners mentally immersed themselves in the luxury and glamor of movieland's fabled existence. And the popularity of films made motion pictures the fourth largest industry in the country.

In 1936, *Variety* reported that Hollywood had helped the New Deal to the extent of $100 million in taxes.[1] Filmgoing, after a severe slump, picked up, and studios hastened to accommodate the public need for escapist fare, mostly musicals, many of them the lavish spectaculars of the Busby Berkeley genre. Million-dollar movies were now commonplace.

Corwin's job thrust him more and more into refined circles—contacts which called for tact and social aplomb. He met incoming film stars at train depots and ship piers and escorted them to their hotels. These encounters were normally brief and businesslike. Only once, he remembered, did anyone actually notice him. Loretta Young, upon meeting Corwin, gasped and said to a friend, "Doesn't he remind you of Father Brown?"[2]

New York offered sophisticated surroundings that challenged Corwin's New England conservatism. He had not been at his job very long when Leonard Gaynor invited him to lunch, at a French restaurant whose menu held Gallic mysteries for Corwin. So, as Gaynor ordered, he followed suit. What was served, however, was not what he expected. Of his first contact with cold madrilène, he remembered, "I could not have been more surprised by its texture and taste . . . if it had been made of the puréed ink sacs of squids."[3]

Al also joined the Fox organization. Again, it was family connections, for as Emil had helped Norman acquire his job, Al was informed by Norman of an opening in the company's international department. Al, who was fluent in languages, was interviewed for the position and employed to edit a house publication for overseas sales representatives.

Working in separate departments, the brothers seldom saw each other and, unknowingly, they developed mutual interest in a pretty, vivacious Latin girl who wrote Spanish titles for Fox films distributed abroad. Her name was Consuelo de Cordova, but since childhood her godmother had called her Sarita—"Little Sarah"—an allusion to Sarah Bernhardt. Young Consuelo had fancied herself an actress.

She first met Norman the day she delivered informational copy to the Fox publicity department. She thought him intense, and not very suave. "He had a lot of rough edges," she observed.[4] Al, in her view, fared better. As soon as he came to work in Sarita's department, she liked him—"the Harvard type." So began a courtship which led to Al's marriage in 1942, ten days before he was to enter the army.

Corwin kept busy. At work each day, he joined other members of the promotion department in an ornate, upper-floor theatre to see the latest film releases. He hacked out scripts which highlighted the films of Fox and its stable of stars. But he thought of Springfield, too, and his experience before the microphone. He kept a folder of ideas.

What began as W2XR, a 250-watt experimental transmitter in an electronics laboratory atop a Ford agency garage in Long Island, became in 1936 the dream of two men and materialized into a full-fledged quality station for New York. John V. L. Hogan and Elliott M. Sanger—one an engineer, the other a journalist—set out to broadcast fine music and, in general, offer a station that was "different"—indeed, in later years would proclaim from the pages of *Variety:* "WQXR—The Station for People Who Hate Radio!"[5]

The ultimate call letters, formalized with issuance of a license in February 1936, was the result of no idle decision. Both Hogan and Sanger concluded that, to keep an established audience, they should not venture too far from the experimental designation. They merely changed the 2 to Q, reasoning that they not only sounded alike but that many people wrote them similarly.[6]

Classical music was its mainstay, but WQXR began to offer other programs of the "talk" variety—all designed, of course, for the discriminating listener. Commercials were infrequent and the format endeavored to reflect good taste and intelligence. Corwin surmised that this was a station which might accept a program similar to the one he and Ben Kalman had created in Springfield; so he wrote a letter to WQXR, offering to produce and perform "out of sheer avocational interest in the utterance of poetry and with no commercial object in mind." He ended diplomatically: "Of course you will want to hear my work before committing yourself."[7]

Elliott Sanger, the general manager of WQXR, expressed interest in Corwin's idea and invited him to audition, whereupon Corwin prepared a sample program and, during lunch hour one day, hurried over to the WQXR studios in the Hackscher Building, 57th and Fifth Avenue, to read for him. Sanger was impressed. Many offers had been received by the station to do poetry on the air, but to Sanger, this approach was novel and interesting.

He scheduled the program, and two weeks later the series *Poetic License* began weekly broadcasts on WQXR, each Wednesday evening at 9:45. It was fundamentally *Rhymes and Cadences,* without Kalman and the piano. Corwin, sometimes alone but frequently with friends, introduced a wide range of treatments, from takeoffs on nursery rhymes to lyrical themes like spring—and once, a poetic medley on inebriation.

He wrote the programs at home and each Wednesday went to the studio for the broadcast. Remembering his Springfield experience, he felt confident in his writing and his delivery. He felt that "some were good, some only fair, but I don't think any were bad."[8]

The series, until concluded by Corwin's departure for CBS, ran almost twenty weeks and attracted considerable mail and audience recognition. One letter, with cartoon impressions of Corwin's poetic portraits, prompted a reply that "anyone who draws as well as you shouldn't want for publication very long and I look forward to seeing more of your work." He did not have long to wait, for the following week Corwin opened the Sunday edition of the *New York Times* and he saw on the front page of the drama section a spread of theatrical drawings by his letter-writing fan, an established artist, Don Freeman.

"It was typical of the occasional blind spots which have always plagued me," said Corwin, who recalled a remark made by E. Y. Harburg to a friend, "Poor Corwin. He is out of touch with everything but the world."[9]

Emil continued to watch his brother's progress, admired his efforts on WQXR, and even participated occasionally as an actor. He always spoke highly of Norman's talent. Among the interested listeners was T. Wells Church, a publicist for NBC, who made a point to hear *Poetic License,* thought it extremely creative, and suggested to an NBC producer that he should have Corwin appear on his program. It was the popular NBC variety show *The Magic Key of RCA.*

For his appearance on NBC, Corwin presented a parody based on "Mary Had a Little Lamb." Variations of the familiar nursery rhyme were offered as a radio commercial, as an event covered by the *New York Times*, as written by several well-known poets, and as *Time* magazine might have published it. Although *Variety*, which had reviewed the *Poetic License* presentation earlier, had noted "fine possibilities for the idea-weary networks,"[10] neither the idea nor the man apparently interested NBC. Corwin's first appearance on network radio went virtually unnoticed.

Unaffected by this brief moment in the national limelight, he returned to the WQXR series. He felt a sense of mission in taking verse from the printed page, appreciated by the most literate, to give it more popular appeal through the dimensions of voice, dialogue, and dramatic interplay. He drew heavily upon modern poets and occasionally included works of his own.

His approach to radio, even then, was inventive. Albert N. Williams saw Corwin's work as experimental and influential: "Always, he was less interested in content than in the presentation. A new way to pour old wine has been his constant search, and through that search he has probably contributed as much as any editor or critic towards the popular enjoyment of serious poetry."[11]

Emil, meanwhile, was not content to have Norman languish in the limitations of local radio. He went once more to see his friend Ted Church, in hopes of focusing network attention on his brother's talent. Church agreed that Norman was capable and creative and offered to make contacts in his behalf. He considered his own network an unlikely prospect, but CBS seemed to him a network that was more interested in innovative radio. Besides, he knew Katherine Crane, the secretary to William B. Lewis, vice president of programming at Columbia. He knew her as Kitty.

When Church called Norman at WQXR, it was no surprise. They had met previously through Emil. Corwin was startled, however, when Church asked if he would like to direct the *Columbia Workshop.* Corwin thought he meant a drama workshop at Columbia University and, after taking a moment to bolster his courage, said yes. But then it was made clear that Church was speaking of the highly acclaimed CBS series—that he was, in effect, asking if Corwin would like to join the Columbia Broadcasting System. Corwin was astounded, unbelieving, yet intrigued. He gave Church permission to effect a liaison with the network authorities.

Church, therefore, talked Kitty into persuading Lewis to listen to

Poetic License on WQXR. As it happened, only a few weeks later, Lewis was home nursing a case of influenza and he thought to tune in Corwin's presentation of Edgar Lee Masters' *Spoon River Anthology.* "It was one of my best programs," Corwin said. "Emil was in it, along with Genevieve Taggart, the poet. If Lewis had heard the program before, or the week after, he might not have been interested."[12]

Lewis liked what he heard, and in just a few days Corwin was summoned to 485 Madison Avenue. He recalled that the office of the vice president seemed modest for a network executive and that, behind a mahogany desk, sat the dark-haired, dynamic William B. Lewis. His smile and gracious manner quickly put Corwin at ease.

"Thank you for coming, Norman."

The familiarity of a first-name relationship set the tone for the interview, and indeed defined an enduring characteristic of the man. Corwin would find him a friendly, concerned corporate manager who was never far from the level of his colleagues. Straining the easy, informal atmosphere, however, was the presence of Douglas Coulter, next in the hierarchy of command. Big, bearish looking, he sat close by, surveying the recruit and speaking in a deep, gruff voice with brief, businesslike comments that, though friendly, were guarded.

Lewis led the discussion. He radiated genuine conviction and cordiality, which made Corwin feel that CBS really wanted his talent, that it was only a matter of terms. At no time did they indicate that they knew he was a $50-a-week movie flack; instead, they concentrated on the prospect of directing and performance. Not a word was said about writing.

Corwin had been coached by Ted Church in how he should conduct himself during the interview, even as to the salary he might reasonably request. So when the matter of salary came up, Corwin confidently suggested $150 per week. Lewis and Coulter looked at each other; then the senior executive explained that the network started directors at $125 per week, with a $25 raise at the renewal of each year's contract.

Corwin did not persist. The interview had been amiable, low key, a negotiation without pressure. Obviously, the terms were fair and evidently final. He accepted, and the two men arose to shake Corwin's hand.

As he left the building, Corwin pondered his decision. Only he, it seemed, fully realized how unprepared he was to produce a network program. His meager background of some twenty weeks of poetry broadcasts for WQXR, however unique, hardly provided the experience to meet the standards expected at CBS. Mostly, he had been before the microphone, leaving the technicalities of mixing and levels to the engineering personnel. He was a novice in handling professional talent. He knew nothing of intricate audio production or control room procedure.

That evening, over dinner, Emil assured his brother that he was equal to the task, but Norman picked at his food. It was not easy to share Emil's faith. Nevertheless, he served notice at 20th Century–Fox.

He was almost twenty-eight, unmarried, and eager to engage in the creative challenges of broadcasting. At CBS, he felt, he would have the opportunities, for Ted Church had told him that it was a daring network. He relied on Church for other advice as well. "Remember, you must be in command at all times," Church counseled him. "Never, never betray ignorance of what you are doing."[13]

With only this to go on, Corwin awaited the day, which was April 25, 1938. Corwin was at the CBS studios by nine o'clock and discovered that no one had yet arrived; his apprehension soon dissolved, however. As the staff came in, they extended a warm welcome to the new man. He was assigned a small office and introduced to a tall, attractive young lady who was to assist him.

Betsy Tuthill knew her way around the CBS control rooms. A sister-in-law of William N. Robson, one of the top producer-directors at the network, she once had been an assistant for both Robson and Irving Reis, the latter being the founder of the *Columbia Workshop*. Thus, having learned under two of the best directors in broadcasting, she was considered competent to handle several sustaining programs herself—a radical departure from the network's policy against women directors. (Actually, only one woman had become established at CBS, Nila Mack, and her series, *Let's Pretend*, implied that women directors—if any—should be confined to concerns of women, children, and the home.) Miss Tuthill, having tasted the thrill of production-direction and performed well, resented being returned to the rank of secretary-assistant, especially to serve a beginner.

In the days to follow, Corwin was quickly eased into the network structure, observing, at first, then receiving his first assignment to direct *Living History,* an afternoon drama series produced by Gilbert Seldes. He was faithful to the scripts, written by two CBS staff writers, which dramatized selected historical events. He also heeded the advice of Ted Church and tried to conduct himself with confidence. And for the most part he acquitted himself favorably in the eyes of Seldes and the production staff. His mistakes, however, did not go unnoticed under the scrutiny of Betsy Tuthill. She was careful not to criticize, and kept her place, but neither did she intercept or inform Corwin of anticipated problems. Her silent censure and animosity—not toward Corwin but to the system—made their relationship delicate and strained.

One evening after a show, Corwin asked Betsy to dinner. As they sat across from each other, the conversation was friendly and candid. He said that he admired her abilities and sympathized with her position. It was difficult, he knew, for her to baby-sit a newcomer and be loyal to anyone so inexperienced. "But Betsy, I'm learning. Most of my mistakes are those of technique. Still, it's a little like learning to shift gears in a motorcar—that'll come. As important as it is to learn technique and procedure, I really think they hired me for other things that are more important. I hope you understand. And that you will be patient."[14]

She was touched by Corwin's concern, and from that time on her attitude changed. She became more cooperative as he undertook his next assignment, *Americans at Work,* a series more demanding than his first.

A call from Douglas Coulter requested that Corwin direct a *Workshop* program. This was the ultimate; no other calling equaled a summons to produce for the prestigious *Columbia Workshop.* He was given a radio adaptation of Stephen Crane's *The Red Badge of Courage.* Weeks later, in September, he was assigned to direct another *Workshop* presentation, *The Lighthouse Keepers.*

Norman Corwin, the novice, was now being noticed by the cadre of Columbia producers. They seldom congregated, except at a nearby restaurant-bar or chance meetings in the elevator, or occasional conferences on the eighteenth floor; but company talk began to include references to Corwin's potential. No one felt threatened by the newcomer, of course, for most had convincing credits to their names.

Charles Tazewell, for instance, had demonstrated his inventiveness three years before by producing Edgar Allan Poe's *The Tell-Tale Heart* as a remote from Poe's cottage, using a medical stethoscope to render a magnified heartbeat.[15] There was also Charles Jackson, who would later write the best-selling novel *The Lost Weekend.* Prominent, too, were Earle McGill and the flamboyant, energetic Bill Robson, both of whom carried on the tradition of the *Columbia Workshop* after the departure of Irving Reis.[16]

Radio of the thirties advocated pride and a sense of importance. This esteem was maintained in an obsession for quality which saw insistence by the major networks that all programs be broadcast *live*, rather than risk the doubtful fidelity of recordings. It was evidenced in a well-mannered, articulate concern for accurate speech, and content, and by a policy which limited commercial intrusions.[17] It showed itself, in form and philosophy, by the dignity which surrounded most productions. Tuxedo-clad announcers, for example, were customary—a radio formality exemplified at its height in 1937, when Robert Trout, a CBS reporter, covered the Manhattan Easter Parade in full morning attire and top hat.[18]

Although radio was fast becoming big business, only about a third of the network schedule was sponsored. This meant that many hours of the broadcast day were open to ideas and even experimentation, unencumbered by commercial restrictions. Corwin, now more certain of his ability, longed for the opportunity to express his ingenuity and originality. Deciding the time was ripe for such a request, he proposed to his boss, Bill Lewis, that he develop a series similar to his WQXR effort. Lewis thought it a good idea and consigned $200 for Corwin to hire actors to cut an audition record.

A few days later, Corwin delivered the sample program. The vice president heard the show, then sent for Corwin. He approved the production and suggested that the series follow the weekly Philharmonic Symphony concerts on the CBS schedule. As a title, Lewis offered *Words Without Music*—a plain title, Corwin thought, and painfully honest, since no money had been allocated for music. But to

Corwin's surprise, the CBS executive went further: he prefixed the title with Corwin's name, an honor heretofore unheard of for writers or producers of radio.

> I could hardly believe my ears. He had offered, without being asked, the kind of billing for which a man usually works half a lifetime to get into a *position* to request or demand. He did for me what the highest-powered agent in the business could not have wrung from a major network executive, especially when his client lacked a single important credit to his name.[19]

The fall of 1938 brought tremors of growing restlessness abroad, but New Yorkers paid little heed. Most saw, some with amused indifference, the burlesque of goose-stepping German troops in newsreels at the Rialto and the Paramount, and they read of Hitler's takeover of Austria, with his boast that "no force on earth can shake us."[20] England, it was reported, had begun organizing an air raid alert system. It all seemed so distant, so vague; even unreal. At home, meanwhile, the invincible Yankees walloped the Cubs four straight, to take the World Series. Any prospect of war seemed an ocean away.

And yet, almost subliminally, a deep fear *did* exist and, at times, surfaced. Toward the end of October, two CBS programs exposed the anxiety of the nation. *Air Raid,* a verse play by Archibald MacLeish and directed by William N. Robson, brought home the brutal bombing of helpless citizenry and awakened many listeners to the swift and violent terror advanced by the warplane. A later work by Corwin (*They Fly through the Air with the Greatest of Ease*), on the same theme, would invite comparison.

Three days later on Halloween night, Orson Welles and his Mercury Theatre players panicked the country with his radio drama *The War of the Worlds*. Although adapted from an H. G. Wells story and conceived on the fantastic idea of a Martian invasion, many listeners, primed by international tension and the program's technique of utilizing news bulletins, believed the events to be true.

On November 3, 1938, amid the wake and fury of the Mercury Theatre controversy, Norman Corwin concentrated on directing a pilot show for his proposed series. It was to be broadcast on the *Columbia Workshop,* and bore the familiar title *Poetic License.*

One month later, on December 4, the premiere broadcast of *Nor-*

man Corwin's Words Without Music was aired. It received instant acclaim. Leonard Carlton of the *New York Post* wrote: "Mr. Corwin's method is to dramatize poetry while retaining most of the original lines. We can assure the purists that the first program at least was in the best of taste, and we hasten to add for the lowbrows made darned good entertainment."[21] Dinty Doyle, of the *Journal-American:* "The listening public owes a debt of gratitude to Norman Corwin and executives of CBS for the quarter hour of poetry dramatization introduced last Sunday, because it certainly sounds a new note in radio."[22] Letters, too, praised the series.

As at WQXR, Corwin covered a wide range of poetical subjects— some serious, some satirical, all with a creative touch which made each exciting, unusual, exceptional. In the twenty-six weeks to follow, the series that CBS termed "vitalized poetry" showcased works by Benét, Sandburg, W. S. Gilbert, Browning, Bret Harte, Whitman, Longfellow, Jonathan Swift, Poe, and others—both renowned and little known. Corwin even adapted nursery rhymes with modern implications. Old King Cole, for instance, was envisioned as a youthful snob before becoming a "merry old soul."

MAIN VOICE: Young King Cole was a very young soul
And a very young soul was he.
2nd VOICE: When this little king
Said he didn't like swing
He was only quarter past three.
KING COLE: The first thing I'm gonna do is get all the loud swing
bands out of this kingdom. What I want is three
fiddlers.
MAIN VOICE: He called for his
KING COLE: Knaves!
MAIN VOICE: And he called for his
KING COLE: Slaves!
MAIN VOICE: And he called for his
KING COLE: Fiddlers three
Fiddlers three wanted.[23]

But in growing old, King Cole becomes deaf and, unable to hear anything but trumpets and saxophones, summons swing bands to return to his kingdom.

Corwin did much of his writing at home, often in a lounge chair on the roof of the Riverside apartment. As he developed and produced each program, it became the task of Emil, Freda, and Al to fuel his ego, to lend encouragement, to lift his spirits. Always, upon returning home, he seemed depressed, feeling the week's effort had missed its mark. They would assure him that the program had been excellent, but he was never quite satisfied.

This impatience for perfection was peculiar to his character and was evident throughout his career. Corwin would sentence himself to a regimen that for the next five years would practically exclude all social life. As one colleague put it, "While we were in the bar across the street from CBS, drinking, Norm was at home writing a goddam script!"[24]

Returning to his office one day, Corwin was confronted by a CBS publicity man who reminded him that Christmas day that year fell on a Sunday. He wondered if Corwin had anything special in mind for *Words Without Music*. Offhandedly, because he could not think of an appropriate Christmas poem to adapt, Corwin said he would write one. The publicity man pressed him for a title. Corwin pondered only a moment, then said, *"The Plot to Overthrow Christmas."* With only a title to go on, he set about writing his first network original. It began:

> Did you hear about the plot to overthrow Christmas?
> Well, gather ye now from Maine to the Isthmus
> Of Panama, and listen to the story
> Of the utter inglory
> Of some gory goings-on in Hell.

To Corwin, it was a romp all the way. "I wrote it from line to line, rhyme tumbled upon rhyme, this idea and then that idea—it was fun. There was very little rewriting, and it flowed."[25]

The play in verse concerns an assembly of assorted villains—Nero, Haman, Ivan the Terrible, Simon Legree, Caligula, Lucretia Borgia, the Devil himself—who meet in Hell to plot how they might do away with the holiday of Christmas. Nero's plan (to assassinate Santa Claus) is selected and this noted fiddler of Rome is dispatched to the North Pole. There, St. Nick counters the threat with a boisterous welcome and instructs Nero in the real meaning of the Yuletide, winning over his would-be assassin with the gift of a Stradivarius.

In the script, Corwin commented openly about radio production techniques and procedures—a narrative device he used often in many of his works for the medium. In *The Plot to Overthrow Christmas,* he explained a transition as follows:

> With aid of a fade, a fade on the radio,
> We'll take you there, with a hi and a hey-di-ho,
> To hear first-hand the brewing of the plot
> Down in the deepest Stygian grot.

At this point a second narrator, called Sotto Voce, was introduced:

> Grot is a poetical term for grotto.
> (Whenever you hear my *voce sotto*
> Or sotto voce, whichever you prefer,
> It's just I, taking pains to make quite sure
> That nobody makes a poetical allusion
> Which may in any way create confusion.)
> I return you now to the voice you were hearing
> Before I had to do this interfering.

Later, Sotto Voce pointed out:

> That, my friends, was a big brass gong.
> It is used in this story, right along,
> To indicate that we're about to travel
> To points where the plot will further unravel.[26]

A young Will Geer, the latter-day "grandfather" of television's long-running series *The Waltons,* played the Devil, while House Jameson was Santa Claus. When the program was repeated two years later on the *Columbia Workshop,* Martin Gabel performed the role of the Devil, with Ray Collins as Santa.

The premiere performance of *The Plot to Overthrow Christmas* was not reviewed, but considerable listener response convinced Corwin and his CBS superiors that the show had been an unequivocal success. The most warming compliment of all, however, came in a personal visit from Edward R. Murrow. The CBS newsman, home from Europe on a brief sabbatical, had heard the broadcast and was deeply impressed. The next morning, he took the elevator to the eighteenth floor and knocked at Corwin's office door. Entering, he introduced himself—the beginning of a long and close friendship—and told Corwin how much he had enjoyed the program. He was convinced, he said, that there had not been anything like it since W. S. Gilbert.

Corwin, obviously, had met the most exacting demands of the nation's epicenter of broadcasting. A goal was within reach. He would, within months, prove his place among the leading innovators of radio and, in time, be called a "genius of the medium" by William S. Paley himself.[27]

4. The Network:
A Liberal Mountain

An experiment in radio is something nobody ever tries except strange people with a funny look.

—*Radio Primer*

"We were at the top of a liberal mountain . . . !"[1]

Almost thirty years after the fact, William N. Robson, in a mood of nostalgia, exultantly described the network policy and the eminent position he and Corwin shared at CBS. He had reached the summit early, having followed the footsteps of Reis and others to attain premier standing as a producer. It seemed evident that Corwin, given his creative bent, would make the ascent in due time. Their success, Robson recalled, was possible only because of a prevailing network attitude which openly encouraged experimentation.

The "mountain" had once been a molehill, compared to an older, expansive NBC. William S. Paley, who had taken over the Columbia Broadcasting System at the brink of bankruptcy in 1928, inspired growth through executive foresight and clever management. He lured affiliates into the fold by offering, without charge, a wealth of sustaining programs—programs subsidized by the network. And then he endeavored to make these programs better. He saw a mass of unsold time, 77 percent of the CBS schedule in 1933,[2] as a frontier of development. To implement a plan for broadcasting prominence, therefore, he sought a strong, energetic executive who could direct a concerted effort for progressive programming.

William Bennett Lewis thus became a principal figure in the creative evolution that was to occur at CBS. With no experience in show business and only a brief background in advertising, Lewis nevertheless possessed two infallible traits: an uncanny ability to recognize talent and the courage to try new ideas. As vice president of programming, Bill Lewis listened and was alert to new suggestions; he added his enthusiasm to each new programming scheme; he aided its development. He assembled and supported a remarkable group of writers and producers, Corwin included, and gave them free rein to experiment. Moreover, he gave them credit.

Such largess was less an act of gentlemanly generosity than a strategy of good business, yet he was both generous and a gentleman. "If they get their credit, I know I'll get mine," he said, and in a speech before a conference of advertising men at White Sulphur Springs he outlined his theory as a viable show business maxim:

> What can management do to encourage the superb craftsmanship that this business so desperately needs? Mainly it is in the wise and sympathetic handling of the creative people you have developed. Make them feel cherished and important; praise good work or extraordinary effort on the part of creative people, and—above all—see that they get credit for it.[3]

CBS became a center of excitement as ideas flourished at 485 Madison Avenue. Ed Klauber, executive vice president and principal aide to Paley, one day called Lewis to his office. "Bill, I know I gave you carte blanche to do what needed to be done. But would you mind once in a while telling me what in the hell's going on?"[4]

To Lewis, it was obvious. CBS was fast becoming a network known for creative, original, competitive programming. NBC, so long superior in the power struggle among networks, now abandoned its smug indifference and tried to counter Columbia's approach by offering similar program efforts. To oppose Corwin's *Words Without Music,* for instance, NBC presented Alfred Kreymborg in a series called *Fables in Verse.* The big concern remained the *Columbia Workshop,* with which CBS had garnered much good will. NBC, nevertheless, thought it might have the answer in a prolific and enterprising young writer-producer by the name of Arch Oboler.

It was only a matter of weeks after his Christmas show that Corwin wrote and directed an original which would have a notable impact on his career. It was conceived in anger. Haunted by daily headlines of deteriorating peace in Europe, Corwin was aroused against fascism. And the event which fired his indignation was the deliberate bombing of the "open" town of Guernica, Spain. Corwin fumed over the innocent lives lost in this cowardly act and seethed at the fact that little was said about the atrocity—for, as he put it, "It was not yet fashionable to be anti-fascist."[5]

Corwin scripted a poetic, hard-hitting play for his *Words Without Music,* a play which, without mentioning names, hardly disguised his feelings toward the Fascists and their heartless actions of indiscriminate bombing. Indeed, the object of his wrath was Vittorio Mussolini, son of Il Duce, who as a pilot had written an unfeeling observation of slaughter amid the burst of his bombs. The target had been a band of Ethiopian cavalrymen, about whom he said, "One group of horsemen gave me the impression of a budding rose unfolding, as the bombs fell in their midst and blew them up. It was exceptionally good fun."[6]

Corwin decided to dedicate the program to young Mussolini, then changed his mind. He instead broadened its accusation to present the drama in the names of "all aviators who have bombed civilian populations and machine-gunned refugees."[7]

Like *The Plot to Overthrow Christmas,* the program came easy. Enforced by his outrage, ideas crystallized one after another. The script, given the long and ironical title *They Fly through the Air with the Greatest of Ease,* dramatized the unconcern of a bomber crew which methodically carries out a mission of destroying homes and strafing fleeing families. It begins quietly:

> Assume it is morning.
> You know what mornings are.
> You have seen thousands of them:
> They rise out of the East, huge as the universe
> And stand in the sky till noon.
> Oh, you've seen all kinds of them.
> Some come up dirty-faced, as though they had spent the night in a
>   gutter between two stars;
> Some bluster, brandishing big winds . . .

On this morning, airmen board a bomb-laden plane to take off, and the listener is rushed ahead to eavesdrop on the anticipated target: the tenements of a city.

> Just think:
> Ten thousand savage rooftops, tarred and tiled,
> Against a single plane!

The mission completed, they sight a column of fleeing civilians and gun them down. The pilot notes a similarity to the mowing of wheat, to which the radio operator replies, "Nice symmetrical pattern, isn't it?" The narrator agrees:

> It is. It is.
> A symmetry of unborn generations,
> Of cancelled seed.
> The dead below, spread fanlike in their blood,
> Will bear no more.
> The pattern is symmetrical indeed—
> Of ciphers linked, repeating down infinity.

But then the bomber is intercepted by an enemy plane. The action builds. The bomber is struck, loses control.

> There's apoplexy in your motors now
> And they will not recover.
> Sirs, I speak to you:
> Be calm!
> Sit back:
> There still is time
> To see
> A final symmetry:
> The spiral of your spinning
> Is a corkscrew in the sky.

The intensity, backed by the scream of a falling plane, mounts as the bomber plummets to the earth and crashes. Several seconds of silence. Then:

> That's all.
> That's all the fighting they will care to do.
> They have a treaty with the earth
> That never will be broken.
> They are unbeautiful in death
> Their bodies scattered and bestrewn
> Amid the shattered theorem.
> There is a little oil and blood
> Slow draining in the ground.
> The metal still is hot, but it will cool.
> You need not bother picking up the parts.

> The sun has reached meridian.
> The day is warm.
> There's not a ripple in the air.[8]

"The very calmness of the approach, the apparently dispassionate narration, packed a wallop twice as effective as a scream," was the opinion of House Jameson.[9] Jameson, who narrated the program, was greatly admired by Corwin, who used him often and found him to be a reliable performer, a man of modesty who had a sense of dignity, without being stiff. It was Jameson who provided the paradox which made the message so powerful, in a voice described as "a mellow instrument . . . master of language cadences . . . a fine gift of irony."[10]

They Fly through the Air, by Corwin's acknowledgment, was a turning point in his career. Broadcast on February 19, 1939, the program brought him instant national recognition. A thousand letters poured into CBS, all favorable but one—a dissenting Harvard student. Press reaction was mixed. Ben Gross, of the *New York Daily News,* considered it "the best radio play ever written in America." Ruth Lechlitner of the *Herald-Tribune,* on the other hand, did not think much of the effort. Allen Smith praised the play in the news columns of the *World-Telegram,* while Harry Hansen, in the book review section of the same paper, panned it. *Theatre Arts Monthly* hailed it as "steps ahead" of previous radio poetry "on every count."[11]

It was, in truth, bold radio at a time when growing isolationism made even the mention of war a matter of controversy. Broadcasting, in particular, tried to maintain a balance between the two factions of public sentiment. The fact that CBS made no attempt to censor the broadcast was evidence again of the network's liberal leaning. Still, seven months later, the network decided it best to cancel a repeat of the program upon the news that England and France had declared war.

The show's aesthetic impact, as well as its indictment of war's ruthlessness, made *They Fly through the Air* a significant entry in the annals of radio poetry. Jack Sher, of the *Detroit Free Press,* even alluded to the work in his "portrait" of Corwin, titled "Poet with a Punch":

> He writes of mornings—and you see mornings everywhere. He writes of people—and they have the humility and hopes and feelings of people everywhere. He writes of war—and it is war.[12]

Warner Brothers purchased the film rights to the play, but after subsequent delays and the rush of world developments, it was never made into a movie. In May 1939, the Ohio State Institute for Education by Radio awarded *Norman Corwin's Words Without Music* top honors, citing it as the series "best demonstrating the cultural, artistic, and social uses of radio." *They Fly through the Air with the Greatest of Ease* received a first award for the best individual dramatic program of 1938–39.

Shortly after the broadcast of *They Fly through the Air,* House Jameson met Corwin in a restaurant near the CBS building and surprised the producer with a simple observation. "You've become famous."

The actor explained that people now seemed anxious to know about Corwin—what he looked like, what he wore, what it was like to work for him. The idea of fame had not occurred to Corwin; success, perhaps, in terms of achievement, recognition, even awards—but hardly the realization of fame. He entertained the thought for awhile, then dismissed it in the face of an upcoming show.

Words Without Music was a week-to-week challenge. Each show had a singular significance, but one with special meaning was the re-creation of the program that had catapulted him into CBS, *Spoon River Anthology.* The aged author and poet, Edgar Lee Masters, had been invited to observe the broadcast and was ushered into an audition booth adjoining Corwin's control room. He seemed gentle and subdued, but interested. As the program progressed, Corwin noticed his actors casting furtive but frequent glances at the booth's window, and he was curious. At the conclusion of the broadcast, he opened the door and found Masters hunched over in his chair, his face bathed in tears. Corwin's first thought was fear that the old man had been disturbed by the interpretation of his work, but after the poet regained his composure, he explained that it had been the *voices* of the cast. By an uncanny coincidence, they matched the vocal personalities of the people Masters had known and about whom he had written his free-verse epitaphs.

In April 1939 the CBS administration circulated an interoffice memo that requested ideas in a campaign to make people "radio conscious," sponsored by the National Association of Broadcasters.

No other producers seemed interested except Corwin, who decided to tackle the task, and within two weeks had written *Seems Radio Is Here to Stay*.

Do we come on you unaware,
Your set untended?
Do you put down your paper to lift an ear,
Suspend what you were just about to say,
Or stay the finger tip that could snap shut
The traps of night between us?

Were you expecting us?
Your dial deputized to let us in
At thirty minutes after ten along the seaboard on the east,
Nine-thirty inland by a thousand miles,
A mountain's half-past eight,
And dinner dishes still uncleared on shores that face Japan?

In either case, good evening or good afternoon, good morning or
    good night,
Whichever best becomes the sector of the sky
Arched over your antenna.

We wish a thousand words with you
Concerning magics that would make a Merlin turn pistachio with
    envy:
The miracle, worn ordinary now, of just such business as this
Between your ears and us, and oceantides of ether.
We mean the genii of radio,
Kowtowing to Aladdins everywhere,
As flashy on the run as Light, and full of services to ships at sea and
    planes in air and people in their living rooms, resembling you.

All this by way of prologue, listener;
And prologues should not be prolonged.
Let our announcer do what he's engaged to do:
Announce
What this is all about.
And let there be, when he is done, some interest expressed
By brasses and by strings.
A little music, as they say,
To start an introspective program on its way . . .[13]

House Jameson narrated. Cleared for broadcast on the *Columbia Workshop* April 24, the half-hour program created much excitement in the radio industry. Station personnel in Boston, Utica, Davenport, and San Diego wrote to thank Corwin for making their jobs "seem more important and dignified."[14] The NAB, swamped by requests, decided to make 400 records of the program for distribution to stations throughout the country, then shelved the idea in view of the cost. Instead, CBS released an expensive brochure heralding the program and quoting the script. Dinty Doyle, radio editor of the *New York Journal-American,* dared to uphold the show as the best writing ever to go on the American air[15]—a bold, but recurring, evaluation of Corwin's work.

Corwin was well established now, at the crest of the liberal mountain. His name was well known. He received invitations to attend social affairs, was asked to speak at functions, became the subject of newspaper and magazine articles. His boss, Bill Lewis, joked, "Seems Corwin is here to stay."[16] And there was talk of turning his "classic" about radio into a series.

Corwin dared not allow one milestone to obscure the next. He applied himself with diligence and ceaseless energy. He now shared an apartment with his brother Al at 510 West 110th Street, Freda and Emil having moved to roomier quarters a few blocks away at the birth of their first child. He often labored late into the night, usually at the office, so as not to disturb Al.

To Corwin, *Words Without Music,* with its infinite variety of challenges, was a fulfilling experience, and he might have wished the series to continue indefinitely. But Lewis had other ideas. He saw an extension of *Seems Radio Is Here to Stay* as an effective way to persuade potential clients and the general public of radio's tremendous power, and the CBS sales department enthusiastically endorsed Lewis's plan. Corwin was asked to conclude his poetry series within the month to develop and produce six programs promoting the medium.

The first effort of what *Variety* described as "a CBS sales promotion brochure set to music" was aired in July under the title *So This Is Radio.* It featured House Jameson and Everett Sloane, with music by Bernard Herrmann. This is the way *Variety* reviewed the event:

> Radio has not been much loved. Most of its earlier years were spent apologizing. And its recent prosperity has been so sensational and in some ways so effortless that hints of complacency can be found by looking no further than the . . . sales promotion department. Nev-

ertheless, radio could not be the eating-sleeping-living companion of millions and the energy-releasing channel of vigorous personalities, without, along the way, inspiring some eloquence. This is it.[17]

Corwin found the assignment difficult. He was certain that no industry should be showered with three and one-half hours of self-centered praise. Happy to move on to something else, he did not have long to wait.

Bill Lewis called a conference in which he expressed to Corwin his concern over world developments. He felt a compelling need, he said, to reinforce the American ideal. He wanted Corwin to direct a new series, which he envisioned as a variety program to promote national self-awareness and pride among Americans. It was to be supported by front-line performers, a full orchestra, original music, and Corwin would more or less have a free hand in its development.

Lewis chose Davidson Taylor, a lean, ministerial-looking executive, to be the producer and George Faulkner to write the program's continuity. For health reasons, however, Faulkner soon left the series and was replaced by Erik Parnouw as editor-writer. Burgess Meredith was signed to emcee. Mark Warnow and his orchestra, then featured on the Lucky Strike program, would provide the music. The first official CBS announcement read:

> PURSUIT OF HAPPINESS, a special series of programs dedicated to the brighter side of the American scene, has been scheduled by CBS for Sunday afternoons beginning October 22nd. These broadcasts of newsworthy entertainment are slated for approximately 4:30 p.m., immediately following the Philharmonic Symphony programs. The world is at war. Columbia will continue to bring you comprehensive news of this war and its attended circumstances here and abroad, but PURSUIT OF HAPPINESS will not deal with war or with issues growing out of the war which divide our minds. Instead, these new programs each Sunday for a little while will turn aside from the stream of grave events and bring us reminders that today, with thankfulness and humility, we Americans still enjoy our constitutional rights to life, liberty, and the PURSUIT OF HAPPINESS.[18]

The first program introduced three small-town editors—one from Alabama, another from Kansas, the third from Vermont—purportedly to lend a little grass-roots philosophy to this exemplar of Americana. Solemnly, Burgess Meredith linked the program elements with frequent references to democracy, and singer Ray Middleton performed a lusty number from the musical *Knickerbocker Holiday:* "How Can You Tell an American?" Virginia Verrill sang "Having Any Fun?" In a skit, black comedian Eddie Green played the part of Columbus, and the featured star of the show, Raymond Massey, delivered a reading from the play *Abe Lincoln in Illinois.*

In its review, *Variety* acknowledged that the opening program signaled a series that was "off the beaten path," but said that "the idea behind the show, whatever it was, did not manage to make itself known to the listeners."[19]

Lewis remained optimistic; he felt his idea was sound, its purpose valid. He was accustomed to wobbly starts; after all, *Columbia Workshop* had begun with a failure[20] and righted itself to be the network's most respected series. His *modus operandi* was patience: never to panic, or apply undue pressure, to the people who create. As for *Pursuit of Happiness,* he showed his interest through visits to the studio, an occasional suggestion, but mostly by constant and complete faith in Corwin and a company of concerned individuals. For Corwin, to work with several program advisers was a new experience.

Pursuit of Happiness was only three weeks old when, on the evening of November 5, 1939, it generated exceptional excitement. The singer Paul Robeson elicited a thunderous, standing ovation with his performance of *Ballad for Americans,* a miniature musical by Earl Robinson and John Latouche. The CBS switchboards were swamped by calls, mail was extremely heavy, and *Broadcasting Magazine* called the performance "an American epic."[21]

Strangely, the work had come to the attention of Corwin as a theatrical failure. Originally titled *Ballad for Uncle Sam,* the piece had been part of a Federal Theatre musical revue, *Sing for Your Supper,* which had lasted but six weeks on Broadway. Its composer, Earl Robinson, suggested to Corwin that it might nevertheless be appropriate for *Pursuit of Happiness.* He had sat down at the piano to play it and sing the words. Corwin had listened, and considered it folksy and a bit rambling. It was much too long, perhaps, for it covered four periods of American history, and it often seemed to interrupt itself.

Corwin advised Robinson to shorten the work, give it focus, drop the "cantata" label, and change its title; and Robinson agreed. Corwin also urged him to make the changes as soon as possible, so that the revised work might be auditioned for Bill Lewis and Davidson Taylor. Both men liked it, and it was Lewis who suggested Robeson for the leading role.

Robeson, a singer with an imposing voice and physique, had been openly critical of America's treatment of the Negro and would later become a controversial figure through his political empathy for communism. He was, nevertheless, a world-famous concert artist who, Lewis reasoned, would give *Ballad for Americans* its essential strength and momentum. So certain was the CBS hierarchy that Robeson was needed, the network offered him more than the normal fee of $500 for top-featured personnel.

Despite the emotional impact of *Ballad for Americans*, it was a small part of the program. The show opened with Gertrude Niesen singing a Hawaiian song, followed by Robert Benchley's humorous talk, "How to Help Your Wife Buy Clothes." Carl Carmer then reported the latest lore on rattlesnake oil, and Carl Van Doren portrayed Benjamin Franklin in a vignette he had written. Then the climax: Robeson's virtuoso baritone, which made *Ballad for Americans* a powerful finale.

The studio audience, which had crowded the 55th Street Playhouse, arose as one to cheer the production. The ovation lasted long after the program had gone off the air.

By the end of the year, *Variety* reported that *Pursuit of Happiness* was "gradually slipping into the groove that should make it a sound candidate for a commercial spot."²² Although it failed to find a sponsor, the projected ten-week series was extended, and in time tripled its run.

Corwin, however, was not satisfied. He wanted the shows to be more innovative, and he devoted many hours and much attention to the series. Miffed at a memo from Douglas Coulter, which suggested that directors account for their time, Corwin typed a reply, dated January 12, 1940:

> Maybe I should acknowledge it myself since everything you've discussed in the memo fits my case precisely. I should like to go on record that the exigencies of my particular work are such that since the inauguration of *Pursuit of Happiness* last October I have had but three days away from the office. Two of these were occasioned by illness and on both of these days I was in constant telephone communication with the

office. The third was Christmas day spent at Buzz Meredith's and even there the occasion turned into a program conference . . .

The memo also detailed long hours of evening rehearsals, late-night interviews and conferences with Broadway stars, the irregular pattern of work time to accommodate certain performers, the amount of material left for his secretary, Sally Austin, at the end of each day. "Frankly," he wrote, "I am trying to operate on the basis of getting the least amount of rest necessary to keep running." Writing the memo was a catharsis, and he decided not to send it; instead, he filed it away and forgot it.[23]

But what bothered Corwin most was the *direction* of the series. He showed his usual aggressiveness in another memo, to William B. Lewis—a ten-page document which began:

As it now stands, Pursuit is merely a new framework for old and conventional and outworn elements. Its emcee bears the same relationship to the show as all emcees to all variety shows since radio began. There is no by-play, no surprise, no sense of fun in progress, no use made of the running device, no outstanding cohesive force, no esprit de corps, but instead an esprit de Meredith, which is not enough. It's a straight show, a dignified and sincere show, but it's also the kind of show that cannot come off unless it has the courage to turn its back on those qualities which identify most other variety shows. I feel most strongly that part of the risk we take on a program of this calibre should be the material as well as the overall concept—risks such as we are taking with Robeson singing an untried composition and Van Doren writing and performing an untried sketch. Let's get Ray Scott to write a "Pursuit of Happiness Blues" right away. Let's get some satire on American foibles, like sitting through a football game in a pouring rain. Let's get one of our Hollywood people to read a concoction out of the writings of Whitman, instead of a scene from an old play that is tried and true, but not particularly exciting. Let's try putting the show together differently each week, instead of by formula. Let's open the windows and let some big ideas flow through. Let's not stereotype our routine so that it goes from Meredith to music to comedy to remote to dramatization invariably each week. Let's systematize idea conferences and organize stimulation channels. Let's keep the show moving as if each program were the beginning of a new series . . .

He implored his colleagues to provide "entertainment plus" in a program that should be "polished, smart, solid, understandable, and never obvious." Corwin complained that he was unable to apply his personal talents because he had too many "helpers," too many kibitzers. "I long ago made a ruling," he wrote, "that no author ever be allowed at my rehearsals where I could help it."

The memo was divided into sections, the first labeled "format," the second "director," and the third "remotes." Of the latter, he stated a hope "that you have not permanently abandoned my earlier idea of American sound patterns and phenomena" in fast-moving montages involving subjects such as

A. The bells of the nation—the carillon of the Bok Peace Tower in Florida, the Liberty Bell in Philadelphia, a bell buoy off the coast of Maine, the bell of a community church in a prairie town, mission bells in California.

B. Arteries of the nation—the rush of traffic in the Holland Tunnel, steamship whistle in the Erie Canal, train pulling out of a station in Santa Fe, the noise of traffic across the Golden Gate Bridge.

C. The pulse of the nation—pick up mechanisms of great and little time pieces, including the wrist watch on Burgess Meredith's wrist, the wheels humming inside the biggest clock in the country, the clicking meter inside a Chicago traffic light control.

D. The energy of the nation—a giant dynamo in the Manhattan power house, water pouring over Boulder Dam, a steam turbine inside a locomotive cabin in Kansas City, a diesel engine aboard an ocean liner on the west coast, the throb of an airplane engine over Buffalo.

Corwin was critical of Meredith's role in the series and, under the heading "master of ceremonies," concluded that "his performance seems to take two directions: one, the solemn, funereal oration form you heard on the first show and in yesterday's dress, and two, the contrived punch he had in yesterday's show." Corwin maintained that Meredith was "a great actor" but "at the moment lacked authority as an emcee."[24]

The memo aptly demonstrated Corwin's detailed, aggressive approach to matters of concern. It typified his personality—an intrepid, impatient response to the ordinary, the commonplace. He was intensely involved and unblushingly forthright in his insistence that the medium meet its potential.

Many of Corwin's suggestions were observed, and in the weeks to follow, *Pursuit of Happiness* took on a fresh, unpredictable air of inventiveness and aural surprise. Burgess Meredith broadened his participation as an occasional actor. Bolstered by the success of *Ballad for Americans*, the series furthered the trend to radio musicals, and introduced a short opera by Maxwell Anderson and Kurt Weill, *Magna Carta*, which was broadcast February 4, 1940, with Walter Huston as a singing narrator. Marc Blitzstein even asked to write a musical based on Hemingway's "The Killers," but the work never materialized.[25] And Corwin found time, while confined with the flu, to write an original, *The Oracle of Philadelphi*. Indeed, he arose from his sickbed to direct it, with Gale Sondergaard in the starring role.

Norman Corwin read the unpublished short story that Douglas Coulter handed him. It had been written by a former CBS publicity writer, Lucille Fletcher, who would become a top radio dramatist—with such powerful suspense plays as *Sorry, Wrong Number* and *The Hitch Hiker*—and was now the wife of CBS composer-conductor Bernard Herrmann. It was a delightful story about a caterpillar, named Curley, who danced to the tune of "Yes Sir, That's My Baby"[26] and created a sensation in Hollywood. Coulter thought it unique and charming, and suggested that Corwin adapt it for the *Columbia Workshop*.

At first, Corwin was reluctant. Involved in the logistics of *Pursuit* and depressed by the political pyrotechnics abroad, he was in no mood for fantasy. On the assumption that a lighthearted venture might be good for the morale of the people, Corwin eventually succumbed to Coulter's persuasion and adapted the story, switching locales from Hollywood to New York and broadening its concept to satire. He added much material to the original and related a chance meeting between a theatrical agent and two young boys, one of whom owns a trained caterpillar. The agent persuades the owner, Stinky, to join him in exploiting the caterpillar's talents and soon the insect, called Curley, is a national sensation—an inspiration for a dance craze named "The Curley Crawl," the object of a hit tune titled "The Caterpillar Creep," and the starring role in a Disney cartoon feature. Success is clouded by complaints from sociologists and editorial writers, accusing inhumane treatment and commercial misuse of Curley.

In the midst of the controversy, with the caterpillar's talent at a premium, Curley disappears. Stinky and the agent are terror stricken, then heartbroken. Then, while the agent idles away at the piano, playing "Yes Sir, That's My Baby," Curley reappears in metamorphosis to "flutter goodbye." He has turned into a butterfly.

When Everett Sloane, cast as the crafty agent, saw the script for the first time at table rehearsal, he could hardly read his lines for laughing, and at the final rehearsal on the evening of broadcast (March 7, 1940), Corwin had to warn his cast. He recorded in his diary:

> Produced *My Client Curley* for *Workshop* tonight and it went off without a hitch. The cast and the orchestra and even spinsterish Howard Barlow, who was the conductor, seemed on the point of breaking into laughter at times. And I had to caution the studio not to giggle on the air.[27]

Mrs. Herrmann and her husband heard the program on the West Coast in an audition booth at KNX. She later told Corwin how pleased and amazed they were at the number of clever twists he had conceived in his adaptation to enhance the humor and pathos of the story.

My Client Curley was immediately acclaimed a fast and funny program, a sensitive and satirical look at show business. The *World-Telegram* hailed Corwin as "a pixie running wild in the CBS production department."[28] *Variety*'s radio editor, Robert J. Landry, headed a two-column box review with the caption "Curley the Caterpillar Clicko."[29] Max Wylie selected the script as one of the year's best for his annual anthology of broadcasts.[30]

The series *Pursuit of Happiness* ended May 5, 1940. It had presented many outstanding people, some for the first time on radio, including Danny Kaye, Bert Lahr, Ethel Barrymore, Beatrice Kaye, Betty Comden, Adolph Green, Clifton Fadiman, Jimmy Durante, Abbott and Costello, Gene Autry, Ethel Merman, and Miriam Hopkins. Additionally, Charles Laughton had been featured in a Corwin adaptation of Stephen Vincent Benét's *John Brown's Body*, which marked the beginning of a remarkable friendship.

In Corwin, Charles Laughton found gentle guidance and strength and the comforting knowledge that he was nurtured in a rare province of quality radio. Laughton, to Corwin, was a kindly giant whose combination of awesome talent and trepidation often made him vulnerable. Laughton liked Corwin and unhesitatingly accepted a second invitation to appear on *Pursuit of Happiness,* to narrate a script based on works by Thomas Wolfe.

Upon Laughton's return to Hollywood, the actor spoke highly of the radio writer and persuaded his RKO producer, Eric Pommer, to have Corwin adapt for film a newly acquired property, *Two on an Island,* a play by Elmer Rice. Laughton himself relayed the offer, and invited Corwin to stay at his home while he was on the West Coast.

CBS was amenable. The network proposed that, in addition to the film commitment, Corwin write, and possibly direct, several programs for the CBS summer series *Forecast,* which was being originated from the West Coast. *Forecast* was envisioned as an experimental showcase of broadcast ideas, from which, CBS hoped, would evolve client interest and the basis for marketable series. Each program was to serve as a pilot.

Columbia was a commercial network, and to remain viable, progressive, and competitive it needed the support of popular programming and sponsorship. The pressure was ever present. But William S. Paley knew the other side of the coin as well: "From the beginning I saw that the business side of broadcasting required us to reflect in our programming the taste of the majority. But at the same time I also realized that we should balance popular entertainment with programs which would attract minority tastes."[31]

It was in this concept of artistic liberalism that Corwin found comfort and opportunity.

5. The Series: Deadline Times Twenty-Six

Now then—let's talk about time; that which we have so much of, yet so little.

—*Good Heavens*

The Laughtons lived in a Spanish-stucco, ranch-type house on Rockingham Drive. It had the conventional swimming pool and privacy associated with Hollywood stars, but by Brentwood standards it was a modest home. Corwin occupied the guesthouse, and during his visit of several months enjoyed relative independence. He came and went as work demanded. The Laughtons likewise moved freely, and once, during Corwin's stay, departed east for a publicity tour.

Corwin was comfortable in the company of Charles Laughton and his wife Elsa. The trio often spent evenings discussing the arts: theatre, music, literature, painting—especially painting, for Laughton was fond of art and firm in his prejudices regarding works he knew well. But it was Corwin who introduced the noted actor to the pleasures of classical music, and he frequently brought albums home for Laughton.

Hollywood, however, was disappointing. Corwin left each morning for the RKO lot, only to find the moviemaking process embroiled in committee bureaucracy. He could not accustom himself to "the country club pace of movie work"; he found it frustrating, lacking in stimulation. It was hard to endure Hollywood's assembly line scrutiny, having experienced the freedom and individual control of radio. In spite of his disenchantment, however, he completed the screenplay of *Two on an Island* in July 1940.

The association with the Laughtons brought Corwin ever closer to the war abroad. Both Charles and Elsa, who confided deep concern for friends and relatives in England, were especially worried about their personal secretary, Renée Rubin, who at the time was in London, experiencing nightly Nazi air raids.

Moved by their anxiety, Corwin wrote a short radio play especially for them. It was a poignant story of an RAF gunner who awaits a dawn mission from which there can be no return. He writes to his five-year-old son—a letter to be opened and read when the boy reaches twenty. In flashbacks, *To Tim at Twenty* reveals the happy relationship between the airman and his wife, and their anticipation of a child. The Laughtons loved the script, thought it tender, filled with pathos, and they approached their roles with dedication—even rehearsing their parts before Corwin at home.

To Tim at Twenty was the second part of a double-feature program for *Forecast* and was broadcast before a live audience in a theatre studio at KNX. Special lighting was planned for the radio drama. Corwin explained:

> I seated Laughton at a table, with a spot directly overhead, and put Miss Lanchester on a separate standing mike perpendicular to the first mike. During the direct address to Tim, Miss Lanchester stood in darkness, but in the flashback Laughton arose and took a single step to his wife's mike while the table spotlight went out and the standing spot went on.[1]

The production was aired on the evening of August 19, 1940, preceded by Keith Fowler's light comedy *Ever After,* directed by Earle McGill.

A week later, again as part of his commitment to the CBS series *Forecast,* Corwin directed Margaret Sullavan in one of her rare radio appearances. The play was *Bethel Merriday,* a Sinclair Lewis story of backstage life, adapted for radio by Helen Deutsch. It was the thirteenth presentation of the limited summer series, which ended the following week.

His Hollywood sojourn only convinced Corwin more strongly of his infatuation with radio. He understood it, enjoyed its challenges, and was endowed with the temperament and talent suited to broadcasting. Edith Isaacs, editor of *Theatre Arts Monthly,* upheld Corwin as "perhaps the first poet for whom the radio seems to be a natural medium, who seems to have the rhythm and sweep of radio in his own blood."[2]

Corwin's career, not unexpectedly, gathered momentum in the months to come, and the first hint of a unique broadcasting achievement involving Corwin was revealed in his letter to William B. Lewis, dated September 13, 1940:

Okay, okay, you are absolutely right, Bill. The fact you think I am a great director and a terrific writer shows that your vacation has not softened the keenness of your judgment. To hell with money, anyway!

I expect to be back in town within two weeks and will let you and Sarah invite me to dinner for a slight charge. Numerous things I want to discuss with you—my plans for the fall, providing I am not indispensable to the armed might of the nation or gravitating toward pictures because of interest shown in me recently, both here and at Paramount. But I have signed nothing and have declined another long-term offer from RKO, and am perfectly free to do what I want after October 15th. RKO has asked me to stay on through the production of *Two On an Island*,[3] but I have deferred giving them a definite answer.

I have lately been approached by a New York stage producer on a proposition I cannot divulge at the moment because of its confidential nature. But here again, no decision will be made until after I meet him in New York.

But I should like you to know as far as radio is concerned, I would be interested in any good 26-week setup—even though it paid less than movies—providing I could do a show that would make us all happy and self-respecting rather than rich. I mean a whopper of a prestige show in which I might be given resources and a free hand to write and produce the best goddamned show on any air. That, sir, would be worth more to me than the Hollywood lucre which, mind you, feels very nice on the inner lining of the pocket.

If the show sells, then include me out and I will return to pictures. The satisfaction of having built it, plus a royalty or two of course, will be sufficient reward for me. While such a show remains sustaining, Uncle Norman would hold its hand.[4]

On September 26, 1940, he wrote from Hollywood to Mildred Cohen, an aunt in New Hampshire: "I have been here three months and am leaving for New York tomorrow with what is familiarly known as a sigh of relief and expect to unsigh in about three weeks."[5]

Autumn in New York was a restless season of casual social and professional encounters for Corwin. He had lunch one day with an editor from Henry Holt to discuss the possible publication of a "collected Corwin." And after writing *Ann Rutledge*, a radio drama commissioned by Du Pont's *Cavalcade of America,* he was invited by the program's director, Homer Fickett, to sit in on the rehearsal. Against his better judgment and violating his own principle decreeing writers *persona non grata,* Corwin accepted. In his diary, he recorded the event as "very painful."

In December, Corwin returned to the West Coast at the request of a group which was organizing development of a film in behalf of British war charities. Upon his arrival he discovered, to his dismay, a very complex committee arrangement—some one hundred motion picture personalities, including Alfred Hitchcock and Sir Cedric Hardwicke, masterminding the movie. "It ended up with literally twenty writers on the project."[6]

He escaped the imbroglio briefly by being recalled to New York to direct a repeat of *The Plot to Overthrow Christmas.* At the point where Nero embarks on his journey to assassinate Santa Claus, the program was suddenly interrupted by a news bulletin reporting the assassination of the commander of the Vichy fleet, Admiral Jean-François Darlan. It was a disquieting parallel.

Immediately after the broadcast, Corwin returned by plane to Hollywood, to resume work on the war charities film. But two months later CBS approved Corwin's proposal to produce a twenty-six-week series, and on February 23, 1940, he wrote to Bill Lewis in New York:

> I'm leaving here Tuesday and will be in to see you Friday, if the train is not held up by bandits. I am in a fine mood of rolling up sleeves and want to do you a job that will make you proud of your protégé.

He wrote that he welcomed the hard work he knew it would entail, but "after the soft work and easy money out here, that's what I want." He asked to do his work away from the interruptions of the eighteenth floor, and informed Lewis that he could expect him the third of March.[7]

To create and produce, from script to final broadcast, twenty-six original plays in as many consecutive weeks was a formidable task, and yet, typically, Corwin seemed unperturbed. He gave little thought to a requisite backlog of scripts and submitted to other duties and distractions. In a letter to Lewis, he even offered to direct several programs in the network sustaining drama series *Free Company,* "because I think it is important at this hour to CBS and USA, both of which cover a lot of territory."[8] He witnessed a special showing of Orson Welles' *Citizen Kane*, and took time to devise a singing telegram to celebrate Max Wylie's departure from CBS. It was written to the tune of "Auld Lang Syne":

> When Wylie goes, we blow our nose
> And wipe a weeping eye,
> Because we think New York will stink,
> When Maxy says goodbye.[9]

Toward the middle of March, he directed an adaptation of Stephen Vincent Benét's *Freedom's a Hard Bought Thing.* The day after the broadcast, Corwin left for the Palisades, to take up residence in the peace and seclusion of the country.

The series, which Lewis had titled *26 by Corwin,* was scheduled as a *Columbia Workshop* presentation. The premiere was less than a month away, and Corwin had not written a word.

Corwin's idyll was at Sneden's Landing, near Nyack. He had leased a thatched cottage (he called it "Booby Thatch") in the garden and greenery of a sloping lawn overlooking the Hudson River. He had selected the site in the belief that its quiet and natural setting would aid inspiration. It was only thirty-five minutes from New York; and he would commute on Sundays to produce his programs, driving a newly acquired Buick convertible.

He relished the solitude. A housekeeper came in the mornings to do his housecleaning and prepare meals. He would arise around nine, work outside among the garden flowers, or walk by the river with a clipboard in hand. He considered it his Walden—"It was my Thoreau year."

Occasionally there were visitors, and one of the earliest was Earl Robinson, whom Corwin had invited to help create a musical version of Carl Sandburg's *The People, Yes.* The composer slept in the extra bedroom, and they labored through the long hours of each day. It came hard, as Corwin revealed in his diary entry of March 26, 1941:

> Worked all day, laboring like a mountain and bringing forth a mouse. By the way, there is a mouse who feels very much at home in the bookcase of the living room. It came out and looked at us at dinner tonight.

Corwin did not intend the musical to open the series; instead he imagined the premiere of *Twenty-Six* to be a poetic *tour de force,* not unlike *They Fly through the Air.* So, along with the preparation of *The People, Yes,* he was also writing a play, to be titled *Appointment.* Its theme of vengeance against a prison commandant was, in reality, an allusion to Hitler; but he could not "get into" the piece and soon shelved the effort.

After several days of arduous collaboration, Robinson and Corwin completed their adaptation of *The People, Yes* and dispatched a script to Carl Sandburg. It was not a literal translation of Sandburg's work; rather, Corwin had embellished the original with ideas of his own, even added other Sandburg lines, and immersed it in Robinson's catchy music. Sandburg was "pleasantly surprised," and in a letter to Corwin called it "a touch of miracle."[10]

On April 6, Corwin finally decided that he would begin the series with a lighter script. He began writing *Radio Primer,* a playful, alphabet-like look at broadcasting. Heavily musical in concept, the program ended with a soloist singing

> Having thus come
> From A to Z
> Our Primer has prum
> The Radio Indust-ry![11]

Lyn Murray, commissioned to do the score, made several trips to Corwin's country retreat to confer about the music. He admired the pleasant, peaceful environment so much that he soon became Norman's neighbor, moving into a nearby baronial house once occupied by Orson Welles.

With only two scripts completed and several in various stages of development, Corwin inaugurated *26 by Corwin* on Sunday, May 4, 1941. The broadcast, *Radio Primer,* was well received, with radio critics calling it a refreshing satire, a very witty roasting of radio with overtones of Gilbert and Sullivan. *Time* magazine said it demonstrated "that there is room for sensitivity as well as soap in radio."[12] The *New York Post* proclaimed it fun, and wondered how Corwin could keep up the pace.[13] Corwin also received congratulatory telegrams from Fred Allen, Erik Barnouw, Ted Church, Ezra Stone, and Deems Taylor.[14]

But Bill Lewis had reservations. After the program, the CBS vice president forwarded a memo to Corwin:

> I thought *Radio Primer* a lot of fun and enjoyed it very much. My only criticism of it as the opening show of *26 by Corwin* is that it is pretty much a show for the trade. If you really have ambitions to sell Corwin and the series, I believe you have got to come closer to hitting the nail on the head with the audience and forget the trade.[15]

Variety agreed. The trade paper referred to it as an "in" program, likely to be appreciated only by those involved in broadcasting.[16]

A week later, Corwin directed Frank Lovejoy in *Log of the R-77,* a drama about a submarine crew trapped at the bottom of the ocean. Then, as the third program of the series, he offered *The People, Yes.* In it, Burl Ives sang with an orchestra for the first time and was featured in his first major acting role. CBS received 150 calls commending the broadcast.

Three days later, Corwin completed *Appointment* and showed the script to Martin Gabel, who liked it. The next Sunday, four days later, Corwin produced *Lip Service* with Larry Adler, the world's leading harmonica virtuoso. The play was about a hillbilly harmonica player from Tennessee who became the sensation of New York and ultimately, as a good-will envoy to a Latin American president, helped cement Pan-American relations. Of the shows to date, Corwin considered *Lip Service* least effective, and blamed himself. In his diary, he bemoaned the fact that "among the other great mistakes I made on the show was not giving Larry enough time for just playing the harmonica."

Appointment, produced June 1, 1941, became the fifth program of the series. Corwin wrote in his diary: "I acted in it, God help me. However, I tried three men in the role before taking it myself." And because of his participation, he called on his assistant, Perry Lafferty (who thirty years later became a key executive for CBS, and later NBC), to manage technical matters from the control room.

Corwin would become known for his imaginative excursions into radio fantasy, and no effort would be applauded more than *The Odyssey of Runyon Jones,* created for this series. It was a delightful story about a boy who searches for his dog Pootzy among the bureaucratic red tape of Dog Heaven and "Curgatory." Corwin had wanted to do a dog story for weeks. He had been inspired by Nick, an English setter who lived down the hill and often accompanied him on long walks.

> Nick was erratic and irregular, a Grand Hotel of fleas, and all things a well-bred dog shouldn't be, but his personality was so winning that, had he been Pootzy, an odyssey such as Jones' would seem well worth the effort.[17]

On those infrequent occasions when Nick happened to be at his own home, he would hear the bell above Corwin's door and come lumbering up the hill, panting eagerly, prepared to follow his new-found friend on his customary walk. To honor his canine companion, Corwin thought he would write a program which he might title *A Walk with Nick*.

The idea for *Odyssey* came to him the evening of May 28, shortly after dinner. He had not been feeling well, but the prospect of this plot improved his mood and made it possible for him to sleep better that night. He started writing the next day, but it came slowly, "which I charitably attribute to the grippe." The next day he completed almost a third of the script before succumbing to fatigue. He wrote in his diary: "I've never been as late as this before."

Joel O'Brien, Corwin's secretary-assistant, came to the cottage the next afternoon to type the script as it came off the author's clipboard. Corwin finished *The Odyssey of Runyon Jones* around 10:30 that evening. Then, after a night of insomnia, he drove into the city to rehearse and produce *Appointment*.

CBS secretaries or production assistants were normally women, but O'Brien best suited Corwin's needs because the duties demanded long and irregular hours, with frequent trips at night between the Palisades and Madison Avenue. O'Brien was eminently efficient and was called on to act as a liaison with the network and to make certain production arrangements. And when Corwin worked late into the night, as he often did, O'Brien would let himself into the cottage the next morning to pick up the completed pages of a new script. He would act on any instructions left by the writer: clear an actor's schedule for a given role, arrange copyright permission, make studio reservations, or relay information to Lewis or Coulter.

When the first six programs of *26 by Corwin* ran well over budget,

Corwin decided that he might recoup by writing a simple show for one performer. He thought of calling it *Soliloquy*, or as he explained to Davidson Taylor, a "soliloquy to balance the budget." The CBS vice president said it was a very good idea and suggested that he use the entire phrase as a title: a soliloquy to balance the budget.

Intrigued by its experimental dimension, Corwin set about to create a half-hour show with only one narrator and the support of a few sound effects. And with typical capriciousness, he made light of radio and its fiscal concerns as he computed the cost of *Columbia Workshop*:

> Now get this:
> We are standing just outside the house that lack of jack built:
> A house called Corwin's Folly . . .[18]

Although adventurous, it was not easy to write. His first day at the script produced only five pages. The next day, he was forced to take time out when a former girl friend and her fiancé stopped by for a visit; the man, a Boston University professor, wanted to get into radio and he sought Corwin's advice. The day after, Corwin wrote until very late and was pleased with what he termed "fair lines." He complained that it came slowly, and again, in his diary, expressed concern that he had "never been so far behind."

When he drove into New York on Sunday, June 8, to produce *The Odyssey of Runyon Jones*, he had written only about two-thirds of *A Soliloquy to Balance the Budget*, and he acknowledged that "for the first time I have failed to finish a script a week ahead." Despite the diminishing time span between deadlines, Corwin would not concede that his commitment was impractical. Only once did he experience doubt, he said, and that was at the beginning. "It was like driving into a desert and seeing a mountain ahead. It looked a ninety-degree climb straight up to the sky, and you wondered how your car would make it. Yet, as you got there, mile by mile, it flattened out."[19]

On this particular Sunday, Corwin's parents had come down by train from Boston to see him direct *The Odyssey of Runyon Jones*. Sam, an extrovert, enjoyed the city and association with the elite of show business; Rose, on the other hand, was more reserved and self-contained. She hovered at the edge of excitement, smiling, quietly pleased at her son's success. Corwin of course had little time to spend with them, and leaving his parents to visit with Emil and Alfred, he hurried back to Sneden's Landing.

A Soliloquy to Balance the Budget was readied for production the following week, with House Jameson as the monologist. Reactions to the show were mixed, but among those impressed by the program was Howard Smith, CBS assistant treasurer and comptroller of the budget. Smith requested—and William B. Lewis arranged it for him—to receive an autographed copy of the script.

In an article he wrote years later, in 1973, Corwin declared: "If there is any kind of printed and folded document more fascinating, inch by inch, than a good road map, I will agree to shred it, and eat the resulting paper coleslaw in a public ceremony."[20]

The same implicit passion of discovery prompted him to write the eighth program of his series, *Daybreak*. For a week, he pored over atlases spread on the cottage floor, plotting a hypothetical journey around the globe, beginning and ending at latitude 40° north, longitude 25° west. The script was a mélange of moods through word imagery and music, and Corwin called on his neighbor, Lyn Murray, for a supportive score. The script and the music sheets were shuttled back and forth across the lawn between the two houses.

It was a fun show. Still, on June 17 he complained in his diary about its limitation of form: "Somehow, it does not feel solid to me." He also felt slowed by an accumulation of fatigue. And to complicate matters, the next day was taken up by photographers. So, with his routine interrupted, he resolved that night to finish the show. He found composing on the typewriter more satisfactory than longhand. As he put it, "My attention wanders less that way." He finally completed the program at 3:30 in the morning.

It was not until a day before the production of *Daybreak,* only eight days before another broadcast deadline, that Corwin began his next script. It was a desperately induced inspiration which occurred during an outing with Al and Sarita. Al had felt Norman was working too hard and, with Sarita, persuaded him to join them for a day at Jones Beach. Even there, however, Norman could not dismiss the pressure, and when the day turned cool and breezy, he retired to the car to scribble four pages of a new script. It was the beginning of *Old Salt,* a lighthearted yarn about a whiskey-loving sea captain who baby-sits his grandson with tall tales.

By midweek he completed the script, with production just four days away. On Wednesday evening Corwin was invited, with Carl Van Doren and his wife, to have dinner at Lyn Murray's house. The Van Dorens had not heard *Radio Primer*, so Murray played his recording of the program. In a subsequent discussion of the *Twenty-Six* series, Corwin described his latest effort and Van Doren suggested a noted character actor, Dudley Digges, as an ideal lead for *Old Salt*. Van Doren even left the conversation to call Digges, but the performer wanted more money than had been allocated for the role.

The next day, June 26, 1941, Corwin experienced an unusual burst of creative energy. He finished *Old Salt* and moved well into an idea that had been incubating for some time. The script began:

> This program is between Americans. That's where the title comes in. We hope you like it, but you don't have to. At any rate, nobody's goin' to make you stick around and listen to it. That's one of the advantages of being an American.
> We invite you to think that one over for a moment; and while you're exercising your inalienable right to tune us out or let us ride, we'll help ourselves to a music cue.[21]

He wrote the final pages of *Between Americans* the following day, and began blocking out another script. He jotted down ideas for *Job*, which would eventually be the third program of a Biblical trilogy. After finishing the notes, he gave thought to one more program in the trilogy, a script based on the Book of Esther.

Then it was Saturday. He drove into Nyack for a shampoo and, according to his diary, was quite concerned that he had not had more people out from the city to enjoy the country air. On Sunday he directed *Old Salt,* and Carl and Jean Van Doren watched the production from the control room. It featured Everett Sloane as "Gramp" (the retired sea captain), Larry Robinson as the grandson, and June Havoc as the main siren, an antagonist in one of Gramp's tall tales. Miss Havoc, although a leading Broadway star, performed her small role for scale.[22]

Corwin now concentrated on his Biblical trilogy. The pressure he had felt with mounting intensity was eased somewhat with the inclusion of a script already written. On July 13 he resurrected and produced, with minor revisions, *Ann Rutledge*. And while the trilogy, which now included the story of Samson, occupied most of his attention, Corwin met the deadline of *Twenty-Six* by quickly conceiving a comedy called *Double Concerto.* Paul Stewart and Peter Donald were starred as two musicians who jealously tried to undo each other with practical jokes, only to have each prank backfire into boosting the other's career.

On Sunday, the 27th, the *Workshop* was preempted for an address by an Iowa archbishop, Francis J. L. Beckman, originating from Chicago on a topic of timely concern: "Effects of the World Crisis on America." In spite of the week's reprieve, Corwin still found it difficult to keep pace, as indicated by his diary entry for July 29:

> Had one of those days of fruitless searching for an idea. The concentration on the trilogy, especially *Samson,* resulted in a situation of falling farther back against deadline than ever before. Tuesday night, and no script begun.

That evening he had dinner with Lyn Murray, and returned home to confront an absolute deadline. At length, he began *Descent of the Gods,* a piece of gentle humor about a visit of several Greek gods to America. He wrote one page before retiring; the next day, five pages; then he struck an impasse. The weather was hot—"steamy, like a Turkish bath"—and he fretted over the awkwardness of the show. That night, he decided to drop the script and exploit another idea. "But there wasn't an idea in the house."

On the day after, August 1, he tackled *Descent of the Gods* with renewed determination. He had Nick, the "God of Trivia," narrate the program, and the cynical nature of the character suggested to Corwin the dour comedy of Henry Morgan. But casting the popular comedian might prove difficult, it was thought; Morgan might demand a prohibitive price. Corwin contacted him, nevertheless, and Morgan surprised everyone by eagerly accepting the role. Corwin then stayed up all night to finish the script, typing the final sentence at 4:30 in the morning.

Much of August 1941 was occupied with the preparation and production of the trilogy. And always, the specter of a deadline hovered constant and close. On August 9, just one day before production, he finished *Samson* and telephoned in the balance of the script. A partial script had made possible the casting of the play—Martin Gabel as Samson, with Mady Christians as Delilah—and provided a basis for Bernard Herrmann's original score.

Music for the trilogy was composed by three close friends of Corwin: Herrmann (*Samson*), Lyn Murray (*Esther*), and Deems Taylor (*Job*). Of the three, Herrmann proved most independent, recalcitrant, individualistic—and, certainly, innovative. He was offered the full facilities of a large orchestra to score *Samson*, but he chose to write music for four harps, a flute, a mandolin, and a drummer-xylophonist. Corwin conceded "it had an astonishingly ancient feeling."[23]

The music opened the program, with Delilah studying her man:

> Lift the curtain.
> See: the moon is on the face he wears at night.
>
> He smiles like a thumb-sucking babe
> And turns a half-turn in his love crib.
>
> Sleep is good news to bone and sinew,
> Therefore to Samson, who is bone and sinew;
> Therefore he smiles.
>
> Sleep, Samson, sleep your gifted sleep . . .

There follows Delilah's treachery, the cutting of Samson's hair, his capture, his ultimate torture and humiliation. At the end, Samson, blinded and beside a small boy, awaits his final confrontation with the crowd:

> SAMSON: Boy, where's the door to my humiliation?
> BOY: Here. I will open it and lead you through. They're jeering you
> and saying, "Bring him on."
> SAMSON: Then bring me on.
> I'll have the last to say of what is said today.[24]

Corwin immediately sensed that it had been one of his better programs. After the show, Deems Taylor and his actress girlfriend, Giuliana Taberna, accompanied Corwin to the home of Carl Van Doren. The host confirmed Corwin's feelings; *Samson* had been exceptional, he said.

Such respites as Van Doren's postproduction party and an evening at the Stork Club with Deems Taylor and Giuliana hardly obscured the ever-present pressure to meet the weekly deadlines of *Twenty-Six*. Corwin, however, had completed the trilogy, having worked on all three scripts simultaneously, and no doubt felt momentary relief. He even took time to write an article of 1,500 words for the *New York Times* at the request of the radio editor, John K. Hutchens.

On Wednesday, after conferring with Lyn Murray about *Esther*, the second of the Old Testament scripts, he held auditions. The next day, August 14, he became absorbed in Demosthenes while reading about Philip of Macedon and Alexander the Great. He saw the Athenian statesman as a possible subject for a future script.

Friday began an unprecedented two-day rehearsal for *Esther*, at Liederkranz Hall on 58th Street. Corwin recorded a runthrough and complained about the acoustics—"a frightful studio"—and then, finding the show nine minutes too long, he spent the next four hours cutting the script in an adjoining audition room with Lyn Murray. After the Sunday broadcast of *Esther*, he stopped by Deems Taylor's apartment to pick up the score for *Job*, the third program of the trilogy, and left the next day for Hollywood.

Almost from the beginning, Corwin had envisioned Charles Laughton as Job. So, upon receiving the actor's agreement to play the role, he took a flight to the West Coast to arrange production. Laughton, of course, invited his friend to stay at his house. Ruth Gordon, the actress, was also a houseguest, and one evening, while dining with Charles and Elsa Laughton, Ruth, and Renée Rubin, Corwin became suddenly ill. He was confined several days to his room, attended by the Laughton staff, and while in bed wrote a script especially for the talents of Elsa Lanchester and Ruth Gordon. A comedy-fantasy, it was titled *Mary and the Fairy* and concerned a gullible working girl who entered the Crinkly-Crunkly Bread Contest to win five wishes. The wishes were then personally delivered by an "exploitation department" fairy, who appeared complete with wings and a special wand in a zipper bag. It was a touching story, timely and quite humorous. It followed *Job* as the seventeenth program of *26 by Corwin*.

Before leaving for New York, Corwin produced another program in Hollywood for the series. It was an essay on sound, an experimental exercise that required 8 microphones, 4 sound men, 32 live effects, 21 recorded effects, 63 distinct cues, and "the patience of two saints."[25] It featured the solo performance of Gale Sondergaard, who, against a frenetic background of busy technicians, stood forlornly on an empty theatre stage amid a forest of microphones and sound equipment.

On his eastbound train, Corwin resumed his study of Athenian history and wrote *Fragments of a Lost Cause*—fondly remembered as a fine show which received little attention. For his twentieth program,

Corwin adapted an unpublished short story by Hollywood's Dore Schary. *The Human Angle* concerned an undersea diver—which prompted Corwin, in remembrance of his production of *Log of the R-77*, to remark that hereafter he hoped to keep his head above water. He did, by writing a lighthearted piece about astronomy. *Good Heavens*, number twenty-one in the series, was written at the invitation of the University of Chicago, as part of the institution's fiftieth anniversary celebration. After a quick fact-finding visit to Yerkes Observatory at Williams Bay, Wisconsin, he developed and directed the program from New York.

The descriptive insight of Thomas Wolfe had always impressed Norman Corwin. Thus it was natural that he turn to the works of this outstanding author to create a mood piece for radio, which became the next offering of *Twenty-Six*. Corwin himself narrated, Perry Lafferty assisted, and Alexander Semmler composed the music. *Wolfeiana*, as it was titled, drew favorable response—even a congratulatory telegram from a listener on an island off the coast of Alaska.

The next program was disappointing. Corwin conceded an error in casting Ruth Gordon in a mystery-comedy, *Murder in Studio One*. "I guess I was seduced by the success of *Mary and the Fairy*," he explained. It was, Corwin confessed, a study in the clichés of murder mysteries and designed to bring to the microphone what he termed "the funniest comedians of our unfunny era," notably Gordon, Eddie Mayehoff, and Minerva Pious. He admitted it was a half-hour "as subtle as a Sears, Roebuck catalogue." As for Miss Gordon, "I could not seem to get her away from a characterization that did not fit the role. Not her fault; rather, mine for not seeing the material as unsuited to her particular talent. A man might have been better in the part."[26]

Because of the tremendous audience reaction to *Descent of the Gods*, Corwin decided to repeat it with Henry Morgan and the original cast. He thought he might offer the program as an "extra," so he had Nick, the God of Trivia, explain:

Pardon me while I take a spin on my clavichord. I like to accompany my own narration.

CLAVICHORD MUSIC

Oh, you're surprised, huh? You think this is where you came in? Well, just take it easy, chum, because this is number 23-A of *Twenty-Six by Corwin*—not 24 or 23, but the *Columbia Workshop* blue plate special 23-A.

And it doesn't count as one of the 26. That's what I said, it doesn't count—period.[27]

In the final analysis, it *did* count. Pressure to complete the series did not permit the luxury of additional efforts, and Corwin set about to plan program number twenty-five. He really wanted to do another program with Henry Morgan, and he devised a musical comedy called *The Rise and Fall of Henry Morgan*. The comedian, however, got his dates mixed; so Corwin hurriedly revamped the show for Budd Hulick (of *Stoopnagle and Budd*) and retitled it *A Man with a Platform*. At the last minute, Morgan found time to take a lesser role in the cast and appeared with Arlene Francis and Eddie Mayehoff.

The lease on his cottage to Sneden's Landing had now expired; so Corwin returned to the city to share an apartment with Al. He had one more program to go in the series; he wanted desperately to make it significant.

With Thanksgiving only weeks away, he thought he might develop a "service" based on the premise that "thankfulness need not be somber and genuflective, but upstanding, straightforward, good-humored, positive; need not necessarily be cast in the dim light of stained-glass windows, but out in the open, in the sunlight of an Arizona morning, under the one dome not yet equaled in the architecture of the church."[28]

But the script came hard, and after a fruitless afternoon he decided he had to get out of the apartment. On impulse, he tossed his typewriter in the back of his convertible and drove to Atlantic City. He arrived well after dark. His hope was to secure a quiet room in a seaside hotel to work overnight. As soon as he checked in, however, he discovered a Coca-Cola convention in progress. Obviously, the featured product was not the staple beverage of the evening, and the corridors and lobby rocked with revelry. It took him only twenty minutes to realize that no work was possible; so he checked out and drove back that night to Manhattan.

Arriving in the early hours of the morning, Corwin let himself into the apartment quietly. Not wishing to disturb Al, he retired to the bathroom. There, sitting in the bathtub, he wrote the concluding program of *26 by Corwin*.

In his foreword to the second compilation of his published plays for radio, Corwin spoke of *Twenty-Six* as a "once in a lifetime" experience which prescribed "Spartan" conditions: "no parties, no movies, no late bull sessions, no smoking, drinking or distractions. I gave up all but a few distractions."[29]

The final broadcast, *Psalm for a Dark Year,* was aired on November 9, 1941. The author himself narrated, with production assistance by Joel O'Brien and Perry Lafferty.

Immediately after the program, participants of the seven-month series assembled to celebrate. At the cast party were Eddie Mayehoff, Henry Morgan, Lucille Meredith, Ann Shepherd, Everett Sloane, Hester Sondergaard, Luis Van Rooten, Frank Lovejoy, Minerva Pious, Arlene Francis, Beatrice Kaye, Joel O'Brien, Perry Lafferty, Lyn Murray, Clifford Carpenter, Ted de Corsia, Arnold Moss, Winston O'Keefe, Alexander Semmler, Gale Sondergaard, Burl Ives, Martin Gabel, Parker Fennelly, and Larry Robinson.

Corwin was presented with two brightly wrapped gifts. One of them contained twenty-six towels, each beautifully embroidered with a program title of the series. The other package was a box-within-a-box, to heighten suspense. As Corwin opened the final box, the company exploded in laughter. It was a book, handsomely embossed with the title *How to Write a Radio Play,* by Arch Oboler. Its pages were blank.

Still in the euphoria of having finished a highly acclaimed series, Corwin was totally unprepared for the visit of Douglas Coulter the following day. He thought the network executive had dropped by to tender his congratulations. Corwin offered him a chair, but he said he preferred to stand.

Coulter had succeeded Bill Lewis as vice president of programming, the latter having left CBS for Washington to head the radio division of the newly organized Office of Facts and Figures.[30] Coulter, obviously concerned, did not compliment the series. His voice became grave and serious as he talked of Corwin and the network. He spoke of the expense of producing sustaining drama and emphasized the expediency of commercial subsidy. Columbia, he felt, had to draw the line, had to become more competitive. He pointed out that CBS was not as well heeled as its competition and that, contrary to its past, the network could not indulge in speculative, unsponsored, experimental programming.

He seemed to feel that Corwin had boxed himself into a professional stance that had diminished his viability in the burgeoning business world of broadcasting. And he left Corwin with the impression that his talents, although impressive and proven, had become too expensive[31] for practical value in the future course of the network.

Improbable as it seemed, it was obvious that Corwin was being dismissed. After all the awards, industry plaudits, and public praise, he was being phased out—fired!

6. The Anniversary: Bill of Rights Show

There are more oracles
In Washington already
Than one can shake a scepter at.
And as for Hollywood,
No oracle would sign
A contract for a span of seven years
With options.

—The Oracle of Philadelphi

Have you ever been to Washington, your capital?
Have you been there lately?
Well, let me tell you, it's a place of buildings and of boom and bustle,
of the fever of emergency, of workers working overtime, of
windows lighted late into the night . . .[1]

In early December 1941, America had at last committed herself to the conflict, and this description of wartime Washington was the opening of a momentous Corwin achievement. It not only marked an impressive milestone in radio aestheticism and documentary drama but, more importantly, proved to be the prototype of a new role for radio.

The program, *We Hold These Truths*, had been created to commemorate the 150th anniversary of the nation's Bill of Rights, and under governmental sponsorship was aired in prime time on all four major networks: NBC (red and blue), CBS, and MBS. This coast-to-coast coverage reached half the population of the United States, the largest audience ever to hear a dramatic performance.[2]

With poetic allusions, image, insight, Corwin exploited the attributes of radio in bringing to life the persistent, often painful course of constitutional development in the United States. He blended past with present and evoked aural excitement, which made history timely, relevant, rewarding. He melded an all-star Hollywood cast into a moving, compelling performance that transcended the identity of famous and familiar personalities.

Still, it was the program's uncanny timing—just eight days after Pearl Harbor—which gave it historic significance. Its nationalistic theme, intensified by the shocking attack and subsequent declaration of war, kindled within the people an indignant patriotism and renewed dedication. Its timely statement was heightened even more by a short, concluding talk by President Franklin D. Roosevelt. It was almost as if the broadcast had been created for the moment, yet it had been months in planning.

In the fall of 1941, Corwin had no way of knowing the ultimate importance of the endeavor. He could not envision the program's impact on the people—or, for that matter, on his own career. He was drained, exhausted, after the long and grueling *26 by Corwin*. And when William B. Lewis, who now directed the radio division of the government's Office of Facts and Figures, asked him to develop the special, Corwin at first resisted. But Lewis was adamant. He finally persuaded Corwin that the effort was vital, that his participation was essential.

So, wearily, Corwin came to Washington, with mixed emotions.

It really began at a birthday party. With his children attending a New York school, Bill Lewis had not immediately moved his family to Washington. He commuted, to be with his wife on weekends, and on the occasion of her birthday he joined Sarah in hosting a party for a few close friends. Corwin was included.

It was the first time in months the two broadcasters had seen each other, and Lewis asked how things were going at 485 Madison. Corwin brought him up to date on developments at CBS, then told him of Coulter's conversation the week before. Lewis was surprised at the network's attitude, but told Corwin not to worry. He would be getting in touch within the next few days "about something big," and several days later he telephoned Corwin to explain the plans at the Office of Facts and Figures to celebrate the sesquicentennial of the American Bill of Rights. The occasion was to be highlighted by speeches, special

musical programs, and displays. The director of OFF, Archibald Mac-
Leish, had named a planning committee, which included Philip Cohen, Joe Liss, Alan Lomax, David Mearns, and Jerome Wiesner (the
latter to become president of M.I.T.).

Lewis had urged the committee to think in terms of radio. In fact,
he proposed a monumental media effort that would be aired on all
national networks in prime time. Moreover, he made known his feelings that only one person, Norman Corwin, was capable of creating
the program he had in mind. Corwin, though flattered by the faith of
his former boss, did not greet the proposition with enthusiasm, but
Lewis persisted.

"Remember, the chance to celebrate a hundred-and-fiftieth anniversary comes only once in a hundred-and-fifty years."[3]

So, on November 17, 1941, Corwin arrived in the nation's capital
and went directly to the Claridge Hotel. It had been arranged that he
would share a room with Lewis. That evening, they had a lengthy
bedtime discussion about the proposed broadcast and Corwin
learned, for the first time, details of the program's dimension and
importance. He learned, for instance, of the President's direct involvement and of a possibility that Roosevelt himself might conclude
the presentation with a short talk. Lewis admitted that the President's
participation had been sought primarily "to bludgeon the networks
into releasing prime time." Also, because the program seemed of
national interest, he indicated that star Hollywood talent might be
available.[4]

Political ramifications, nevertheless, posed problems that made the
project sensitive and uncertain. Prior to Pearl Harbor, radio had been
virtually caught in a vise of opposing public sentiment. A world at war
awaited America's decision, while isolationists and pro-Allied factions
argued the issue of involvement. Radio was the forum, but had no
legal right to editorialize, and therefore walked a narrow line in its
effort to be unbiased. Some feared a dramatized "salute" to the Bill of
Rights might, in its patriotic temper, be inflammatory and offensive to
anti-war elements. But MacLeish, who maintained a close liaison with
the President, reported that the program should go ahead as
planned.

With the deadline only twenty-six days away, Corwin again found
himself facing pressure. Moreover, the difficulty of the task became

quite clear upon his first visit to the Library of Congress. After several hours of poking through files to unravel the bibliography of the Bill of Rights, he found the evolution of the first ten amendments a complicated, often fragmentary story. To his dismay, research often dead-ended and left him frustrated.

At lunch with MacLeish on November 21, he told the OFF director of his problem. MacLeish, who was also librarian for the Library of Congress, was sympathetic and granted Corwin's request to remain in the library after closing time. He wished Corwin well in his research and suggested that President Roosevelt had been most impressed by the phrase "in full faith and credit," which the New York Assembly had written into the ratification of the Constitution. Corwin agreed that it was a striking phrase and later included it in the script.

The library was a cold and lonely place after hours. Corwin searched through countless cross-references and pored over volumes of history until the early hours of the morning. At last he quit, to return to his hotel for sleep.

He awoke with a sore throat. As he feared, a summer of accumulated fatigue had lowered his resistance, and he fell victim to the grippe. Now ill, his struggle to meet the pending deadline became even more difficult. He forced himself to work, but his diary defined his difficulty in cryptic comments:

> Nov. 23—Fruitless day.
> Nov. 26—Terrific nose bleed.
> Nov. 27—Horrible day of no work done.

At Corwin's request, Bernard Herrmann was commissioned to compose an original score for the Bill of Rights drama. But when Herrmann arrived in Washington, he found the script only half finished. He conferred with Corwin and returned to New York. *Variety* would later report that his music was to the production "what a good shortstop is to a baseball team," and commended it as "a full-scale collaboration."[5]

December 4, with the script only three-quarters complete, Corwin met with Lewis and his assistant, Douglas Merservey, in Bill's new and sparsely furnished Washington apartment. They sat among unopened packing cases and discussed both the script and Corwin's imminent departure for Hollywood. The production was only eleven days away. It was conceded that the remainder of the program would have to be written en route to the West Coast. Lewis urged Corwin ("a blood vow it was") to rush the script back to him as soon as it was finished. "Unless my memory fails me," Lewis later recalled, "the next time I saw the script was in published form six weeks *after* the broadcast."[6]

Two days after his meeting with Lewis, Corwin made the following entry in his diary:

> Frantic day of shopping, packing, and leave-taking on the *Century*. Worn to a frazzle. Getting nowhere on the Bill of Rights show. I nevertheless had to plug until very late on the article which I promised I would write for Hutchens of the *Times*.

Corwin's article concerned the project, and was published the day before the broadcast in the Sunday edition of the *New York Times*. He wrote that being asked to do the program was "a happy privilege, and yet a super embarrassment of riches." He referred to the honor of depicting the famous document, the participation of the President, the accompaniment of two great symphony orchestras, the assembly of a distinguished cast of cinema stars. And he added: "All these riches, all these modifying and reconditioning circumstances, may have something to do with the fact that at the moment these notes are being written, a few days ahead of broadcast (a few days in radio being the equivalent of eighteen years in other professions), I have just destroyed the fourth complete script and am starting on a fifth."[7]

Aboard the *Twentieth Century Limited*, Corwin closeted himself in a compartment to complete the script. But he was concerned about reimbursement, having waived his fee. He had volunteered to do the show for only expenses, and now was short of travel compensation; so at Cleveland he wired Lewis:

> Despite voluminous sheaf of vouchers, no allowance was made for compartment and I am having to underwrite the difference. Please straighten this out with Washington so I am not left holding the bag. May I once again emphasize urgency of information regarding Stewart.[8]

The reference was to actor James Stewart, whom Corwin had early envisioned as his narrator. Stewart, who had joined the U.S. Army Air

Corps eight months before, held the rank of corporal and was stationed at March Field in California. Negotiations had gone forward to gain his release for an appearance on the Bill of Rights program.

As he wrote and rewrote the script, from Washington to the West Coast, Corwin mentally cast a star in each part. At almost every stop along the way, he sent telegrams to secure outstanding performers, such as Marjorie Main, Edward Arnold, Orson Welles—a million-dollar assemblage of talent who, due to the program's national significance, waived their fee as well.

In Chicago, Corwin made connections with the *Chief* at the Santa Fe terminal and again, confined in his compartment, pecked away at a portable typewriter as the script slowly, agonizingly took shape. He did not leave his accommodations, not even to see his agent, Nat Wolff, who with his wife, actress Edna Best, happened to be on the same train. He sat alone with his thoughts and notes as he tried to piece together the poetry of a hope and struggle and deep concern for a country that was, even then, passing his window in a panoramic blur. It was Sunday, December 7.

That afternoon, Corwin rang for the porter. He wanted to rent a radio to hear the *Screen Guild Theatre*, which on this Sunday evening had scheduled a broadcast from Hollywood of his play *Between Americans*, with Orson Welles. The porter, however, shook his head; there was not a radio to be had. The porter was surprised that Corwin had not heard the news. "Why, suh, th' Japs have bombed Pearl Harbor!"[9]

Speculation coursed through the train as passengers hovered in groups to listen to late developments or discuss the news. Corwin joined Nat and Edna Wolff to listen to their radio. They sat quietly as repeated bulletins and successive programs detailed every known fact about the attack. By evening, the news was no longer news and regular programming resumed. *Between Americans* was the first uninterrupted half-hour on CBS after the bombing of Pearl Harbor.

At the next stop, Kansas City, Corwin tried to telephone Lewis, but all lines to Washington were busy; so he dispatched a telegram. His question: Was the Bill of Rights show still on?

Lewis, at the receipt of Corwin's query, immediately contacted MacLeish, who had a hurried conference with the President. MacLeish then notified Lewis of the decision, and Lewis wired Corwin:

For your guidance we believe it is of even greater importance now than before to carry on with the Bill of Rights broadcast. Emphasis of course should be on the Bill of Rights as a symbol of what we are defending, but should not be a fighting piece. It is hard to advise you without knowing your thoughts or seeing the script, so please rush the script to us the first opportunity and then call me when you get to Hollywood. Great danger at the moment is that everyone is getting a bit hysterical, so try to keep a reasonable perspective on the overall issue.[10]

With the awesome responsibility of representing his country at war, Norman Corwin was spurred by an added incentive. Now it was more than a commemorative piece. It embodied an ideal and a purpose for fighting that was both timely and urgent.

At Albuquerque, Corwin received these instructions:

A Roberts car will be ready for you at the depot upon your arrival and I have reserved comfortable and quiet quarters for you at the Beverly Hills Hotel. Sterling Tracy, with whom you have previously worked, has been assigned as your aide.[11]

The *Chief* arrived in Los Angeles on December 9 and Corwin found the limousine waiting. At the Beverly Hills Hotel, he made several telephone calls that afternoon—one to Lewis, who again pleaded to see the script as soon as possible. Corwin was weary, so he had dinner and retired early.

He was up at dawn, for there was much to be done. He summoned Tracy, his assistant, and outlined preparations for the production. These involved cast commitments, studio schedules, clearances, coordinating the network feed, formulating effects, and keeping Washington informed. Corwin then conferred with Herrmann about music for the program and promised him the remainder of the script by the next day.

To make good his promise, Corwin decided to stay up that night, and locked himself in his hotel suite with the intention of completing the final pages of *We Hold These Truths* (despite the title, it was more commonly referred to as the "Bill of Rights Show"). Los Angeles, somewhat paranoiac by its perceived proximity to Japan, had its first blackout that evening. Corwin worked on through the excitement.

Although the structure of the program emerged easily, chronologically, the close came hard. It took him all night, but he finished the script with a powerful, concluding sequence. It began quietly with a solemn, almost reverential introduction of ordinary citizens ("Ladies and gentlemen, an auto worker . . .") and climaxed with a soaring, emotional acclamation of the citizen-narrator who surveyed the nation ("From men beneath the rocking spars of fishing boats in Gloucester . . .").[12]

The call for first rehearsal was Friday evening, December 12. Earlier that day, Corwin had lunch with Orson Welles' manager, Jack Moss, who said that Welles felt it was "one of the greatest scripts ever written for radio."[13]

Lewis, in consummating the prime-time four-network broadcast, arranged for the program to originate from the CBS Hollywood affiliate, KNX, at Gower and Sunset. There, in a large playhouse studio of the station, Corwin assembled an impressive cast, which included Edward Arnold, Lionel Barrymore, Walter Brennan, Bob Burns, Walter Huston, Marjorie Main, Edward G. Robinson, Rudy Vallee, Orson Welles, Corporal James Stewart, and a supporting complement of American Federation of Radio Artists performers.

As customary, Corwin's approach was a blend of informality and businesslike dedication. He sat on the edge of the stage, his feet dangling, and spoke to the actors, who occupied the first several rows of seats in the empty theatre. He told them of the event, the purpose of the play, and the rehearsal schedule. He assigned parts and directed the first reading of *We Hold These Truths*.

Corwin listened, interjecting comments only to clarify procedure or characterization. Mostly, he sat silently, listening. At last, when Jimmy Stewart completed the final speech of the play, there was a brief hush. Then, suddenly, spontaneous applause erupted as the entire cast showed its approval. "It was not until then," Corwin said, "that I really felt I had something."[14]

The next day, Bob Burns and Edward G. Robinson expressed excitement over the program, and Orson Welles, who repeated what Moss had already told Corwin, backed his enthusiasm with an inspired performance in rehearsal. In his role as an interior narrator, Welles occupied stage center in a declaration that depicted the pain and oppression that had cried all through history for a bill of rights.

Emotionally, he recalled times of tyrants and matters of suffering, suggesting:

> . . . The men of Congress were collaborated with. They added up the gains and losses and the brave words spoken and the brave songs sung; they weighed the drawn and quartered flesh, they took into account the hemlock and the crucifix, the faggot and the garrote. And then they framed amendments to the Constitution.
>
> MUSIC: STOPS
>
> Out of the agonies, out of the crisscrossed scars of all the human race, they made a bill of rights for their own people—for a new, a willful and hopeful nation—made a bill of rights to stand against the enemies within: connivers, fakers, those who lust for power, those who make of their authority an insolence . . .[15]

We Hold These Truths was to involve originations from three cities. The program proper was to come from Hollywood, which would be followed by a live remote from the White House in Washington, then conclude with the playing of the national anthem in New York. While Corwin trusted the feasibility of engineering to effect the relay without difficulty, he was much concerned about continuity and the emotional impact of the switch—especially the transcontinental link with the President.

On Sunday the 14th—the day before broadcast—he sent a telegram to Douglas Coulter at CBS in New York:

> Trust it is definitely understood that there will be no further introduction to the President when control switches to Washington, inasmuch as Stewart's cue line "Ladies and gentlemen, the President of the people of the United States" is ample and must be allowed to carry full formality of introduction; otherwise, whole dramatic development and intention of show will be wasted. Therefore, please make sure no announcer in the White House unnecessarily repeats the introductory line or is any way interposed between the cue line and the voice of the President.[16]

That afternoon, he held a rehearsal for Jimmy Stewart alone.

On the day of the broadcast, December 15, 1941, most newspapers printed the normal Monday night schedule of radio listings without reference to any change in regular programming. The few that accommodated the change simply noted it as a "Bill of Rights Special," a generic indication given to other events, including several political speeches which marked the occasion. One notable exception, though fraught with errors, was published by the *Washington Post:*

> 10:00—All stations. President Roosevelt is heard in an hour-long, all-network dedication to Bill of Rights Day. He is introduced by former Chief Justice of the Supreme Court, Charles Evans Hughes. [Incorrect: The introduction would be by actor James Stewart] Leopold Stokowski leads the Philadelphia Orchestra [Incorrect: It would be the NBC Symphony Orchestra] in "The Star Spangled Banner." Helen Hayes reads the Bill of Rights [Incorrect: She would not appear on the program] and Norman Corwin's playlet "We Hold These Truths" is acted by Lionel Barrymore, Walter Huston, Edward G. Robinson, and Bob Burns.[17]

Around midafternoon, the cast assembled in Studio A at KNX. Corwin first ran through several difficult sections of the script, then directed a dress rehearsal which reached a peak of near perfection. Corwin was elated, of course, yet concerned. He knew the theatrical tradition that a fine dress rehearsal forecast a bad show. He emerged from the control room to express tempered praise, seasoned with suggestions which, he hoped, might inspire a new plateau of performance. He then called a break before air time.

A few minutes before seven o'clock, Pacific Coast Time, the cast stood ready on the stage of the KNX playhouse studio. Some sat in metal folding chairs, others stood quietly, talking or staring into the darkness of the empty theatre. At length, Corwin raised his arms. Stand by. A hush engulfed the group. Corwin cued the announcer.

"We—Hold—These—Truths!"

Herrmann's baton brought forth a fanfare, which segued into a mood version of "America, the Beautiful." Over this, Walter Huston spoke a prologue which heralded this as a program "about the making of a promise and the keeping of a promise," a program about the rights of people, on which would be heard the voices of Americans and the voice of the President. It would be a program, he said, about the Bill of Rights.

The music ended; then the strong voice of a great actor announced: "My name is [Lionel] Barrymore. I'm one of several actors gathered in a studio in California near shores that face an enemy across an ocean pacific in name only. . ."[18] He named the participants in alphabetical order.

After a full statement, the music alternately rose and dipped for some of Corwin's finest poetical images, as read by Elliott Lewis:

> One hundred fifty years is not long in the reckoning of a hill. But to a man it's long enough.
> One hundred fifty years is a weekend to a redwood tree, but to a man it's two full lifetimes.
> One hundred fifty years is a twinkle to a star, but to a man it's time enough to teach six generations what the meaning is of Liberty, how to use it, when to fight for it!

There was a sharp punctuation in music and the orchestra quickly assumed an energetic beat, mixing with the mingled sounds of the city as Corporal Stewart (the "Citizen") asked, "Have you ever been to Washington, your capital?" His narrative surveyed the city, its monuments, its sayings, and soon involved the musings of a tourist:

> CITIZEN: The tourist thinks that over . . .
> TOURIST: "The noblest motive is the public good."
> CITIZEN: . . . and with this in mind, he climbs the marble stairs inside the library—to come at length upon a case containing a handwritten document.
> TOURIST: (reading slowly) "The engrossed original of the Constitution of the United States of America."
> CITIZEN: He sees the manuscript is aging, that its words are worn as though from use. The writing's dim; it's hard to make it out—it's getting on in years . . .[19]

A voice, as faint as the document itself, began low, beneath, speaking the hallowed language, "We, the People of the United States . . . ," as the Citizen observed in intimate perspective the nature and importance of the manuscript. But the "voice of the document" finally surfaced, to become the actual reading of the paper at the Confederation Congress, the listener being witness to a flashback. Thus Corwin fused the present with the past and brought to life the atmosphere and events of an earlier time.

As Corwin feared, the excellent dress rehearsal had been an ill omen; the program was just under way when things began to go wrong. One actor "stretched" a speech, another began an emotional passage at a pitch too high, a third surprised Corwin with a reading not heard in rehearsal. And once, Stewart misinterpreted the director's signal and, having left his isolation booth, missed a line when he was unable to return in time.

For sixty million people, however, the errors went unnoticed as the emotion and momentum of the program swept the country with profound meaning. For them, *We Hold These Truths* translated a historical document into a living, timely, pragmatic attitude toward a new experience: a state of war. And significantly, they saw a soldier cast as a citizen, a symbol of national transition.

Corporal James Stewart entered the closing moments of the docudrama with emphasis and sincerity. Backed by an expansive musical mood that brimmed with expectation, Stewart's voice trembled as he reached the climax:

> —affirmation! Yes! United proudly in a solemn day! Knit more strongly than we were a hundred fifty years ago! Can it be progress if our Bill of Rights is stronger now than when it was conceived?

On this line, Stewart's voice broke. However, without losing stride, he pounded home the conclusion:

> Americans shall answer. For they alone, they know the answer. The people of America: from east, from west, from north, from south![20]

The orchestra swelled to a triumphant ending; then Stewart stepped back to the microphone. As a personification of an abiding Corwin concern, the "Common Man," the actor introduced, with quiet dignity, "the President of the people of the United States." It was another note of effective irony: an army corporal introducing his Commander-in-Chief.

President Roosevelt had not heard the program. He had been in conference with several top advisors, and when an aide informed him that the radio drama was concluding, he took his place before the microphone, installed in his office. At Stewart's introduction, the President spoke:

> Free Americans—no date in the long history of freedom means more to liberty-loving men in all liberty-loving countries than the fifteenth day of December, 1791. On that day 150 years ago, a new nation through an

elected congress adopted a Declaration of Human Rights which has influenced the thinking of all mankind from one end of the world to the other . . .

There were exceptions to this concern for liberty and the individual pursuit of happiness, the President noted, and he named the enemies of the nation as Germany, Italy, and Japan. He singled out Germany and the policy of Hitler and he declared that "the issue of our time, the issue of the war in which we are engaged is the issue forced upon the decent, self-respecting peoples of the earth by the aggressive dogmas of this attempted revival of barbarism." FDR then sounded a challenge to "secure these liberties" in the world and, he said, it was "for that security we pray, for that security we act, now and forevermore."[21]

The switch was made to New York, where the program was completed with the playing of the national anthem by the NBC Symphony Orchestra under the direction of Leopold Stokowski.

In Hollywood, Corwin breathed a sigh of relief. In spite of its complex three-city pickup, the program had gone reasonably well. There had been mistakes, but Corwin was confident that his production had effectively represented the occasion. And yet, the CBS control room telephone—of which Corwin observed that "few barometers of success are more dependable"[22]—was silent.

Nat and Edna Wolff had observed the production from the control room and, reading Corwin's uncertainty, hastened to assure him that the show had been an unequivocal success. He was not convinced. In times past, Corwin had been involved for hours fielding congratulatory calls, and for efforts far less significant than this four-network colossus. He felt miserable, and later remembered, "I was sure the show had been a flop, and I burned with shame and disappointment."[23]

Then, suddenly, the phone rang. To Corwin's dismay, it was a young lady, a brief acquaintance from some long-forgotten Hollywood *soirée* who had heard the program and was calling only to invite him to a party.

The Wolffs urged Corwin to join them at Romanoff's for a drink. Actor Herbert Marshall and his wife happened to be at the restaurant when they arrived, and he came over to tell Corwin that they had been much impressed by the program. This, the first appraisal from an impartial source, made Corwin feel somewhat better. The Marshalls joined them and they talked of the program and sundry things, but Corwin found himself drifting to the edge of the discussion. At length, he excused himself to make several telephone calls. He needed reassurance.

He first called his brother in New York. Al thought the show was first rate, truly outstanding. Corwin then telephoned his friend Charles Laughton, who seemed noncommittal and somewhat "indifferent." Neither call brought satisfaction.

He rejoined the group, but he could not become absorbed in the conversation and soon decided to return to the hotel for some sleep. He was very tired.

Corwin awoke the next morning to one of the most memorable days of his life. For the first time, he learned why there had been little reaction the night before. Listeners, confused because of the three-city origination and the four-network transmission, simply had not known where to call. There had been an overwhelming response, nevertheless. Western Union had labored through the night, delivering sacks of telegrams to Stewart, Herrmann, and to Corwin.

Bill Lewis had not heard the broadcast. He and Merservey had tried desperately to pick up the program on a portable radio in his Dorchester House apartment, but reception was terrible. According to Lewis, "Interference was so bad, you couldn't distinguish sound effects from static."[24] Not knowing exactly what to say, he had not bothered to call the night of the show, and the next day, after learning of its success, he sent belated congratulations for what he then knew to be "an epochal program."

President Roosevelt also learned the following day, from Archibald MacLeish, that the program had been widely acclaimed. In discussing it, he canted his cigarette holder at a rakish angle and joked, "So you've made an actor of me!"[25]

MacLeish wired Corwin:

> Never in my life have I so wholeheartedly congratulated a man on a magnificent job done as I do you and all those associated with you on last night's broadcast. The reaction here in Washington and in all quar-

ters is all and more than you could have imagined in your wildest dreams. All my regards.[26]

Composer Jerome Kern, whom Corwin had never met, sent the following message:

This emotionally shaken household, together with every American within earshot of a radio, thanks and blesses you for that miracle program.[27]

Irving S. Cobb, well-known philosopher, writer, and humorist, had not absorbed the credits, but he wired the Don Lee Network:

Praise God from Whom all blessings flow! Whoever wrote tonight's Bill of Rights broadcast wrote the enlistment papers for a hundred thousand free American volunteers tomorrow morning.[28]

And Clifton Fadiman:

Your job last night made radio history. I listened with a large group of friends, widely assorted in background. There was not one who was not almost moved to tears.[29]

Literally thousands of telegrams and letters poured into Hollywood, Washington, and New York. Corwin even received a letter from a prisoner in Sing Sing, who sent the writer-producer a handsome hand-carved box. And while there appeared to be no negative response to the broadcast, there were a few letters from people of dubious motive. One suggested that Corwin team with him "to rule the world."

A few newspapers hailed the Corwin work, but most concentrated on the President's "address to the nation." Many carried detailed accounts of Roosevelt's comments, and several, notably the *New York Times,* included the complete text of Mr. Roosevelt's eight-and-one-half-minute talk.[30]

We Hold These Truths had touched a sensitive nerve of nationalism and was perceived as the model for a new, wartime challenge confronting the medium. *Variety* noted that the program typified "a modern attempt to translate into the vernacular the abstract idealism of ideas exemplified on the screen by Frank Capra, on the stage by

Robert Sherwood, in poetry by Carl Sandburg, Stephen Vincent Benét, and Corwin himself."[31] Robert J. Landry wrote:

> Actually, Norman Corwin and his documentary-type of program had
> both been familiar phenomena of the American radio scene, but it was
> on this night of December 15, 1941 that millions of Americans and
> myriads of government functionaries first really discovered the man
> and his talent. Both were promptly adopted as the archetypes, and the
> future of hundreds of war-message programs to come thereby prede-
> termined.[32]

The afternoon of December 16, the day after the broadcast, Nat
Wolff stopped by his client's hotel to pick up Corwin for an appointment with Dore Schary. Schary, head of production at MGM, had
made known his interest in Corwin as a film writer. In the car, Wolff
informed Corwin that the radio writer's salary had doubled since the
Bill of Rights show.

Schary was stoic when told; he obviously wanted Corwin at any price,
and he immediately offered a seven-year contract at a salary twice what
Metro-Goldwyn-Mayer had previously mentioned—almost four times
what Corwin was making at CBS. It was tempting, but Corwin weighed
the artistic restraints which he knew were inevitable in the motion
picture industry. He chose to remain in radio.

The mecca of moviemaking, however, was not without attraction.
Corwin enjoyed the West Coast weather and he had made a number
of friends in Hollywood. The very next day, in fact, he had dinner
with Clark Gable and Carole Lombard. He felt relaxed, at ease, and
thought he might stay on a week or so.

CBS, meanwhile, courted him intensively after his recent triumph.
Network officials urged him to return to New York as soon as possible.
He decided he would let them wait.

THE CORWIN BROTHERS. Sixteen-year-old Norman, left, sits with brothers Emil and Al on the front steps of their Winthrop home. (Corwin Collection)

SAM AND ROSE. Corwin's parents "pretend," posed before a network microphone by son Emil, an NBC publicist. (Corwin Collection)

WE HOLD THESE TRUTHS. Corwin rehearses Cpl. Jimmy Stewart, his narrator, for one of America's most significant broadcasts. (CBS)

WE HOLD THESE TRUTHS. The cast, including such Hollywood luminaries as (left to right) Orson Welles, Rudy Vallee, Edward G. Robinson, Bob Burns, Jimmy Stewart, Walter Brennan, Edward Arnold, (seated, left to right) Lionel Barrymore, Marjorie Main, and Walter Huston, posed with Norman Corwin (center). (CBS)

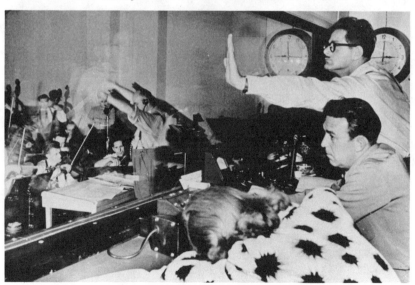

CORWIN IN ACTION. Norman Corwin directs, while Lud Gluskin, the orchestra leader, awaits his cue. (CBS)

THE CONTROL ROOM TELEPHONE. "Few barometers of success are more dependable." Corwin fields a congratulatory call. (CBS)

7. The War: Radio to Arms

There are no barefoot pleasures in these hobnailed times.
The world is burning; it is burning.

—Psalm for a Dark Year

With war, American radio took on new meaning. Its pervasive influence, as proven by the Axis, was regarded more with alarm than optimism by U.S. leaders. And yet it was acknowledged that should war become a reality, the medium might be mobilized as a prime mover of home-front readiness and morale. It had been decided by broadcast executives, even months before Pearl Harbor, that if the country entered the fray, domestic radio would observe three objectives: maintain normal programming, provide prompt and adequate news, and air governmental appeals and provocations of patriotic action.[1]

Yet, with the advent of war that fateful December 1941, both government and broadcasting seemed without an operable plan or strategy. Radio, bound by commercial commitments and entwined in a profusion of governmental controls, was slow to act in any meaningful way to reinforce the nation's resolve.

In Washington, the Office of Facts and Figures viewed with trepidation the lethargy of radio's transition. Hobbled by its self-imposed policy of neutrality toward issues, the medium seemed shy and uncertain. Regular programming only gently absorbed a sense of crisis. There were, of course, pointed references to conditions of war in the commentary or discussion programs. Soap operas assumed postures of patriotism and dealt with problems related to the conflict. Comedians continued to ridicule Hitler, and began reaping laughs from the citizen-trials of army training. But the steel-trap, hard-line, brutally frank approach to the cruel realities of war was missing.

Robert J. Landry, radio editor of *Variety,* offered an explanation. "Of course, American radio had no plans for war. We had no blueprints, no spare antennae, no passwords, no sealed orders. Above all, we had no corps of propaganda masterminds standing by complete with directives for psychological blitzkriegs. To have possessed these things would have been, in a very subtle sense, profoundly un-American."[2]

To fill an obvious and critical void, OFF officials Archibald Mac-Leish and William B. Lewis met with other concerned leaders of government and industry to discuss the mobilization of radio. And with the recent *We Hold These Truths* as an object lesson, the group agreed that a major effort of emotional programming should saturate the country; indeed, would air on all networks, with telling, candid, authentic impressions of war and the enemy the nation now faced.[3]

It was decided that Norman Corwin should direct the series. By his work and his belief, Corwin obviously harbored an intense antagonism toward fascism—an important requisite for the task. And to organize America's first war-effort radio series, OFF authorities asked an advertising executive of N. W. Ayer and Sons, H. L. McClinton, to be the producer. The series would be called *This Is War!*

Corwin celebrated his return to CBS by directing a repeat of *The Plot to Overthrow Christmas,* from California on the eve of Christmas 1941, then retired to the C-Bar-G Ranch in Victorville for a much needed rest. The vacation was cut short, however, when, on New Year's Day, he was summoned East for "an important assignment." He took a train as far as Chicago, then flew to New York. At 485 Madison Avenue, he was briefed on the OFF plan to institute a domestic indoctrination series concerning the war. He left immediately for Washington.

On the evening of January 5, 1942, Corwin, in company with Bill Lewis and "Hay" (for Harold) McClinton, attended a wrestling match. They were relaxing after a long day of conferences, which had been attended by representatives of various government agencies. The Washington meetings had formulated policy and plans for the proposed series of broadcasts, which, according to McClinton, would depart "radically in style and character from any previous formula, in an attempt to make an honest and convincing presentation of the issues of the war to America."[4]

For the next few weeks, Corwin shuttled back and forth between New York and Washington as details to implement the series were worked out. On January 10 he interviewed writers in New York, only to decide later, with McClinton, to abandon the idea of non-name writers and seek proven authors, among them George Faulkner, Philip Wylie, Ranald MacDougall, Maxwell Anderson, and Stephen Vincent Benét.

Again in Washington, on January 20, Corwin visited the White House to meet Alexander Woollcott. The noted critic and raconteur was at the time residing at the executive mansion as the "court jester" and confidant of the President.[5] The meeting led to an invitation to write a speech for President Roosevelt, a task which occupied Corwin until 3:15 the following morning. To his knowledge, it was never used.

Both OFF and the networks wanted the series to start immediately, but Corwin strongly felt that it should be delayed until adequate research and preparations had been completed—at least another two months. "I felt *This Is War!* was such a large undertaking that it would have been better to have studied the subjects much more thoroughly before starting the series."[6] Government principals, however, were adamant in their expressed need for immediate radio action.

Although the Office of Facts and Figures had officially defined the objective of *This Is War!*, McClinton made sure, at Corwin's urging, that only those directly involved would decide program subjects, the style of presentation, and matters of aesthetics. Advice and counsel of the OFF would of course be observed, but timeliness might dictate schedule or topic changes.

The inauguration of this historic series occurred on St. Valentine's Day. According to Sherman Dryer of the University of Chicago, on the night of February 14, 1942, "America put aside lace and sentiment and got tough."[7] The introductory program, written by Norman Corwin, was titled *America at War*. It opened with unconventional candor:

> What we say tonight has to do with blood and with love and with anger, and also with a big job in the making. Laughter can wait. Soft music can have the evening off. No one is invited to sit down and take it easy. Later, later. There's a war on.[8]

Variety joined a chorus of approving reviews by describing the program as "a hypodermic of emotional vitamins" that had been "written, acted, and directed with angry intensity." The show business journal called it "a tough-talking, spade-calling, spine-walloping propaganda of pugnacity."[9] The program was narrated by Lieutenant Robert Montgomery, Hollywood actor turned naval officer.

To most listeners, unaccustomed to this courageous stand by radio, it was an electric, awesome experience. One account told of passengers listening in a clubcar crossing the Rockies—of being so gripped by the program's intensity that absolute silence existed throughout the thirty-minute broadcast; of the porter who, for the sake of the listeners, stood ready to increase the volume of the radio should the train enter a tunnel.[10]

Despite the promising premiere, the second show of the series proved disappointing. Titled *The White House,* it tried to depict the executive mansion as a significant symbol and centerpiece of America's war policy. But problems beset the effort early.

William N. Robson, who had been commissioned to write the program, was denied the privilege of doing his research in the White House. Within the aura of wartime secrecy and without such cooperation, he found the assignment difficult. The script, moreover, was subjected to policy revisions. The mutilated remains ultimately reached production with little resemblance to Robson's work. He asked to have his name removed from the credits.

Variety observed, "In the general letdown, even so fine an actor as Paul Muni sounded, when handed such wet cornflakes, about as animated as, say, Albert Spalding."[11] (Spalding, the first internationally recognized U.S.-born violin virtuoso, was known as an "exquisite and restrained" stylist.)

Critics considered the third program, *Your Navy,* "fair." Scripted by Maxwell Anderson, it relied heavily on sound as it offered a composite of facts and effects portraying naval power. And once again, *Variety's* review was written with reservation. It called the program "a collaboration between Maxwell Anderson and the vice president in charge of noise."[12]

Corwin was never "comfortable" directing *This Is War!* He always faced the exigencies of multiple control imposed by the series' four-network, government-sponsored status. He found himself worrying about his writers as well, a few of whom seemed intimidated by their inexperience in radio. Some actually feared the medium—as, for instance, playwright Lillian Hellman, who withdrew from her commitment at the last minute.

But *This Is War!* soon caught fire under the craftsmanship of accomplished writers who knew the medium well. Poet Stephen Vincent Benét contributed the fourth program of the series, *Your Army,* which starred Tyrone Power, and this was followed by *The United Nations,* "a brilliant, scorching script" by George Faulkner. Thomas Mitchell narrated this tribute to America's allies, a drama which bared bitter resentment toward those who sneered at the country's relationship with other nations. *Variety* commented: "The gentle listeners must have been startled, if not refreshed, by the series' sudden turn for the virile and the tough."[13]

On March 21, Corwin directed Philip Wylie's script, *You're On Your Own,* number six of *This Is War!* It featured Ezra Stone and Claude Rains.

Not unlike the series *Twenty-Six,* Corwin faced arduous deadlines as the weekly commitments of *This Is War!* came and went—policy meetings, script conferences, casting, rehearsing, and directing two live shows—one for the East, the other for the West. Each program originated from an NBC studio, and Corwin called on his assistant, Howard Nussbaum, to assume more and more responsibility. Despite the heavy production schedule, Corwin took it upon himself to write six of the thirteen programs.

One of these, *It's in the Works,* was quickly moved forward as number seven because of "the critical state of war production."[14] It minced no words in stressing the individual's responsibility (labor and management) to increase the supplies needed to subsidize the country's cause. The program, to Corwin, meant more than a statement of national priority; it was an occasion of personal interest.

Having admired the talent of Katherine Locke, a young actress who had just completed a Broadway run of Clifford Odets' *Clash by Night,* he cast her as a Signal Corps officer's wife in the upcoming radio play. This meeting marked the beginning of a long friendship which, in time, grew in devotion. At the time of this professional encounter, however, Corwin little realized that Kate was the girl he would marry.

With Miss Locke, John Garfield appeared in the play as a worker,

Henry Hull as an industrialist. John Carradine narrated. But between the first and second production, Carradine became inebriated. Panic ensued, and there was much scurrying about and forced coffee-drinking before the repeat broadcast (for the West Coast) could be managed. The crisis, which ended only seconds before air time, left Corwin quite unsettled.

With over half the programs of *This Is War!* broadcast, Corwin showed signs of exhaustion, and McClinton feared for his health. It was arranged that Glenhall Taylor would direct program eight from Hollywood, and Corwin would be granted a leave of absence. The show, titled *Your Air Force,* featured a most distinguished member of the service, Jimmy Stewart, who was then a lieutenant in the Army Air Force. The script was written by Ranald MacDougall, who with this show launched a successful career as a radio playwright.[15]

Corwin, meanwhile, accepted an invitation to join Joel O'Brien at the cottage of O'Brien's mother in Provincetown, at the tip of the Cape Cod peninsula. He flew to Provincetown, where O'Brien met him in a rented car. At the cottage, Corwin retired to enjoy twelve hours of uninterrupted sleep. He awoke refreshed, played scrub baseball, then sat down to a splendid New England boiled dinner prepared by Joel himself.

Work was never far from mind, and a few days later—April 7—he was at an awards dinner on the Starlight Roof of the Waldorf-Astoria. Thomas Dewey presented him with the coveted Peabody Award for *We Hold These Truths.* Immediately afterward, he resumed production of *This Is War!* On April 11 he directed *The Enemy,* a program which dramatized Axis attitudes and atrocities. Narrated in the intelligent, considered tones of Clifton Fadiman, this Corwin script rivaled the premiere broadcast in its bitter, propagandistic mood.

David O. Selznick, in New York for a visit, asked Corwin to his Waldorf Towers suite to confer about a series of film shorts he was planning for the war effort. For the first time, Corwin revealed possible CBS plans to send him abroad to produce a series promoting Anglo-American relations. Despite his need of Corwin, Selznick agreed that the radio artist should not leave his medium at this critical time.

This Is War! concluded with three of the final four shows by Corwin.

Concerning Propaganda (April 18) spoke of truth and the dangers of rumor mongering, and was narrated by Donald Crisp. The eleventh program was *Jimmy Smith against the Axis* (April 25), written by Ranald MacDougall and featuring James Cagney. Corwin's script *To the Young* (May 2) told of a young boy leaving home for the war. It starred Joseph Julian.

The Institute for Education by Radio was meeting in Columbus, Ohio, and Corwin had committed himself to address the institute on "The Role of Radio in Wartime." He found himself, however, too involved and too weary, and he asked McClinton to get him off the hook. McClinton then sent a telegram to Keith Tyler at Ohio State University, which began:

> When Corwin promised a year ago, he did not know that we would be at war and getting a bad licking now; nor did he know that on May 5 he would be trying to make the last program of *This Is War!* the best of the series. He has been working like a beaver for months and is very tired . . .[16]

Corwin, nonetheless, *did* appear. He spoke to 600 educators and radiomen in the gilt ballroom of the Deshler-Walleck Hotel in Columbus. He shared the program with writer-director Arch Oboler, who on this occasion created a mild controversy by his advocacy of anger and hatred as pragmatic attitudes for radio and people at war.[17]

Corwin concluded *This Is War!* on May 9, 1942, with his script *Yours Received and Contents Noted.* Narrated by Raymond Massey, it looked at mail response for the series, letters both approving and critical. *Variety,* which had reviewed almost all the programs, observed that the final show was not unlike the series itself: "less effective than well-wishers must have hoped, but nevertheless enlightening, at times stimulating, and at the close, fairly exalted and inspiring."[18]

There were complaints about the series. It had been, as promised, a radical departure from radio's long-standing position of impartiality. Archibald MacLeish, who appeared on the first program as a representative of the Office of Facts and Figures, had established the theory and theme of the effort as "the United People's strategy of truth";[19] still, many saw a dangerous parallel to the propaganda techniques of Nazi minister Joseph Goebbels. For one thing, they looked upon the four-network utilization of American air time as *forced* listening. Further, they felt revulsion at what seemed an "official" government series—although there seemed confusion among many as to the precise sponsorship. But the most serious allegation suggested the series preached hatred.

MacLeish maintained that "there is a clear difference between the hatred of persons and the hatred of evil."[20] Corwin contended that to reveal the shocking realities of fascism, to reconstruct bluntly and vividly the horrors of Nazism, was to aid the understanding of principles for which Americans were fighting. "We cannot be too squeamish about our references to the enemy," Corwin said.[21] And Robert Heller, consultant and chief researcher for the series, issued a summary report to the committee, dated May 9, 1942, which pointed out that "our attacks upon the enemy and upon the system of fascism were more vitriolic and more competently documented than on any previous American programs."[22]

This Is War! was carried on the largest national hookup ever used for a radio series—more than 700 of the country's 924 stations. The series was also shortwaved throughout the world, in as many as seven languages. People who heard the broadcasts in the United States—an estimated weekly audience of 20 million[23]—were stunned by the straightforward assault on wartime issues which pointedly involved everyone. It was courageously candid and, stripped of subtlety, assailed the Axis as "murderers, the assassin with the swagger and the smoking gun, the stumblebum set up in business by the patron state." Beyond name calling, it pointed the finger: "The fight is on, and you are in it, whether you handle a bayonet or a monkeywrench." It underscored the significance of citizen support, it heralded the fighting forces, it stressed the need for production, for perseverance, for personal alertness.

Assuredly, the effort had jolted America's nominally neutral stance. And while it was criticized for being unduly aggressive (especially with regard to "enemies within," who a few believed should be placated for the sake of unity), a summary thought suggested:

> We cannot help but conclude that appeasement is and should be a dead issue, and that American radio of the rest of the war must serve the function of seeking the truth, of speaking it boldly, and of leaving it to our enemies to worry about the possible consequences.[24]

This Is War! had been, in every instance, historic. It was America's first comprehensive attempt to use radio as a wartime tool, to inform, exhort, inspire civilian morale. Its approach had been bold, sometimes headstrong, intense, often oversentimental; but it had aroused the attention of a populace and given purpose. It had evoked individual understanding of the conflict, its needs, its urgency. And most importantly, it had posed a challenge for the radio industry to accept a more active role in furthering the aims of a country at war.

It was June 1942.

> A summer storm came down the Potomac on its way to the sea. It was a pelting, sweet-smelling rain, having picked up fine qualities on its way over the Blue Ridge mountains. I watched the downpour with the kind of acuteness that comes after forty-eight hours without sleep, when the mind goes antic with skittering impressions. Somehow, it resembled a movie storm, for the people on the street ran like extras to get out of it, and the Capitol dome loomed like a process-shot through the curtain of rain. It seemed utterly impossible to me, riding in a cab to the State Department, that the space between Pennsylvania Avenue and Charing Cross could be compressed into thirty hours.[25]

Corwin was in Washington to validate a passport and visas, preparatory to leaving for an important overseas assignment arranged by CBS and William B. Lewis of the Office of Facts and Figures.[26] The radio industry and government were again cooperatively sponsoring a special series, this time to foster a better understanding of an important American ally, Great Britain. Corwin was to spend several months in England, observing, researching, and writing a short summer series of six programs. He was to produce them in London, to be shortwaved live to America and broadcast over the national network of the Columbia Broadcasting System.

The idea had been received with special interest by the BBC and the British government. Britons had been introduced to the work of Corwin by a broadcast of *This Is War!* A recording had been flown to England by bomber and aired by the BBC, and the resulting response, as described by CBS correspondent Robert Trout, was "electrifying."[27]

It was no small task to seek unity of nations through the medium of radio. The assignment called for sensitive probing into the plight of people and a full comprehension of the country's course and its struggle for survival. In addition, he had to orient these facts to American understanding. He knew by the experience of *This Is War!* that a straightforward, honest portrayal was needed, that he could not and should not rely on "the niceties of production."

Corwin took two brief vacations—a week at Ponte Vedra, Florida, then several days of relaxation at Montauk Point, Long Island—before embarking on his adventure. Meanwhile, he was informed by Nat Wolff, his agent, that Columbia Pictures wanted to purchase the rights to *My Client Curley* for $2,600, an "incredibly low" amount, but he and Lucille Fletcher accepted ("We were both babes in the woods about Hollywood then").[28]

At approximately six o'clock in the morning of June 27, he boarded an eastbound Pan Am clipper with thirteen other passengers. After a slight delay, the big flying boat took off into the sunrise for its nonstop flight across the Atlantic, and some hours later landed in Ireland. They were transported by bus through the town of Limerick to an airdrome; from there, an English plane completed the journey to Bristol.

Typically, Corwin approached the project with definitive guidelines of authority and control. He titled the series *An American in England,* and issued a policy memo which read in part:

> There should be a clear understanding at the outset that once general agreement has been reached on the directives, scope, and form of this series, the author-director and the producer shall not be answerable to American or British governmental or any other agencies on aesthetic or other grounds, beyond the ordinary and reasonable requisites of military necessity and good taste; further, that they will not be responsible to radio agencies other than CBS; and that while counsel and cooperation from qualified sources will of course be welcome and necessary, no attempt shall be made to influence the writer and producer against their scruples.[29]

Edward R. Murrow, considered by many "the most important American in London,"[30] had been named producer. Corwin was pleased at the alliance, not only because of their long friendship but also because Murrow knew influential figures intimately and had contacts within both the government and the military in Britain.

At his arrival, clearance through customs was delayed for Corwin when the attending official became concerned about a letter addressed to the radio producer from David O. Selznick. Its contents contained openly critical views of Britain's war policies and the customs officer wanted to confiscate it. Corwin was upset. He argued that Selznick's opinions were no proper business of the British government and, after eventually making his point, was released. The delay, however, caused Corwin to miss the special nonstop train to London. Hot, tired, and hungry, he was more than a little miffed as he boarded a "local." Despite the inconvenience and discomfort, the incident proved providential.

Jammed in a train compartment with stoical Britons, Corwin soon sensed a quiet patience and determination. He studied the faces about him as the train rattled through the countryside, pausing at almost every hamlet and crossroad. The compartment was airless and the window so frosted by grime and dirt he could only vaguely see the summer scenery. He observed his fellow passengers, for these were the people he was expected to meet, to know, to tell about. Indeed, this encounter was to become a part of his first script.

As the train neared London, he struck up a conversation with an RAF flying officer. The dialogue would be remembered and included in the premiere broadcast of *An American in England*. In the program, the officer would be referred to as Hill (his real name was Smith, but "what listener would have believed that?").[31]

At Paddington Station, the flying officer parted with these words: "One thing I wish you'd keep in mind when you're looking about the country. Don't judge us by the occasional bounder you may come across—there's that kind in every country. And don't judge us by the lobbies of a few hotels in London. See us as we are—see us in the towns and villages and on the streets and aerodromes and schools. I think you'll like us."[32]

After Corwin was met by CBS correspondent Robert Trout and his wife Kitty (the former Katherine Crane, once secretary to William B. Lewis), each dispersed separately in search of a cab. At length, Trout returned with a London taxi, triumphantly riding its running board. They then deposited Corwin at the Savoy, where he retired immediately. However, his thoughts were of the people and the country he was to personify, and although weary, he could not sleep.

The next morning he conferred with Ed Murrow, and together they began the search for a suitable studio. He discovered that, due to the war, BBC had decentralized, that studios were relocated in various parts of the city. He also learned that, with the depletion of manpower within the corporation of London, to serve heavy drafts for the armed forces, it might be a problem to assemble personnel to adequately staff his productions. Indeed, it was suggested that the series might have to originate from another city—Birmingham, Manchester, or Bristol.

Obtaining an orchestra was a critical issue, for musicians seemed unavailable. On word of a possible prospect, Corwin accompanied two BBC men to Bedford, some 50 miles away, only to find the orchestra already committed. They were about to despair when someone remembered a Royal Air Force orchestra made up mostly of members of the peacetime London Philharmonic. A sixty-two-piece organization under the baton of Wing Commander R. P. McDonnel, therefore, was contracted to do the series.

To cap this good fortune, Corwin managed to secure England's preeminent composer, Benjamin Britten, to score the series, and on June 6, 1942, he had lunch with Britten to discuss the project. He found that the composer looked younger than his years—lean, thin faced, with curly hair. Britten was a mild, pleasant man and agreeable to Corwin's production requests. Corwin was to be so impressed with Britten's music that he later encouraged the composer to assemble several selections of the score into a suite.

Much of the greatness and grandeur of this extraordinary musical talent was wasted in the wanton ways of shortwave transmission. Quite early, Corwin recognized the difficulties inherent in distant, transatlantic communication and tried to test the feasibility of certain sound effects. Linked by special telephonic circuit to Davidson Taylor in New York, Corwin played records in London for the vice president's evaluation—door slamming, for instance. "No good," said Taylor, "sounds like a bomb going off." To other effects, Taylor gave cryptic comments: "Good . . . bad . . . impossible . . . fair . . . try a higher frequency . . . no, no better . . . mushy . . . very clear . . . too much echo . . ." Two-thirds of the assembled sound effects were ruled out.[33]

To cast his programs, Corwin went to great pains to familiarize himself with the dialects and intonations of British speech. He auditioned fifty actors. And though authenticity in English voices was vital, it was equally important that his narrator ("Joe," an inquiring reporter from the States) be truly American. When he failed to find an American actor in London to fill the role, Corwin asked CBS to acquire Joseph Julian. Julian, a young actor who had appeared mostly in soap operas, was known to Corwin by only one major role, a soldier in *To the Young*. He jumped at the chance: "I practically flew over to CBS to sign the contract. It didn't occur to me to bargain over my fee." The network paid him $250 per program, out of which came living expenses in London.[34]

CBS expedited clearance for the actor and arranged travel by bomber ferry, a B-25 departing from Montreal, Canada. Bad weather delayed the flight and Julian arrived in London barely twenty-four hours before the first broadcast of *An American in England*.

After midnight, July 28, more than a hundred people journeyed through the blackout to a BBC studio in Maida Vale, near the outskirts of London. The first show, *London by Clipper*, had attracted much attention and a number of visitors were present, including several correspondents from Murrow's CBS bureau. In fact, because Corwin was short of American voices, Charles Collingwood was called into service to give a one-line performance as a bishop aboard the London-bound Pan Am clipper.

Rehearsals went well for the premiere broadcast, but as air time approached—4:00 a.m. London time, July 28, to be heard live the previous evening in New York at 10:00 p.m.—an air raid alert sounded. As the sirens screamed, guns were heard nearby, and BBC representatives quickly evacuated the cast of *London by Clipper* into a small, emergency studio. It was crowded, and it looked for awhile as if Corwin might have to omit music, even some sound effects. Only minutes before the broadcast, the all-clear sounded.

Despite the tension and momentary confusion, Corwin was pleased that the show met his expectation. There were congratulations all around. Later, Murrow and D. H. Monroe (of BBC) informed Corwin that, unfortunately, the broadcast had failed to get through. The show had opened with the reporter-narrator (Joseph Julian) jiggling a telephone hook and anxiously demanding, "Hello! Hello! What's the matter with this line?" CBS engineers in New York, not familiar with the introduction, took the dialogue literally and pulled some plugs to investigate. Only when they heard what seemed a dramatic program did they resume the circuit, but by then the shortwave signal had disintegrated. A standby dance band was installed. A week later, they tried again, and the following are excerpts from the *Variety* review:

> Norman Corwin's series, after a complete failure the week before, had a practically complete success Monday night when the reception was remarkably satisfactory.
>
> . . . A fifty-piece RAF orchestra . . . was unnecessary as a small unit would have sufficed and shortwave transmission is not the ideal medium for big orchestras. Joseph Julian, who followed Corwin to England to enact the narrator role, proved an excellent choice . . .
>
> The soliloquizing was especially adroit in allowing the tourist to first mention and then have enacted the typical American misconceptions of English character, the silly ass lord, the variety hall cockney singer. Amusing, too, was Corwin's use of the quaint conceit which appeals to Americans, namely, that the BBC would remain impeccably itself in announcing one evening on the 11 p.m. newscast that the world had come to an end but the Government was, for the moment, withholding comment.
>
> Corwin continues to discharge difficult tasks of rare tact, feeling, and imagination with great artistry.[35]

Corwin had little time for leisurely tours of Britain during his first month on the isle (July 1942) and, as suggested by Murrow, he confined his research to short junkets. He avoided offices of authority and concentrated on interviews with commonplace people. He was occupied of course by diplomatic obligations, imposed by his position as a leading artist in American radio. He was invited to luncheon meetings of the BBC Board of Governors; he met socially with prominent BBC personnel, such as Lawrence Gilliam, Val Gielgud, and D. G. Bridson;[36] he was interviewed by Fleet Street columnists; and he was entertained by leading political figures. J. B. Priestley, noted author and dramatist, had Corwin to dinner several times.

One day, Corwin received a telephone call from Lady Astor, the Virginia-born viscountess, who requested his presence at her Buckinghamshire estate to meet her husband and the venerable George Bernard Shaw. A pressing schedule made it impossible to accept, which he deemed regrettable in that he missed meeting a great man of literature. On the other hand, he did not admire Lady Astor's

"Cliveden Set" politics; after all, she had pandered to the architects of Britain's appeasement policy.

Corwin's second program, *London to Dover*, was heard Stateside on August 10. John K. Hutchens wrote in the *New York Sunday Times:*

> *An American in England* finds Mr. Corwin once more writing with a poet's vision, a good reporter's clarity, and a technician's precise knowledge of his craft—three attributes that have made him preeminent in radio literature.[37]

Hutchens commended its common touch, its realistic intimacy, and called it a "major work in a minor key."

Corwin wrote his scripts at CBS headquarters in London (49 Hallam Street) with the assistance of a secretary and the occasional company of Bob Trout, Charles Collingwood, and Howard K. Smith. Upon returning to the office one day, he was told by Murrow that BBC's director general, R. W. Foot, had called to personally praise the series. *An American in England* was being transmitted to English audiences by BBC two weeks after the live origination for CBS.

Corwin was deeply troubled about his third script, *Ration Island,* and offered Murrow the option of removing his name from the credits. But after returning from an assignment, only hours before the production, Murrow read the script, thought it better than Corwin imagined, and suggested a summary paragraph to improve its potential. Corwin's diary that night indicated that "by furious cutting, tightening, and recasting, succeeded in making it a decent show."

Women of Britain, the fourth program, related the courage and dedication of Britain's distaff side. The fifth program of the series, *The Yanks Are Here,* examined the effect of the arrival of the American fighting forces in England. For this latter program, CBS president William S. Paley was present in the control room. He was in England for the summer,[38] to be escorted through official circles by Edward R. Murrow.

Two days later, September 2, Corwin approached Murrow with an idea. In the United States, Wendell Willkie had been invited by his political nemesis, FDR, to represent the President on a worldwide tour of good will. Corwin's idea was to accompany the Hoosier Republican and report developments and impressions through a series of docudramas for radio. Murrow felt, though, that it was too late to be arranged. At the time, neither could realize that four years later Corwin would indeed memorialize this historic journey by retracing the route of diplomacy as the first recipient of the Wendell Willkie One World Award.

An American in England was ending. The series had been received warmly in Britain and the BBC planned a cast party at the conclusion of the sixth and final program. In writing the final show, Corwin found it troublesome and fussed over the finale of *An Anglo-American Angle* for several days, writing and rewriting it on a bench in Hyde Park. It ultimately read:

> ... The Britons I have met were proud people, and they asked no quarter, and they asked no pity. They'd been through the fire, and they'd been tempered by it. And I thought: Americans are proud people too, asking nothing but the time and place to meet the enemy.
>
> We're a good deal farther from the flame, and therefore we temper slower, but that's not our fault. Fire's fire and this one's spreading. And whether it's to be the funeral pyre of all freedom or the forge in which is shaped the hopeful new world of the common man, was what common men were dying for that night.
>
> The train sped on. England slipped past me in the dusk. I was leaving a strong and valiant people to return to one.[39]

The broadcast, to be heard in the States the evening of September 7, seemed to go well, and the BBC celebration struck a happy note of relaxation and revelry. Lawrence Gilliam proposed a toast, with Benjamin Britten, Corwin, BBC personnel, the entire company of actors and orchestra members, and involved technicians joining in the rejoicing.

After a few hours of sleep, Corwin was awakened to the news that the show had been garbled in transmission—that it had not been received at all. The ironic fact that the final program, like the first, had succumbed to the unpredictability of shortwave atmospherics was too much to bear. And to add to Corwin's depression, he learned from a letter, received the same day, that his brother Al had joined the army. The two events made him wonder, with growing doubt, if he really was doing anything of value to serve his country.

CBS, nevertheless, placed great importance in the English project and immediately proposed extending the series. Both network and producer agreed that it would be unwise to shortwave additional broadcasts, so CBS recommended that Corwin remain another month in England to assemble program materials, then produce the shows in New York.

Free of weekly deadlines, Corwin traveled the length and breadth of England, from London to Liverpool to King's Lynn, and recorded his experiences. He watched, with Paley, from an airfield near Cambridge the takeoff and return of a squadron of British bombers on a mission to Wilhelmshaven, Germany. He had dinner with a family that he and Emil had met in Fontainebleau, France, in 1931 (they had recognized Corwin's name on one of his programs and visited him in London). He spent time with several English families, too, learning of life on the farm and in the city, and he wrote of the country as a home for the soldier: "the last house on the street, this side of Liberty." This, in fact, was the concluding thought in *Home Is Where You Hang Your Helmet*, the second of four programs in the extended series produced upon his return to America. The first, aired on December 1, was titled *Cromer.*

> Cromer is a town on the east coast of England, and this is a program about it. The program has to do with bombs and a postmaster and a rescue squad and an old church and a Spitfire and several other matters, and it takes a half hour.[40]

In it, Corwin documented small human details which characterized the warmth and courage of a not atypical English village, one which faced the North Sea and a constant threat of enemy invasion. The accuracy of the program was corroborated by a special BBC poll of the town's citizenry following the broadcast in Britain. Of the program, John K. Hutchens of the *New York Times* wrote:

> The device is simple: Mr. Corwin, in words finely recited by Joseph Julian, is looking at a foreign land with that special perception a stranger brings to a scene that is new to him. A broken clock, a doll's head in the rubble after an air raid; an old man's voice in a pub; the smell of the weather on the North Sea coast, sixteen and a half minutes flying time from a Nazi base. As you listen, a village comes suddenly alive, and with it a nation. Mr. Corwin had done more ambitious and perhaps more enduring work than this, but nothing that in its way was finer.[41]

Since *An Anglo-American Angle* had not been heard in the States, Corwin repeated the show as the third program of the special CBS series, and on December 22 concluded *An American in England* with *Clipper Home*. These latter programs were performed by American casts, with musical scores by Lyn Murray.

The assignment was observed by Corwin as more than an assemblage of notes. He had absorbed memories of a gallant, determined, reserved, and resourceful folk. He had seen a country which had kept its grace and beauty in the midst of rubble and retrenchment. He had discovered strength and resolve, which needed to be a part of the American objective. And he brought back a new regard for radio and its role in uniting nations in a time of global conflict.

The flight back took a circuitous route, landing in Lisbon, Liberia, Brazil, Trinidad, and five days later in Miami. The Pan Am clipper had no seats, and Corwin slept with his head against a shipment of hard rubber which had been onloaded at an African port. As the big flying boat settled onto the green-blue waters of a Florida bay, Corwin looked out on familiar peace and luxury. He had just left the actuality of war, and now he faced a new and different battlefront.

8. The Challenge:
Dedication and Dreams

I'm vice president in charge of a new public utility—a service dealing in dreams.

—*You Can Dream, Inc.*

The first flush of righteous indignation and optimism for an early victory had faded from the American scene by the end of the war's first year. Each day's bulletin about heavy losses and a setback somewhere in the world made clear that the conflict would be an extended challenge.

To all, it was a time of commitment. Living room windows displayed a blue, star-centered banner, symbolizing a family member in the forces. Women donned dungarees to replace drafted men in war plants and shipyards. Citizens bought war bonds, $49 billion worth,[1] and joined in countless war-effort activities: the Civilian Defense Corps, Victory gardens, serving and entertaining servicemen, even scavenging for scrap metal or other castoff commodities deemed useful to the cause.

Everybody was subjected to the rigors of rationing, through a War Production Board directive to the Office of Price Administration, limiting food and gasoline by the issuance of ration books and stamps and a complex system of points. The windshields of many automobiles bore an "A" sticker, entitling the owners to three gallons of gas per week.

Privations, yes, but the war brought prosperity too. The 1943 standard of living for the United States was one-sixth higher than in 1938.[2] Manufacturing firms expanded under the affluence of government contracts. There was a job for everyone. And Americans saw in the massive financing and production of armament not only prosperity but eventual victory.

Against this backdrop, broadcasting was an indispensable benefactor which helped ameliorate the oppression of expectancy and frustration felt by the people. As the war encompassed the lifestyle of all Americans, radio linked each neighborhood with the world, issued bulletins tempered with optimism of action on far-flung battlefronts, offered incentives for sacrifice and dedication, and assuaged concern through lighthearted entertainment and drama.

Network radio rode the crest of the war boom with increased revenue from a growing list of sponsors. Some patrons of the medium sought domestic sales with the closing of foreign markets, but many— even large companies with little to sell, in view of the monopolization of war needs—preferred advertising to paying the high excess-profits tax.[3] The windfall was exuberantly expressed in *Broadcasting:* "Business is wonderful!"[4]

Corwin, however, was concerned. He saw the onslaught of commercialism as a threat to the integrity of broadcasting. More sponsors meant less time for sustaining programs, less time for public service and experimental pursuits. Above all, he feared that the deluge of time-buying would usurp radio's essential responsibility to the war effort.

In the fall of 1943, while in Hollywood, he addressed his concern to Davidson Taylor at CBS in New York, in a letter dated September 16:

> First, let me say that I am an ingrained and sentimental fool about my feeling for CBS. I think it is the greatest conglomeration of radio people in the world, and my respect for the genius of its top men is something I have already expressed in print and spoken of in public. But the greatness of CBS has always been in the boldness of its enterprise, its readiness to gamble, to pioneer, its high social conscience; the combination of these qualities is what has made my experience at 485 such a happy one. This, and the personal charm and integrity and intelligence of men like Paley, Coulter, Kesten, Stanton, and yourself. But now we are at war. More than ever, the qualities which have made CBS great need to be reaffirmed and assimilated in and by its work. There may never be another time when so much constructive work needs to be done for the United States and the world around it. There may never again be such an enormous opportunity to help out.[5]

The new year, 1943, ushered in another busy time for Norman Corwin. The network, acknowledging a need to interpret the differing cultures and common cause of America's allies, called on Corwin twice: to supervise a series similar to his English venture, to be titled *An American in Russia;* then to write the American programs of a collaborative series between CBS and the BBC. For the Russian series, CBS correspondent Larry Lesueur was returned from Moscow to act as advisor and to narrate. The programs, to be based on Lesueur's experiences in the Soviet Union, were written by Sylvia Berger and directed by Guy Della Cioppa.

Corwin was also commissioned in 1943 to write three scripts which attracted considerable attention. One sparked a mild but meaningful confrontation with his own network, another helped celebrate the President's birthday, and the third dramatized an emotional plea in behalf of the Czechoslovakian cause for a special audience at Carnegie Hall.

CBS became concerned when Corwin accepted an invitation to write a short script espousing world peace for a commercial variety program on another network (Mutual). He had agreed to contribute to the show, *The Cresta Blanca Carnival,* because he was intrigued that an advertising agency (William H. Weintraub) was interested in radio fare which might be considered "good and ambitious."[6] He complied by writing *A Program to Be Opened in a Hundred Years.* It ran for fewer than ten minutes and was filled with prognostication:

> Ladies and gentlemen, what follows now is not to be heard today. This is a program for a date as yet unfixed; roughly, one hundred years hence . . .

It expressed an ideal, a hope for brotherhood, based on the victory of free people, and ended:

> Let us continue to remember and, remembering, continue.[7]

Columbia did not take kindly to its top artist's lending prestige to another network, and quickly reminded Corwin's agent, Nat Wolff, of a contract clause which restricted his client's outside services. Although it held the trump card, CBS was reluctant to play its hand, in view of the extensive promotion the program had received. For obvious PR reasons, the network did not want to appear spiteful; so negotiations ensued in search of a compromise. On January 13 the program went on as scheduled, but, as agreed, Corwin received no air credit.

As for Corwin's contribution to the half-hour program, the critics were divided. The *Variety* reviewer called it "the only air bubble" in an otherwise solid show.[8] Others felt the premise "not so fantastic," and one writer, Robert Lasch of the *Chicago Sun*, suggested that "if we can banish or only subdue the prejudice which nationalism has implanted in our minds, the logic of the United Nations is irresistible."[9] It is interesting to note that this short script was undoubtedly the embryo from which developed the latter-day UN program by Corwin, *Could Be.*

The President's Birthday Ball Committee, meanwhile, was planning an hour-long, all-network, star-studded radio salute to climax the March of Dimes campaign of the Warm Springs Foundation for combating infantile paralysis. The committee asked Corwin to prepare and produce a five-minute script on the "four freedoms." He consented, although he indicated that "a minute-and-a-quarter per freedom isn't much," and he wrote *A Moment of the Nation's Time.* It ran precisely six minutes, with an original music score by Bernard Herrmann.

The broadcast, *America Salutes the President's Birthday Party,* also featured Fibber McGee and Molly, Bing Crosby, Dick Powell, and the orchestras of Artie Shaw and Sammy Kaye—among other attractions. It was aired on the combined networks at 11:15 Saturday evening, January 30, 1943. *Variety* felt the program was not up to par, but it singled out Corwin's piece as an "eloquent" addition.[10]

CBS, remembering the success of *An American in England,* proposed yet another collaboration with the British Broadcasting Corporation, this time a series of exchange programs depicting the character of the two countries. It was to be titled *Transatlantic Call: People to People.* Columbia called on Corwin to conceive the Stateside programs, while BBC named D. Geoffrey Bridson as editor and producer of the English editions.

In London, Bridson conferred with England's most respected American journalist, Edward R. Murrow, who agreed to release Bob

Trout to narrate the programs produced in Britain. In the United States, meanwhile, Corwin considered Ronald Colman, but eventually elected to be his own narrator—prompting a *Variety* observation that "his non-professional manner . . . was refreshing."[11]

The premiere broadcast of *Transatlantic Call* emanated from England and was heard in America at noon, EWT, on February 7. Written by Bridson, it introduced Trout, Wilfred Pickles, Warren Sweeney, and the citizens of a North Country industrial town, Oldham, in Lancashire. "I thought the then not-too-familiar northern dialect (later popularized by The Beatles) would be interesting to Americans," Bridson remembered.[12] The program was a revelation of courage and conviction personified by housewives and mill workers, and offered candid actuality which fascinated listeners in the United States.

The American entry, which examined New England the following week, suffered by comparison. *Variety* wrote: "Corwin devoted most of his half-hour to the dead—even if glorious—past, while his BBC counterpart made his contribution of the Sunday before a living, pulsating thing, radiating human warmth and aspiration. Corwin glowed with awe for institutions; the BBC counterpart put representative common people of Britain before his mike, and the stories they told struck a refulgent flow 3,000 miles away. Perhaps, after all, we have much to learn from Corwin's BBC counterpart in how to present people to people."[13]

It was a weary, disheartened Corwin who arrived in Washington to prepare the second U.S. edition of *Transatlantic Call*. Beyond the disappointment of his first effort, he was not feeling well. He even arose from a sickbed to produce and narrate the program about the nation's capital. The show introduced the English to the city's air of emergency, of world concern, its function as an apex of freedom, its historical validity. To many, it was a marked improvement over Corwin's New England program.

The show, however, which excited everyone—the English, Americans, critics, all—was Corwin's third production for *Transatlantic Call*. It originated from Chicago and portrayed the vast expanse and importance of the Midwest. Britons were told of the great Mississippi River and they were taken through an area which spans three time zones. Carl Sandburg appeared on the program to recite his own works, remembering the city he loved as "stormy, husky, brawling . . . the Hog Butcher of the World." Wendell Willkie spoke from New York about his home state of Indiana, and a complex network of remotes heralded scenes of Americana in Cleveland, Detroit, St. Louis, and Duluth. (In Duluth, for instance, a radio reporter atop a tower overlooking Lake Superior described the activity surrounding a body of water which, he pointed out, was larger than many European countries.) It was a provocative essay for the air, proclaiming the sweep and pride of a great country. Corwin would recall this as one of his finest achievements.

It had not come without difficulty, and had almost been aborted. Chicago was bitter and blustery the March day that Corwin arrived. He was still weakened by the previous week's illness, and he immediately succumbed to the fever and aches of a severe cold. He had to write the entire show from his bed in the Drake Hotel. After being attended by Dr. Jake Buchbinder, noted Chicago physician and friend of Carl Sandburg, Corwin managed to appear for the production at WBBM studios. Afterward, still quite sick, he boarded the *20th Century Limited* for New York.

Manhattan, too, was wintry and cold when he returned; so he took to bed in his Central Park South apartment. His doctor diagnosed abscessed ears and was fortunate to obtain penicillin—not normally available to civilians because of military priority. Corwin was confined for a week of convalescence and, living alone, had someone come in to prepare his meals.

The doctor finally concluded that Corwin, due to his rundown condition, needed to move to a drier climate in order to recuperate completely. His friends urged him to take a leave. Nat Wolff, in fact, suggested a guest ranch in California south of Santa Barbara, owned and operated by actor Ronald Colman and his wife. Corwin made arrangements. CBS was notified and Carl Carmer was assigned to write and narrate the finale of *Transatlantic Call*. Corwin then departed for California, anticipating sun, warmth, and rest.

Ironically, it was raining when he arrived. For days, he was dogged by inclement weather. A fine mist and fog made each day miserable. At last, he reluctantly confronted his friend and host, explaining that the weather, with its dampness, was detrimental to his health. He had to seek a place in the sun. Colman understood. So Corwin packed and left for Palm Springs, where he found peace and beauty, and fell in love with the desert. He absorbed the warmth and ease of the arid environment and soon began to feel fit. Knowing the concern of some at CBS, he wrote to Davidson Taylor in New York on May 15, 1943:

> This is more like it . . . never have I seen such brilliant, primary, forthright sunlight day long. I have been out in it and have a good tan. You and your bride would like this country—hot and dry but a breeze stirring, dragon flies by day and bats by night, hummingbirds standing still among the bougainvillaea and oleanders . . .[14]

Such pleasantries seemed incongruous in view of a professional dispute which had taken place only a month before between the two men. Davidson Taylor, motivated by corporate policy, had requested a "modification" upon the renewal of Corwin's contract. The clause in question permitted the network 25 percent of all commercial gains (publications, motion picture or stage rights, and others) by the playwright-producer while in the employ of CBS. Nat Wolff, representing Corwin, had balked at this stipulation and in a letter, dated April 14, 1943, stated his objections:

> Frankly, I didn't expect that I would have to elaborate on my reasons for not permitting Norman to sign the "modification" of his contract. It is, and always has been, my belief that the functions of a network are twofold: one, the sale of determined facilities, two, public service. This belief seems to have been justified at the time that the networks were forced to relinquish their artist service.[15]
>
> As it was deemed that the function of a network did not include the representation of talent, it is my opinion that this so-called modification consists of very little else than a 25% agent's contract.
>
> It is a strange truth that in almost 35 years that radio has developed only three outstanding creative personalities: Norman Corwin, Arch Oboler, and Orson Welles. To retain the exclusive services of one of these men is to own the greatest prestige possible in the medium. Prestige does not have to be reckoned as a completely intangible thing—editorial comment on Norman Corwin alone has been worth thousands of hard American dollars to Columbia. And all of the various awards which he has earned have reflected material credit on the company.
>
> Forgetting completely for the moment the artistic qualities of the man himself, why not consider that he is a salesman for CBS. As a salesman, he is entitled to a weekly salary. I don't think you will question the fact that his weekly salary has been returned to you from the begin-

ning in value received. Now, if in addition to his daily selling of CBS he is sold on a commercial program, he has not only sold CBS but he has sold a tangible half-hour of time—which is the reason CBS is in business.

Norman has operated with you from the beginning in the closest possible manner, as you have with him. And I think you will agree that I have been anything but arbitrary in any discussion of contracts up to now. This modification I consider a shocking thing and, I reiterate, that under no circumstances can Norman have my permission to sign it.[16]

Such contractual disputes seemed symptomatic of a tightening, demanding medium which now, confronted by growing competition and ever-expanding commercial opportunity, saw expediency in departing from its idealistic posture. This time, the network would back down, but the issue would return and give cause for Corwin to leave network radio.

The crisis had been forgotten. For him at the moment, it was sun and leisure and long walks in the late afternoon coolness of his desert paradise—and work. But even here, he could not escape the demands on his talent, and he was soon giving thought to a request by Joseph Losey, a young producer destined to become an internationally famous film director. Losey had been asked by Jan Papanek, Czechoslovakian minister to the United States, to stage an event which would dramatize the courage and fortitude of the Czechoslovakian people. The presentation would mark the occasion of an address by Czechoslovakian President Eduard Beneš on May 29, 1943, in New York's Carnegie Hall. Losey wanted the production to be a powerful and emotional experience. So he turned to Corwin.

In the quiet of Palm Springs, Corwin wrote *The Long Name None Could Spell.* It was a crisp narrative, filled with the same acidulous irony of which Corwin's later end-of-the-war-in-Europe masterpiece, *On a Note of Triumph,* would be created. It was a brief, stirring proclamation of Czechoslovakia's stand in the face of treachery and the triumph of Hitler's will.

It began with questions, which were prefaced by a five-note musical theme which articulated "Czechoslovakia."

Do we now italicize the long name none could spell?
The word attached to no particular earth?
The label under the porcelain dish, the hallmark on the bauble in
the bargain basement?

The introduction was topped by the name of the country, and the narrator then called on his audience to witness, mentally, the image of a nation betrayed:

> Sirs: ladies: sponsors: honorable guests: white collars: countrymen:
> Stand back; make room.
> Into our midst bring now what was dismembered on the bright
>   green table . . .

The script documented the resistance of a nation which refused to die, and the conclusion cried out for retribution:

> And on the high avenging scaffold by the monument,
> The Fascist uniforms bemedaled will appear for the last time before
>   the people
> And at the given signal, they will hang who did the hanging.
>
> And free men and women will begin the taking over once again.
>
> And the long name shall be spelled and lighted in the heartways of
>   the world![17]

In Carnegie Hall, Losey staged it with gallows and placed the narrator, Berry Kroeger, fifteen feet above stage level. A red spotlight cast an eerie glow over the set. Lyn Murray conducted his own, passionate score, utilizing an organ, which the composer-conductor called one of Corwin's "best ideas to date."[18] Corwin's words rang with virility and truth and tremendous emotion, but he could not be present for the effect; he was in California. Corwin could not see the tear-streaked faces or hear the shouts and applause of overwhelming national pride which greeted his work.

By 1943, war dominated America's lifestyle. The course of conflict was followed on maps, the common sight of servicemen was revered and accommodated, posters postulated patriotism, and a dedicatory zeal was everywhere. Radio, while enjoying a record income, contributed more than $6 billion of free time to publicize the Second War Loan. Its stars joined other entertainers in spawning a USO circuit bigger than vaudeville in its heyday. Kate Smith led her show business colleagues in promoting war bond sales, mostly by singing "God Bless America."[19]

The country was united by sentiment. Everyday events and experiences were immortalized by the big-band sounds of Miller and Dorsey and Goodman and James. Listeners, overseas and at home, were linked by Sinatra singing "There Are Such Things," Helen Forrest gingerly embracing "I've Heard That Song Before," Crosby crooning "Moonlight Becomes You," or Peggy Lee performing "Why Don't You Do Right?" Song titles, like life itself, adopted the romance and rhythm of war: "You'd Be So Nice to Come Home To," "When the Lights Go on Again," "I Just Kissed Your Picture Goodnight," "This Is the Army, Mr. Jones," and even "There's an FDR in Freedom."

The motion picture was vogue entertainment for a largely transient audience of war workers and members of the armed forces. Hollywood prospered by producing flag-waving, jingoistic films to satisfy a need for nationalism and escapism. Films were grossing $480 million a year.[20]

And it was to this mecca of money and glamor that Corwin gravitated in the summer of '43—first, briefly, by invitation to serve as a well-paid consultant for a prominent studio; later by preference, as he lived between the lure of Hollywood salaries and loyalty to a newly enacted CBS series.

Columbia Pictures, having optioned *My Client Curley,* asked for Corwin's counsel in a one-day Hollywood conference and paid him $5,000. He returned to Palm Springs to resume his vacation, but not for long. CBS, at the request of the Office of War Information, initiated yet another "good will" series to interpret foreign places of wartime interest and summoned its premier writer-producer.

Passport for Adams was intended to acquaint Americans with their allies, what they were like, how they were fighting a common war. Like many broadcasts of the day, it espoused the prevailing attitude of liberal, democratic ideals which reinforced the "righteousness" of America's involvement in the hostilities.

Corwin wrote the pilot program and established the characters. The series centered on a small-town editor who had been selected by a syndicate to visit the various Allied countries. The editor, Doug Adams, was accompanied by a photographer named Quisinbury. "Quiz," confident in his experience and blunt in his manner, disliked working with what he termed a "hayseed." According to Corwin,

The relationship improved as soon as writer and photographer got to know each other, but throughout the series Quiz remained a foil for Adams. He was essentially as good an egg as he was a cameraman, but his general ignorance about worldly matters and some of the prejudices growing out of that ignorance gave Adams a handy anvil against which to hammer points intended for the instruction and edification of the listener.[21]

In a memo to network and production personnel, Corwin outlined Adams' character, his attitude and his actions. He pictured the editor as an "enlightened, fair, internationally-minded American who hopes for and believes in a better world after victory." He predicted that Adams would be disturbed and shocked at what he saw around the world, that he would acknowledge the mistakes of the past, and that he would see problems abroad as similar to those at home—his home, Centerville. Corwin felt the series should not "sell any concrete plan for world collaboration" but should be "constructive" in the promotion of democratic principles.[22]

Robert Young was cast as Doug Adams, with Dane Clark as Quiz the photographer. Ranald MacDougall, whose *The Man behind the Gun* had just won the Peabody Award, was asked to write the series. Corwin directed from the studios at KNX in Hollywood.

Passport for Adams premiered August 17, 1943, but after a month CBS officials in New York sensed that the series was not following the spirit of the pilot show and requested that Corwin take over the writing. MacDougall made it easy—he joined Warner Brothers; and Corwin wrote the final four programs of the short, eight-week series.

The series ended by mutual consent when Corwin forwarded a lengthy telegram to Davidson Taylor, CBS, New York, dated September 16, 1943:

Dear Dave: MGM offers me following deal—thirteen weeks starting screenplay of *They Were Expendable* at $2,000 weekly. Then, if I remain, contract would run 23 additional weeks at $2,000, constituting first year, with options another 36 second year and another 36 third year at $2,500 weekly. Would work with Sidney Franklin, top Metro producer. Because I wished to make myself available to CBS in case anything important shapes up within the next three months, I insisted on an experimental basis mutually cancellable week-to-week for the first 13 weeks and, beyond that, stipulated four months leave of absence from studio annually. Thus, I would be available to CBS for a total of twelve months out of 36. Am also attempting to secure contractual clause whereby if, after first 13 shows, an extraordinary event requires a big, special show and CBS would like me to handle it, I may be given leave to do so. However, that is difficult to secure unless sufficient advance notice assures the studio of unbottlenecking its own production. Considerations most predisposing to deal are these: first, sustaining time admittedly tight until next spring, commercial sale unlikely before next fall; second would be working on an important war picture for producer of integrity under liberal terms and for unusual money. Have advised Metro regarding the starting date that under no circumstances would I start before CBS felt it would safely and comfortably release me from *Passport for Adams*. Studio hopes the earliest possible in October, but I haven't promised anything . . .[23]

The same day he sent the telegram, Corwin also wrote the letter to Davidson Taylor, expressing his sentiment for CBS and, at the same time, his concern over radio's commercial onrush toward nonentity.[24] In the letter, he suggested that the network had made its sustaining time the substance of greatness in broadcasting:

> I believe the gap between CBS and all other networks must necessarily narrow in direct proportion to the extent to which they resemble each other. If all networks sold all of their time, they would be practically identical. The achievement which has most distinguished CBS from its chief rival has never been a sponsored comedian, or a variety show, or a mystery yarn, but the use it had made of its sustaining time—the *Workshop*, MacLeish, Shakespeare, Welles, Corwin, Robson, MacDougall, Murrow, *Pursuit of Happiness*, *Philharmonic*, Reis, etc. . . .
> . . . I am not one of those who spits kerosene on commercial radio. It is mainly good, it pays the bills, it makes it possible to bring Brahms and MacLeish and Chungking direct to the public. I am not sorry that we are making more and more money and selling more and more time—I rejoice in that. I am just sorry that along the way we may well lose the very stuff that made CBS what it is, a network of character.[25]

In warning his superiors of a self-serving trend which he saw as artistic suicide, Corwin not only stated a view of the medium's future, as he perceived it, but also effected a decision—backed by the Metro offer—as to whether or not he would remain with the medium which had given him singular significance and satisfaction in creative success. It was a momentous juncture.

Three days later, Corwin received a reply by telegram:

PLEASE SIGN NOTHING UNTIL YOU RECEIVE URGENT TELETYPE FROM ME
TOMORROW MORNING.[26]

CBS issued a counteroffer and, ultimately, a compromise which permitted Corwin a leave of absence to write the film adaptation of the book *They Were Expendable*. He worked at the scenario for five weeks, then forwarded a memorandum to the producer, Sidney Franklin, urging him not to make the movie. Corwin felt it could not succeed as a movie, no matter who wrote or directed it. Franklin, after due consideration, agreed with Corwin's assessment and the project was dropped. Interestingly, John Ford later resurrected the production, only to see the film fail badly against a bullish trend at the box office. Corwin's prognosis had been correct.

Without an assignment, Corwin decided to remain on the West Coast through the final months of 1943. He made a brief trip to Texas, at the invitation of the army, to instruct soldiers at Camp Hood on how to use closed-circuit radio in overseas situations. He returned to Hollywood and, as the year ended, retired to Sagehen's Little Verde Ranch in Victorville, California. He wrote to Bill Lewis:

> Your letter of the seventh reached me here at Little Verde after chasing me to Texas and back. Unfortunately, I expect to be getting back to New York just about when you plan to be in Hollywood. I am preparing a new series for Columbia and need to be there at least a month before the opening show on March 14th. If, however, I do stay out here longer, I will be reachable through KNX.[27]

This was the first indication of what would become *Columbia Presents Corwin*—creatively, Corwin's most important series since *Twenty-Six*. Like *26 by Corwin*, the new series was to be an anthology of unique originals, offering a variety of subjects, types, techniques, and avenues of experimentation.

Until now, he had devoted his talent to the exigencies of the war, in a belief that "morale is conviction."[28] He had written almost a dozen hours, and directed many more, emphasizing a need for determination and dedication. Corwin was convinced that radio's real responsibility in wartime was to keep the public attuned to critical issues, to reinforce the rationale for fighting, for seeking a better world.

Yet, he knew, to hammer repeatedly on a theme of anger and urgency might in time be mesmerized into the impotency of a cliché or platitude. Dedication to duty had to be constant, of course, but dreams had to be nourished as well; thus Corwin put aside overt propaganda to undertake a series in which listeners might lose themselves in imagination, fantasy, and fun. There were to be references to the war, nevertheless, for the cause could not be ignored.

On January 12, 1944, Davidson Taylor wired Corwin:

WE NEED TITLE FOR YOUR NEW SERIES AND THINK IT OUGHT TO BE THE NORMAN CORWIN SHOW.[29]

The eventual title, *Columbia Presents Corwin,* was suggested by Douglas Coulter, which Corwin acknowledged in a later message to Taylor confirming the starting date of the series:

DEFINITE STARTING DATE MARCH 14. COULD TRY FOR FEBRUARY 29, BUT PREFER ADDITIONAL SECURITY OF TWO WEEKS PREPARATION TO ASSURE STRONG START AND FOLLOW-THROUGH. I LIKE DOUG'S TITLE VERY MUCH.[30]

For all his good intentions, Corwin began the series in a characteristic dilemma: a backlog of only two scripts.

9. The Assignment:
Pursuit of Peace

A SOLDIER: Peace in the time of our children, and beyond them?
CHORUS: Yes.

—A Moment of the Nation's Time

Norman Corwin, now thirty-four, again found himself in a maelstrom of creative activity. The new series, like the extraordinary *Twenty-Six*, was constant in its weekly pressure, and he found little time for himself. He was still a bachelor, by his inordinate dedication to his profession, but the most telling sacrifice was a deterioration of his health, a state of physical exhaustion that made the seemingly husky six-footer suffer from chronic insomnia, nervous indigestion, and—when he was very tired—nosebleeds.

He was not deterred, however, and he persisted in his obsession. His day began at eight. He cooked his own breakfast, reading all the while, then walked seven blocks to his CBS office. Later, at home, he would write—on a clipboard, sometimes at the typewriter—until the early hours of the morning.

Columbia Presents Corwin started March 7, 1944, one week earlier than proposed, and aside from the fact that it began without a backlog of scripts, the effort suggested other similarities to *26 by Corwin*. The title of the first show, *Movie Primer,* even suggested the same tact taken by the inaugural broadcast of *Twenty-Six:* an "alphabetical" satire of the film industry, instead of radio.

Variety saw a different parallel. Corwin's recent encounter with Hollywood filmmaking made the subject of the first show more than coincidental, thought the show business journal. It commented:

> What heightened the trade anticipation, of course, was his recent resignation from a supposed $2,000-a-week film job to return to CBS at $500 in reported disgust with the celluloid industry.[1]

The paper noted, nevertheless, that it was a gentle spoof, compared to the comedic putdown of *Radio Primer*.

The *New York Post* said it was "possessed of great wit."[2] *Time* liked it and happily welcomed Corwin back,[3] as did *Variety,* which cautioned: "Admittedly, he'll not enjoy the 'circulation' he might prefer—and rates—because of the Bob Hope slot opposite him, but the Pepsodent kid is gonna lose quite a few of the 'wise' bunch if Corwin maintains par for the course."[4]

Newsweek saw in the CBS series a rare reversal of radio's obsession with commercial avarice. The magazine reported:

> More significant than the contents of the programs is the fact that CBS has given Corwin a weekly half-hour of highly salable time (Tues., 10–10:30 p.m., EWT) and has announced that any sponsor who wants to buy the half-hour will have to take the program with it. Coming at a time when almost any half-hour is potential money in the network's pocket, CBS's take-it-or-leave-it stand was evidence of an important and fairly recent change in attitude.[5]

Columbia Presents Corwin showcased a miscellany of subjects and forms and exemplified Corwin's constant search for unexplored themes. But it was more than an urge to experiment that motivated Corwin, for by the time the series had been interrupted in the late summer of '44, all but five programs dealt with current issues—most, more or less, with war. And in response to critics who wondered why he dwelled consistently on social themes and war, he conjectured:

> You have all met representatives of the school that believes there is a dichotomy between what is loosely called Art and what is just as loosely called Propaganda. You may belong to the school yourself. I do not. But then, to me the equation is not one involving art and propaganda, but art and conscience—and I believe the latter pair mix as readily as gin and tonic.[6]

As the second program of his series, Corwin created an extended version of his Czechoslovakian tribute, *The Long Name None Could Spell*. Martin Gabel narrated. About the show, *Billboard* magazine declared:

> When Corwin is good, he is very, very good. When he isn't, you are surprised. So far, no one has been surprised.

To the lowbrow, *The Long Name None Could Spell* was a thriller about Czechoslovakia, with killing and murder, with the sound of whiplash and a corpse being carved up. To the middlebrow, this was a melodrama about Czechoslovakia, with dialogue that shocked them back to the days when they ignored Hitler's speech at Nuremberg. To the highbrows, this is a searing indictment of the laissez faire, the appeasement, the stale diplomacy of the democracy, the blindness that sought to sacrifice Czechoslovakia.

Technically, Corwin was superb.[7]

The Long Name had a long trajectory of emotional impact, igniting first an explosion of fan mail that even included a letter from the Czechoslovakian ambassador to the United States, Vladimir S. Hurban, who wrote: "I want to express to you and to the Columbia Broadcasting System my sincere appreciation for the program honoring the Czechoslovak people on the eve of the fifth anniversary of Nazi occupation of Czechoslovakia. The program was most effective and I was deeply impressed." The consummate reaction came fifteen years later, when, during dinner at the Corwins, actress Shelley Winters and her husband of the moment, Vittorio Gassman, discussed wartime radio with their host. Shelley had not heard the broadcast, and Corwin obliged her by playing a recording of *The Long Name None Could Spell*. She was so moved, she left the room in tears.[8]

Coincidentally, the third program of *Columbia Presents Corwin* also involved a famous lady emotionally. A little more than a year after its broadcast, America's First Lady, Eleanor Roosevelt, rode the train which transported her husband's body back to Washington, and she remembered a haunting refrain from the broadcast:

> A lonesome train on a lonesome track,
> Seven coaches painted black.
> A slow train, a quiet train,
> Carrying Lincoln home again . . .

She wrote:

I lay in my berth all night with the window shade up, watching the faces of the people at stations, and even at the crossroads, who came to pay their last tribute all through the night.

The only recollection I clearly have is thinking about *The Lonesome Train*, the musical poem about Lincoln's death. I had always liked it so well—and now this was so much like it.[9]

The Lonesome Train was the work of Millard Lampell and Earl Robinson. Written in 1942, it was acquired by Warner Brothers, but for two years the movie company did nothing with the property. It remained unproduced until Robinson, in 1944, offered it to Corwin. Robinson, by his experience with *Ballad for Americans* and *The People, Yes,* respected Corwin and welcomed his suggestions. Corwin thought the title *The Lincoln Cantata,* which Lampell and Robinson had called it, rather pompous and recommended they retitle it after the recurring theme, "the lonesome train." He also felt that the work should not start *tutti* or full orchestra, but rather simply, with a single instrument—the banjo. Corwin decided to open with a brief prologue, which he wrote, and he enlisted Earl Robinson as the narrator. Raymond Massey was cast as Lincoln, Burl Ives the ballad singer; Lyn Murray conducted the orchestra and chorus.

The Lonesome Train musically traced the solemn route of Lincoln's funeral train from Washington to Springfield, Illinois, delineating in vignettes a portrait of the gaunt President. But it was more than historical drama; it had timely implications. Its stirring themes matched the mood of America and its thoughts paralleled Roosevelt's hard task of piloting a country at war. With determination and intensity, its chorus—like the voices of the people—soared in triumphant challenge:

> Freedom's a thing that has no ending,
> It needs to be cared for, it needs defending!
> Free–dom![10]

"I know this letter to you will be only one in thousands but, after your broadcast of *The Lonesome Train,* I could not keep silent. I had to write and express my appreciation for that magnificent broadcast." This letter, from Pontiac, Michigan, was typical of the tremendous response. Another fan letter from Cambridge, Massachusetts, stated simply, "I'm not very good at throwing bouquets but, in my own awkward fashion, I feel that I simply have to inform you of how terrific—for lack of a better word—I thought your program representation of Abraham Lincoln was."[11] Hollywood took notice, and one columnist reported that major studio executives were listening to records of the radio broadcast.

As soon as the live broadcast of *The Lonesome Train* ended, at 10:30 the night of March 21, 1944, the cast was transported across town to Decca Studios. There, until 3:30 in the morning, they repeated their performance for the recording of a 78 rpm album, a tedious process that required an interruption of the performance at the end of each side of each record. Because of a prior commitment, Raymond Massey was unable to play the part of Lincoln for the recording, so Corwin called in Raymond Edward Johnson.[12] This was the recording which, as President Roosevelt's funeral train moved through the seaboard lowland of America, radio stations played over and over again:

> A lonesome train on a lonesome track,
> Seven coaches painted black . . .

To avoid the appalling pressure evident in the development of *26 by Corwin*, the network and Corwin concluded that occasional works by other authors might be featured on *Columbia Presents Corwin*. Actually, only two programs in the series were not written by Corwin (*The Lonesome Train* and, later, a play by Jerome Lawrence and Robert E. Lee), but six repeats by Corwin somewhat eased the week-to-week commitment.

The fourth program was a Corwin original; he called it a "far-out fantasy." In it, a pilot bails out over a jungle, to encounter a higher order of natives who speak archaic English and live a paradisiac existence, removed from the faults of "civilization." The experience is respectful, cordial, even romantic, as the pilot meets a beautiful girl named Ara. Native trust is shaken, however, when he reveals that a war exists among nations beyond this place, and he is blamed for being part of the madness. He is brought to trial. The pilot persists in his plea: there is a difference between "the makers of war and the breakers of war."[13]

The play, *Savage Encounter*, had been suggested by a news item which had told of a wartime pilot parachuting among people who had never before seen a white man. Some critics thought Corwin had been influenced by *Lost Horizon* and its episode of Shangri-La, but he dismissed the charge by saying simply that he could not recall that James Hilton claimed all unexplored territories and advanced civilizations for the British crown.

Corwin next repeated *The Odyssey of Runyon Jones*, then followed this fantasy with another, one which depicted a company dealing in daydreams. *You Can Dream, Inc.* was one of the few light scripts offered in the 1944 series, and one of the most innovative and flexible of shows.

> Its structure is so loose that scenes can be removed and substituted like the suspended rooms in Paul Nelson's marvelous modern house. In my first draft I included a dentist who was bored with his work. He was provided with a dream in which Adolf Hitler turned up as his patient. [Corwin included suggestive dialogue and sound, exemplifying painful drilling and dental activity.] . . . This went on, with savage detail, until the dentist called Miss Callaway, his assistant, aside. "Am I seeing things? Was his mustache white when he came in here?"
>
> This particular daydream was frankly an exercise in sadism and much too graphic and tasteless to broadcast, but it felt good to write.[14]

On the basis that human daydreams usually seek practical, if no less fantastic, dimensions, Corwin dramatized the dreams of ordinary individuals: an elevator operator, an aesthete, the announcer of the program (Harry Marble), and a secretary, whose typewriter became a musical instrument on which she performed a "Concerto for Typewriter No. 1 in D."

The special work was created by Alexander Semmler, per detailed instructions from Corwin, to be performed on a tubby-sounding Royal. Immediately after the dress rehearsal, however, Corwin had dashed from the control room to demonstrate for Harry Baker, the drummer in the CBS orchestra, precisely what he wished in the way of a carriage return, to climax the typewriter concerto. In a final flourish, to show what he meant, Corwin broke the tension spring and rendered the machine useless. With only five minutes before air time, an emergency team was dispatched to find a substitute. The nearest office was several floors away, and all CBS typewriters were found to be fastened securely to their supports. The live broadcast started without the all-important typewriter.

At length, only a minute or two before the concerto, two porters rushed in with a replacement. From the control room, Corwin was shocked to see that it was an adding machine. He shouted through the intercom, "For God's sake, get a typewriter, not a comptometer! Do you know the difference?" A sound man nodded, tore off his headphones, disappeared, and returned shortly with a broken-down Royal. Baker, of course, was thoroughly shaken by the time the machine was set before him—barely three seconds before his entrance in the score.[15]

It was now April 1944, and news of the war's dead, commonly unveiled in cold statistics, accompanied progress reports from distant war zones. The price had been paid in capturing ten more atolls in the Marshall Islands; in Italy, the drive on Cassino had left a long list of casualties and the unofficial conclusion that it had been a "temporary" failure.

Corwin followed the morning news and felt a deepening sense of obligation to implement his talent for the cause, to help interpret the personal dimensions of this global conflict. His Common Man now wore battle dress and stalked an enemy on foreign soil, and often died in the effort. So Corwin wrote a simple and poignant narrative about such a soldier, Hank Peters. He called it, simply, *Untitled*.

Fredric March starred. As the narrator, he reviewed the life of a young man recently killed in combat and introduced thoughts and opinions of people who knew the boy best: the army medical officer who determined the cause of death, the obstetrician who had delivered him, his mother, a teacher, his music instructor, his girl, an editor back home, the Nazi soldier who shot him, his buddy. He began by establishing Hank's fate:

> With reference to Hank Peters—he is dead.
> That much is certain.

Later, toward the end, it was to be acknowledged that the narrator was actually Hank Peters himself; and he wondered aloud about his contribution. Hank wanted confirmation:

> From my acre of now undisputed ground I will be listening:
> I will be tuned to clauses in the contract where the word Democracy
>   appears
> And how the freedoms are inflected to a Negro's ear.
> I shall listen for a phrase obliging little peoples of the earth:
> For Partisans and Jews and Puerto Ricans,
> Chinese farmers, miners of tin ore beneath Bolivia;
> I shall listen how the words go easy into Russian
> And the idiom's translated to the tongue of Spain.

I shall wait and I shall wait in a long and long suspense
For the password that the Peace is setting solidly.

On that day, please to let my mother know
Why it had to happen to her boy.[16]

Untitled was more than a tender, tragic story of a wartime victim. It was an eloquent condemnation of home-front apathy, of political immaturity, of innocent and ofttimes overt coddling of the enemy. It cuttingly expressed Corwin's continuing conviction that fascism was something to be hated and fought in every quarter. It sounded a challenge for the architects of an anticipated victory. As Arthur Polleck, drama critic for the *Brooklyn Daily Eagle,* put it: "Corwin pulled the whole world together in that broadcast . . . knitted together this war and the last and the future and all the people and their aspirations everywhere."[17]

The script received wide circulation, appearing in such publications as *Coronet, Reader's Scope, PM, Vogue, Scholastic,* and the *Des Moines Register.* It was adapted for the stage and performed a number of times—especially at armed forces installations throughout the country and overseas and most notably, at Carnegie Hall, to climax a 1944 election campaign rally, attended by Mrs. Franklin D. Roosevelt.

One year later, it was selected by Gilbert Seldes and Worthington Miner for television production on the CBS experimental station, WCBW, in New York. Of this early TV effort, *Variety* felt "it demonstrated how well suited his [Corwin's] writing and style is [for television]" and held that the defects were "minor and inherent in the medium."[18]

The original radio broadcast received more than 1,500 letters; all but three were friendly. Several thought the show "defeatist" and "cynical," but an overwhelming number lauded Corwin and the network for making "democracy a live and wonderful thing." Typical of such fan mail was the letter from Robert W. Murray of Chicago: "It's the only decent epitaph for a war casualty that I've ever heard"; from Mrs. Vivian Fletcher of Washington, D.C.: "As the wife of a soldier overseas, I found it strengthening"; from Mrs. Clifford Gallant of New York City: "[It] affected me to a degree that I feel a real, new, definite responsibility not only to my own husband who is in the service, but to all our boys"; from May Forbes of Philadelphia: "My husband, Hank Forbes, was killed in action at Anzio on February 16. I did not hear the broadcast, but many people have phoned or written to me asking if I heard it."

A longtime friend, Marshall Bragdon of the *Springfield Republican,* wrote to Corwin: "You have a pivotal position in building a decent postwar world because you reach people's minds through their feelings, and unlike most intellectuals you know the limits of the purely rational appeal. Even more important, you stir people deeply, and yet somehow convey to them that they've got to use their beans, hard, to make sure that something will come, this time, from Hank's death."[19]

The most gratifying response of all came from the servicemen themselves. Corwin received letters from soldiers in France and New Guinea and Germany suggesting that Hank Peters was more than a symbol. A pilot, Robert E. McCumber, wrote: "Your Hank Peters still lives. I know, because my Hank Peters by another name, my copilot, still lives, although we saw him crash on enemy territory last spring. He lives within us; and will, unless we quit." A letter from Private Jack Rubin, somewhere in France, declared: "Hank Peters was my brother. I mourn his death as a brother. . . . He was more than a puff of smoke on a hillside; he was everyone fighting oppression, intolerance, and bigotry. . . . To forget Hank in the gay years of peaceful relief to come would be an admission to our children that we have failed them."[20]

Untitled proved one of the more important statements of World War II, for within its personal, emotional theme there existed the malaise of a disquieting and questionable future. People were moved to comment, and mail trickled in for years after. In 1972, the *NET Playhouse* thought it appropriate to present the Corwin show as the third item in a three-part television program, *The Last GI,* and it was telecast nationwide by the Public Broadcasting Service.[21]

Corwin considered his next effort "the most trouble for the least benefit derived." *Dorie Got a Medal* was based on a true incident of a black soldier who received the Congressional Medal of Honor after the bombing of Pearl Harbor. Even though the lead was performed by Eric Burroughs, the fine actor who played Nero in the original *The Plot to Overthrow Christmas,* the show, in Corwin's view, did not come off.

He was happier with the next, the ninth program of *Columbia Presents Corwin*. Titled *The Cliché Expert*, it was a fun show, adapted from amusing *New Yorker* articles by Frank Sullivan, depicting Mr. Arbuthnot, an expert of the cliché, as a courtroom witness. It was highlighted with musical spoofs by Adolph Green and Betty Comden.

Corwin then decided to do a trilogy on cities. He may have been motivated by the opportunity to resurrect two previously written scripts, *Cromer* (from *An American in England*) and *Tel Aviv* (from *Passport for Adams*). In between, he wrote and produced a lyrical essay titled *New York: A Tapestry for Radio*.

Spring days in Central Park and the majesty of a multifaceted city helped inspire the work. Corwin conceived a light, lilting, descriptive piece, spun of memories and moments of urban encounter. He spent much time and thought strolling the park, enjoying the mild weather of May and pondering a possible approach. He first considered writing it from the viewpoint of a visitor, entering the city by train or bus, plane, or perhaps by ship, but he dismissed these as hackneyed and too involved. He then hit upon the "tapestry" idea:

> . . . This tapestry, being dimensioned by a half-hour of your time and
> the arbitrary limits of the city,
> Has for its warp the avenues and for its weft the crosstown streets
> (The shuttle traveling back and forth, as you'd expect between
> Grand Central and Times Square);
> As for loom, that's what ships do on the horizons of the city
> practically continuously . . .
>
> So much for bobbin, shuttle, loom, and weft.
> Regarding individual threads, you will have to follow them by
> listening acutely,
> For there will be excursions and motifs, snatches of native song and
> speech, time signals, bulletins, reflections, and footsteps,
> To say nothing of the retirement of batters at first base and of
> ballerinas from ballet at the age of forty.[22]

New York: A Tapestry for Radio had its serious side, woven with unrest and implications of local "enemies." It advocated world unity, exemplified in the polyglot harmony of New York's people. It possessed threads taut with the strain of war and the urgency of an all-out effort, symptoms of concern that greatly colored Corwin's works with tints of patriotism.

On Sunday, May 14, two days prior to the production of *New York: A Tapestry,* Norman Corwin appeared as Fred Allen's guest. On the comedian's show, he narrated "Jack and Jill" as a burlesqued representation of his own radio production techniques. *Variety* commented that it "provided mirthful listening, while actually being a tacit kudo for the CBS producer."[23]

Columbia Presents Corwin continued with yet another trilogy, as Corwin chose to adapt the writings of three favorite authors: Sandburg, Wolfe, and Whitman. Aside from the vitality of their verbal imagery, he felt their words reinforced the character and ideals of the current struggle. He asked his friend, actor Charles Laughton, to narrate each of the three programs, and Laughton agreed. These occasions would later influence Laughton's interest in "reading" tours, as the actor in years to come would travel the country performing the works of Wolfe and Benét.

The overwhelming response to *Untitled* prompted a decision to repeat the program. So, on May 30, he assembled the original cast and directed a repeat performance. He then left for Hollywood.

While working with Laughton most of the month of June 1944, Corwin spent considerable time at the actor's home. One particular evening, Laughton remembered an old magazine, *Life and Letters,* and took it down from his bookshelf. He recalled buying it at a London "Underground" newspaper kiosk in 1928 and reading it on the train en route home. One article enthralled him: "A Murderer's Confession," the verbatim confession of Samuel Herbert Dougal, who in 1899 clumsily murdered his wife. Laughton, taken by its vivid detail, suggested it might make an interesting radio script, and Corwin agreed.

The result was *The Moat Farm Murder,*[24] a spine-tingling episode for radio which was heightened by a chilling musical score composed by Bernard Herrmann. The program, number eighteen of *Columbia Presents Corwin,* featured Charles Laughton and Elsa Lanchester. It was broadcast on July 18, 1944.

As Corwin boarded the *Chief* for New York, he faced a familiar problem: a network deadline just six days away, and not one idea in mind. His first thought was to fall back on an old impulse to do a rhapsody about trains. Trains had always fascinated him—the complex timetables, the language, the logistics of transporting goods and people from place to place. But he again dismissed the inclination on the basis that there was hardly time to create an essential music score.

As the transcontinental train gathered momentum in its departure from Los Angeles, Corwin settled to the chore of writing his next program. To expedite matters, he chose to dictate, instead of composing on a typewriter or writing in longhand. With his nose stuffed with cotton to offset a flu-inflicted nosebleed, the resulting nasal sound belied the romantic mood engendered in a developing play about a young army corporal who meets a pretty girl on a train—a train called the *El Capitan.* The script took three days to write, or the distance between Pasadena and Pittsburgh.

Casting *El Capitan and the Corporal* was no problem, for Corwin had in mind Joseph Julian as the soldier, Katherine Locke as the girl. In Julian, there was a direct simplicity that had worked very well in other Corwin roles (*To the Young, An American in England*) and would, Corwin knew, make Cal a corporal "as American as corn flakes." As for Kate, their fast-developing friendship (he said he saw her "as regularly as geography permitted") did not obscure his judgment of genuine talent, and he felt she was precisely the person to make the role of Betty "keen, yet warm; discerning and restrained, yet nicely sentimental."[25]

One scene in *El Capitan and the Corporal* characterized a true incident which had involved Corwin and composer Bernard Herrmann. Once, while en route to Hollywood to do a broadcast, the two had left their train to browse through an excellent bookstore at the depot. Time passed quickly; then, they suddenly remembered, their train had been due to depart fully a minute before. Frantically, they rushed up and down stairs and, breathlessly, reached the track, only to find their train still taking on mail.

> CAL: (DOWN) We got to Kansas City and went up the stairs to the station, and Betty took her book. Then we walked around outside the station to get a breath of fresh air, and we stood there looking at the lights. Betty put her arm in mine, and it felt to me as though it belonged there, and I couldn't help thinking to myself how nice it would be if we were married and this was our honeymoon.
>
> BETTY: Cal—how long does the train stop here?
>
> CAL: Huh? Oh—uh—seven minutes. It leaves at 11:22.

BETTY: Well, what time is it now?

CAL: (GALVANIZED) Holy smoke! 11:21! We've only got one minute.

BETTY: (BEGINNING TO RUN) We'd better run for it! What track is it on?

CAL: I think it's Track 4.

BETTY: Well, don't you *know*?

CAL: I'm pretty sure it's four.

BETTY: Well, here's the staircase down for Track 4. I hope you're right.

THEY SCRAMBLE DOWN A FLIGHT OF STAIRS. THE DIALOGUE TAKES PLACE MOSTLY IN FULL FLIGHT.[26]

In rehearsal, Corwin was not content with the synchronization of the soundmen's footsteps, and he chose to have his actors create their own by dashing up and down steps in a stairwell adjoining the studio. It was quite an accomplishment, considering the broadcast was live and the action continuous. With no break in the dialogue, Joe Julian was handed a portable mike as he and Katherine Locke left the standing mike to walk through the studio exit into the stairwell. There, he was relieved of the hand mike and, together, he and Kate ran up and down the steps, the sound being picked up by microphones strategically placed at the top and bottom of the stairs. The ensuing action not only provided realism in running footsteps but the accuracy of a breathless performance as well.

Such attention to detail and authenticity was common with Corwin. Like a composer, he *heard* his works as he wrote them, and labored long in rehearsals to achieve the preciseness he knew possible. As for sound, he never compromised with contrived or phony effects. He once dismissed a soundman's footsteps by informing him, "I know, without looking at you, you're stamping in one place. You sound like a man waiting to get into a public toilet."

Similarly with music, he seemed to reach for memorable heights in conceiving moods and expressionistic moments, and he tried the patience of composers by calling for nonexistent instruments or unusual thematic arrangements. His puckish demands were said to be "one part Corwin foolery and two parts prod of the imagination." His requests often seemed bizarre, as in this introductory cue for *New York: A Tapestry for Radio:*

AN INTRODUCTION DESCRIPTIVE OF THE ANNOYANCE OF FIFTH AVENUE AT HAVING TO CROSS BROADWAY IN FULL VIEW OF TWENTY-THIRD STREET.[27]

Or this musical cue from *Savage Encounter:*

A NOCTURNE EXPRESSING THE SOUTH SEA ISLAND YOU REMEMBER FROM
YOUR FONDEST IMAGININGS. HEALTHY LUSTS AND RED FLOWERS AND BLUE
SKY AND BARE BREASTS ARE ALL MIXED UP IN IT.[28]

On August 1, Corwin directed *A Pitch to Reluctant Buyers,* written especially for the series by Jerome Lawrence and Robert E. Lee.[29] It was a functional play, a special wartime drama to motivate civilians. This, the twentieth program of *Columbia Presents Corwin,* was followed by a romantic comedy written by Corwin solely for the outstanding character actress Minerva Pious. She was best known as "Mrs. Pansy Nussbaum" of Allen's Alley on *The Fred Allen Show,* but she had proven her versatility in many radio dramas.

Meanwhile, the war was going well. Russian troops had reached the Baltic Sea, severing the Nazis in Estonia from the main German army. There were reports of unease in Berlin, of Hitler's desperate plea "to adapt in every respect the entire public life to the necessities of total warfare," of another attempt on *der Führer's* life—this time by members of his own staff. The Americans, having taken Normandy, entered Brittany. The invasion front fanned out and the push north picked up tempo. The liberation of Paris seemed certain. The conquest of Germany appeared only a matter of months.

Such news prompted a visit from Douglas Coulter, the CBS vice president, who stopped by Corwin's office to discuss the war and the network. He surprised Corwin by suggesting that the *Columbia Presents* series end abruptly at twenty-two programs. He wanted Corwin free to develop a special program to commemorate the day of victory in Europe, which now appeared imminent.

For his final show, then, Corwin wrote a valedictory filled with caustic concern that Americans, on the eve of inevitable victory, would be apathetic to the dimensions and demands of a war that still continued. He titled it *There Will Be Time Later.*

> This is the moment to dig in.
> There will be time later for the dish that takes two days to make
> And the collection of stamps from occupied countries . . .

House Jameson, as the soliloquist or narrator, offered what Corwin described as "a clean, cutting intellectual incisiveness" to the script's timely warnings.[30]

> Some things can wait, and some things can't.
> The paint job can hold over, but the blueprints had better move along.
> There will be time later for the dividend and for further findings from a bathysphere.
> The lot on the California hilltop can afford to wait until after the cellars of Warsaw are cleaned out.
> But in the meantime noncommittal mailmen keep distributing familiar Greetings from the President—Form 215, for preinduction physical—
> And the boys who passed their physicals some time ago die on a sand dune. . .[31]

For War Bond drives, the program was to be repeated several times on West Coast radio stations.

The assignment to represent the Columbia Broadcasting System on the evening of a long-awaited armistice loomed large and important. Corwin walked the floor, wondered, worried about a sensible approach. He wanted to do justice to the event. And yet, for three years and more, he had written of war and had, he thought, articulated almost every aspect of the cause. What could be said that was different, revealing, appropriate to such a historic occasion?

He tried to think of his audience. Who might they be, where, under what conditions would they receive the news of victory? Indeed, would there even be an official pronouncement? No one really knew the nature of the end—and, certainly, it was not to be the end, for the Pacific War seemed destined to outlast the conflict in Europe. Under such circumstances, with bloody campaigns yet ahead, would people at home be in a mood to celebrate? Even so, should there be dancing in the street, shouting, drinking of toasts and tears of joy, who would be left to listen to radio?

He walked the park, fed the pigeons, perused the skyline from his apartment window, read, listened to music, even discussed his problems with close friends. He took his clipboard with him wherever he went. He tried out phrases, wrote down thoughts, and filled his waste-paper basket with discarded ideas. With the Allied advance in high gear, a victory in Europe seemed assured, and each battle won moved the deadline closer, magnifying Corwin's frustration.

It was not that he was in want of something to say. Corwin had long felt a responsibility to speak out for the principles of liberty, the moral rectitude of the fight, the fundamental essentials of the democratic process. The war had given him cause to interpret what he termed "an emotional concept of freedom." He had done it with artistry, courage, and conviction. Anger, which once inspired *They Fly through the Air* and asserted itself in *This Is War!*, still consumed him and colored his characterization of an enemy he knew to exist at home as well as abroad. His programs evoked patriotism and the optimism of ultimate victory, but within each there were echoes of concern, for the triumph to come and for the peace to follow. Now, with the end of Nazism in sight, Corwin wanted mightily to add a significant footnote to the great struggle and to voice feelings about the future. In short, he had no wish to be gay, musical, or frivolous, but chose instead to be sober and meaningful.

The fall of 1944 offered more than an expectancy of peace; there was a national election. It was a season of hope for the Republicans who, with a slate headed by Thomas E. Dewey and John W. Bricker, endeavored to end the political monopoly of President Franklin Delano Roosevelt. The incumbent was running for an unprecedented fourth term. But FDR, to the dismay of his advisors, had decided to confine his efforts to the final two weeks of the campaign.

The chairman of the Democratic National Committee, Paul Porter, asked Corwin to contribute his talent in developing an election-eve special for Roosevelt. Porter envisioned an impressive four-network effort, and he outlined his proposal in a six-page, single-spaced memorandum, dated September 15 and marked "personal and confidential." The goal, he advised, would be to create "a sense of urgency" that would get voters to the polls.[32] Porter wanted the emphasis placed not on war needs but on the necessity to press forward for reforms interrupted by the war.

Corwin, at first, was puzzled. He was a dramatist, not a politician, and the network policy of both CBS and NBC barred "dramatization" of political messages. If he accepted, he decided—and he would, for he greatly admired the President—he would make it difficult for the authorities to define "dramatization."

Corwin therefore put aside his VE Day script, despite its critical deadline, and undertook the election-eve special, without pay. "I was the dunce of all time; everybody else got paid. The agency handling the account of the Democratic National Committee, in fact, got 15% of something like $150,000. Imagine, $22,000 for doing nothing."[33] His CBS contract permitted him up to six months of each year to pursue personal projects, providing he fulfilled all assigned CBS commitments.

As usual, Corwin took nothing for granted. He detailed the conditions necessary for him to accept the project. He wanted no political-party interference, so he insisted that he submit a prospectus to the President and that, upon FDR's approval, he would have free rein to formulate the program. After seeing the two-page outline, the President's only reaction was, "My God, can he do all this on one show?"[34]

It was indeed elaborate. Corwin proposed using a number of people—union members, a TVA farmer, a soldier and a sailor returned from action, a World War I veteran who had sold apples during the Depression, an industrialist, a housewife, an old man who had voted in fourteen elections and who was asked to introduce a young girl voting for the first time, and she in turn introducing the President. A few Broadway celebrities were to be heard from New York, but the main program originated from Hollywood under Corwin's direction, with guests and many stars assembled there for the live broadcast. The President was to speak from the White House.

The Hollywood production utilized a music-backed sequence which brought to the microphone a succession of popular personalities. The montage of brief statements formed a dramatic "train" effect:

CHORUS: *All aboard for tomorrow!*

LUCILLE BALL: This is Lucille Ball. I'm on this train.

CHORUS: *Vote!*

TALLULAH: This is Tallulah Bankhead. So am I.

CHORUS: *Vote!*

JOAN BENNETT: Joan Bennett—for the champ.

CHORUS: *Vote!*

IRVING BERLIN: Irving Berlin—

MRS. BERLIN: And Mrs. Berlin.

CHORUS: *For Roosevelt!*[35]

The roster included such reigning stars as Humphrey Bogart, Judy Garland, Claudette Colbert, Rita Hayworth, Paul Muni, Lana Turner, John Garfield, Linda Darnell, Walter Huston, Paulette Goddard, Jane Wyman, Harry Carey, Rex Ingram, and Joseph Cotten—among others. A barbershop trio, consisting of James Cagney, Groucho Marx, and Danny Kaye, sang a devastating satire written by E. Y. Harburg. Jimmy Durante, set for a big spot, pulled out at the last moment—the only defection. All others stars stood fast. Radio would never again see such open commitment to a political candidate by so many top-ranking stars on one show.

The Durante departure was, ironically, a godsend. The Republicans had purchased a period of coast-to-coast air time immediately following, and many Democrats feared their star-studded effort would only serve to build an audience for a Republican last word. As it turned out, though, the Corwin broadcast ran short, after the cancellation of Durante's satirical number, and the time was filled with dreary organ music, which no doubt sent most listeners to bed.

A few days later, Corwin received a letter from the White House, dated November 27, 1944:

> Dear Mr. Corwin: The election-eve broadcast was really outstanding. As a participant, I was of course interested in what preceded me, but was not prepared for the really incredible performance which you had so ably organized. I am personally very grateful to you for your efforts in this truly brilliant program, and wish to ask you to convey to all of your associates who made possible this performance my thanks and best wishes.
>
> Very sincerely yours,
> FRANKLIN D. ROOSEVELT[36]

Corwin returned to his VE Day script in frantic haste, feeling the pressure of a mounting Allied winter offensive in Europe. The Third Army had penetrated the Saar Basin, and the Canadian First Army entered Germany from the Nijmegen area of Holland. The cities of the Reich were aflame from repeated bombings. A Nazi surrender could not be far off, and Corwin, wanting desperately to celebrate the joyous hour with his finest work, worried that he might not be ready.

But suddenly—shockingly—the "defeated" army of Germany arose as a phoenix to muster a last-ditch counteroffensive, striking at the weakest point of the Allied line, the Ardennes, in a final attempt to alter the course of the war. Bastogne was encircled and the bitter days of the Battle of the Bulge dashed hopes of imminent victory.

It was clear. There would be no peace that year.

10. The Victory: On a
Note of Triumph

As to the latest war, what's to become of its victors and their victory?
Their dear-bought, blood begotten, towering and grave victory?
Need the laurel wither?

—*Set Your Clock at U235*

Corwin's quandary as to how precisely to approach the proposed victory broadcast was resolved one evening while he was reading Walt Whitman. In the Whitman poem "Years of the Modern" is the line "Never were such sharp questions ask'd as this day."

There were questions—not only about when and how hostilities might end, but of the fate and future of the world after victory. History had proven peace tentative and fragile. Universal greed and foreshortened distances made war a constant threat. But inevitable?

Corwin pondered the current situation and the concerns which seemed paramount at this point in history, and he decided to structure his script around five common but comprehensive questions: Whom did we beat? How much did it cost to beat him? What have we learned? What do we do now? Is it all going to happen again?

He would open the program on a note of triumph, of course, but he would end with an emphasis on hope, and to effect a forceful and provocative conclusion, Corwin envisioned a prayer. It would be a statement of thanksgiving, a plea for sanity among nations, a petition for brotherhood. He concentrated on the prayer first, but revised it throughout the process of the script's development. Ultimately, it began:

Lord God of trajectory and blast,
Whose terrible sword has laid open the serpent

So it withers in the sun for the just to see,
Sheathe now the swift avenging blade with the names of nations writ
 on it,
And assist in the preparation of the plowshare . . .[1]

During the warm and waning days of Indian summer 1944, Corwin had struggled with the script as a frequent weekend guest of Jack Goodman, a Simon and Schuster editor. Goodman enjoyed company, and often had friends to his summer house in Rowayton, Connecticut. Corwin scribbled at his clipboard while sailing Long Island Sound, and often he read portions of the developing program to Goodman for his reaction. So impressed was Goodman that he negotiated purchase of the work for publication before the script was even finished.

Corwin had shelved the VE Day script immediately after the Ardennes setback to concentrate on other matters. But the assignment was never far from mind, and around the first of the year he began work in earnest. He tried out concepts and phrases on interested listeners. Once, his brother Emil. And Martin Gabel, who would be asked to narrate the program, visited Corwin's apartment on occasion and saw sections of the script in its formative stages. The script was completed near the end of January, and he titled it *On a Note of Triumph*.

The completed script received its first public hearing one evening when Jack Goodman asked Corwin to read his manuscript for a few friends at Goodman's townhouse in Greenwich Village. Among literary notables present were playwrights and producers, including George S. Kaufman, Howard Lindsay, and Russel Crouse.

The next and only other public exposure before broadcast occurred in March. Corwin had attended the inauguration of the President and, returning to New York, stopped over in New Jersey to fulfill a speaking engagement at Rutgers. With no time to prepare a formal speech, he read the VE Day script to five hundred students.

The European war, meanwhile, moved inexorably toward its final showdown in Germany. The Russians pushed into Poland, recapturing Warsaw, while the British and the Americans stood poised at the Rhine. Would the Nazis hold out to the bitter end? No one knew.

For eight days in February, the Big Three held a summit meeting at Yalta. Just over a year before, at Teheran, President Roosevelt, Prime

Minister Churchill, and Premier Stalin had met to shape policy toward an ultimate Allied war effort. Now, on a sunny shore of the Black Sea, the Crimean conclave proposed the formulation of a new world. Among their decisions was the early establishment of "a general organization to maintain peace and security," the foundation of which had already been laid at Dumbarton Oaks. The governmental heads agreed to call a conference of "United Nations" in the United States at San Francisco April 25, 1945, for the purpose of preparing a charter.

With the VE Day script ready, Corwin proposed for CBS a special program to herald the significance of the San Francisco Conference. In Corwin's eyes, however, it was to be no "ordinary" program, and he outlined his intention in a planning memo to CBS executives, which included the following statement of policy:

> There need be no shadow of controversy over any phase of this broadcast. It should be a positive and affirmative and forward-looking show. It will not propose to tell the Conference how to go about its business. It will call nobody a fascist or communist. It will have nothing to do with the mistakes of the past—Spain, Munich, or Greece. The theme will be hope and the future, will attempt to convey in warm and human terms the earnest desire of all freedom-loving peoples for the success of a conference made possible only by a hard-won victory of arms.

Corwin went further to specify his approach:

> The main dramatic values of the show should come from its sheer scope, from the overwhelming effect of unity and solidarity which it is likely to produce, from its broad frontal representation of many people in many lands, from the color and situation of individuals—both by themselves and in juxtaposition to one another, and in relation to the show as a whole.
>
> There will be a sprinkling of well-known people through the program, but . . . they will function as more than mere names: their participation will be logical and organic to the theme and development of our broadcast.[2]

Forsaking his fundamental style of poetic drama, Corwin sought realism in the program of the San Francisco Conference by planning it as a documentary with worldwide dimensions. He arranged remote pickups from foreign countries and from places throughout the nation to feature both ordinary citizens and outstanding celebrities. For the next month, he busied himself organizing split-second connections between professional and amateur participants in a sixty-minute mosaic of commentary and entertainment called *Word from the People*.

Acquisition of appropriate people was not easy. CBS correspondents, in many different lands, enlisted representative spokesmen to herald the hope for world unity: a Soviet officer in Moscow, a Chinese soldier in Chungking, a Cuban newspaperman in Havana. And there were to be greetings and congratulations from Australia, Czechoslovakia, Canada, Manila, Paris, Uruguay, and Mexico. Associate directors Robert Heller and Charles Lewin aided Corwin with logistics. Corwin himself contacted noted men and women of government, of science, of the arts. He carried out his plans with a crusading fervor, convinced of the importance of this global assembly. And when he occasionally encountered conflicts or reluctance, he tactfully but firmly underscored his impatience—as in a letter to his friend Carl Sandburg, addressed to the poet's Chickaming Goat Farm in Harbert, Michigan:

DEAR CARL:

I don't want to coax you to participate in the broadcast concerning which I phoned you night before last. Frankly, I was disappointed that you expressed any hesitation whatever to appear on a program dedicated to what may well be the last remaining hope for a better world coming out of this war.

I realize that you are busy. No doubt the Metro project is important and you have many other pressing commitments. I don't think any of them can compare with the significance and importance and historic stature of the Conference.

I am not asking you do very much. You can pick out the chair in your living room from which you want to make this broadcast. The writing involved would run less than forty-five seconds on the air; you can write it in five minutes. You're the only man in this country through whose lips the words of Lincoln could convincingly be reactivated. And I rather believe that if Abe's spirit is abroad these days, he might be a little miffed with you passing this up for anything else.

I write in this bold vein not for myself, but because I sincerely believe the country needs this minute from you in your living room. I wish I could give you a week to think it over, but I can't. I must have your answer by return wire and I hope it will be YES.

YOURS, NORMAN.

Sandburg acquiesced, and Corwin acknowledged receipt of his broadcast statement in a telegram, which read:

YOUR TEXT JUST ARRIVED AND IS EXCELLENT.[3]

In the days to follow, the CBS offices hummed with activity as the $40,000 San Francisco show took shape. Protocol and procedure to ensure fault-free transmission of a live, widely dispersed, highly complicated program was a heavy responsibility. Leaving little to chance, Corwin dispatched lengthy wires to various participants, detailing every moment, every move. To Thomas Mann, in Pacific Palisades, California, he advised:

TECHNICAL SWITCHING PROBLEMS IN WORLD-WIDE BROADCAST OCCASION REQUEST THAT YOU BE GOOD ENOUGH TO ADD TO YOUR PRESENT TEXT THE FOLLOWING CLOSING WORDS—QUOTE—THIS IS THOMAS MANN IN HOLLY-WOOD TRANSFERRING YOU NOW TO A THEATRE IN DOWNTOWN CHICAGO WHERE YOU WILL HEAR FROM PAUL ROBESON—UNQUOTE—IS IT POSSIBLE FOR YOU TO QUICKEN PACE OR TRIM TEXT TO A READING TIME OF ONE MINUTE FIFTEEN SECONDS RATHER THAN ONE MINUTE THIRTY.

Mann wanted to cooperate, but he had no desire to play the role of radio M.C. He sent a return wire:

SHALL LIMIT STATEMENT TO SEVENTY-FIVE SECONDS BUT WANT AN-NOUNCER TO INTRODUCE NEXT SPEAKER.[4]

Corwin, deeply involved in details of the forthcoming program, was working late on Thursday, April 12, 1945—and not feeling well, either. A touch of flu, he figured, but he remained at his desk that day, for there was much to be done, the big broadcast being only two weeks away. Suddenly, Bob Allison of the Program Department burst into Corwin's office. "Roosevelt is dead," he blurted out.

The first shock was disbelief. Corwin rushed out to find the nearest radio on his floor. Among other CBS personnel crowded around the set, he heard the report, which to his ear came in agonizing phrases: ". . . Warm Springs, Georgia . . . cerebral hemorrhage . . . funeral arrangements in the White House . . ."

It was after six o'clock when he left the building. He walked home, heavy in heart, sick and uncertain. He called Katherine Locke, and they commiserated over the telephone. She knew how much he had admired the President. FDR was to Corwin the persona of his own liberal persuasion. He had been, in Corwin's view, a great and courageous leader, an inspiration in an age of crisis.

CBS, of course, asked Corwin "to write something." So he expunged his grief in a brief eulogy which, although aired, was lost in an avalanche of emotion and tribute which for several days occupied the medium. Sixty percent of radio's broadcast schedule subjugated commercialism to honor the late and long-time President. But Corwin's only lasting memory was of radio stations playing again and again the recording of *The Lonesome Train,* as the President's body was brought northward to Washington.

Lou Ashworth, Corwin's tall, blonde secretarial aide and production assistant, had served him efficiently during the zenith of his career. She arranged appointments, answered fan mail, sheltered him from the persistent pressures of external demands. Now, on the eve of the difficult San Francisco documentary, she was required to organize a multitude of details. She of course joined the CBS contingent as it departed for the West Coast.

The Conference site, at the Civic Center, was a beehive of activity. Twenty-seven newsreel cameras had been mounted, the largest coverage since the British coronation, to operate as a pool under the direction of the Office of Inter-American Affairs. In the Veterans' Memorial Building, space had been allocated to the American networks, to BBC and CBC, and to thirty individual radio stations, all staffed to provide daily, on-the-spot reports of the Conference sessions.

Like a puppeteer, Corwin stood ready on April 25 to manipulate the many elements of his global documentary. But *Word from the People* was more than a mechanical *tour de force* of around-the-world remotes from six continents. It opened with the Navy Chapel Choir singing "The Meeting Song" ("You-gotta-be-united-to-be-invited-to-the-meetin'") and later featured Alfred Drake vocalizing "It's the Same Boat, Brother"—songs written especially for the program by Earl Robinson and E. Y. Harburg. From Chicago, Paul Robeson appeared between the acts of *Othello* to speak backstage at the Erlander Theatre. At the Hollywood Canteen, Bette Davis spoke for the movie industry. Carl Van Doren, Thomas Mann, and Carl Sandburg represented literature. Thomas Hart Benton spoke for the artist and Bruno Walter for the musician. All suggested the arts could flourish only in a free, united world. Indeed, Elmer Roper reported on the program that 72 percent of the nation favored a world security organization.[5]

The show was cast with simple, unspectacular people as well, who expressed feelings about international brotherhood and personified Corwin's characterization of the Common Man. This was dramatically illustrated by the selection of twenty-year-old Marine Sergeant Harry Jackson, just back from the Pacific combat zone, as the narrator.

But the optimism of the hour was best expressed by Sir Alexander Fleming, the codiscoverer of penicillin, who spoke from London, "where it is not yet light, but dawn is very near. And perhaps that phrase can be extended to the whole world."[6]

The end to World War II in Europe appeared only a matter of days, even hours, away. The Russians had already entered Berlin and a bitter battle raged in its streets. The British and the Americans advanced in northern Italy, Mussolini was dead, and a free world awaited word of victory.

Corwin hurried from San Francisco to Hollywood, the working script of *On a Note of Triumph* in his briefcase. Not knowing precisely when the German capitulation would come, contingency plans had been made in New York to accommodate production of the VE Day broadcast on either coast. Photostatic copies of Bernard Herrmann's musical score, for instance, had been dispatched to Hollywood in case the event should occur while Corwin was in California.

E. Y. ("Yip") Harburg, accomplished lyricist of such hit tunes as "Over the Rainbow"and "Brother, Can You Spare a Dime?," invited Corwin to stay at his Brentwood home while he was in Los Angeles. The two friends enjoyed Harburg's spacious garden, and were relaxing by the pool when William H. Fineshriber Jr. appeared. The arrival of the CBS vice president from New York indicated the network's exceptional interest in the Corwin broadcast. Corwin, on the other hand, was numb to its potential and, typically, fussed with lines almost up to the time of production. He made only one major change in the script, however—a factual correction: from "And how do you think those lights look in London?" to "Europe" (the blackout having been lifted two months earlier in the English capital).[7] Fineshriber chatted with the men for awhile before he came to the point and asked Corwin about the script. "Are you satisfied with it?"

Corwin had reread the script only that morning but he could not be certain and asked Fineshriber to read it. The CBS executive sat by the pool to study the manuscript, and Corwin returned to the house, but he could not resist watching Fineshriber from the french doors, waiting for some sign of approval. At last, Fineshriber stood and walked slowly back to the house. Contemplatively, he placed the script on the table and said with quiet feeling, "I think it's marvelous."[8]

Martin Gabel, whom Corwin had named to narrate the program, was notified and flew out from New York in preparation for the production. He relaxed for a week by the Beverly Hills Hotel pool, awaiting his call. He was not to see a script until the first day of rehearsal.

At five o'clock on the morning of May 7, Corwin was awakened by a telephone call from the KNX production department. It was "on," the caller said. A news flash of Germany's surrender, which was said to have taken place in a school building at Rheims, France, had just been received from Associated Press correspondent Edward Kennedy. It was a heart-expanding moment. The first phase of World War II was at last over, and *On a Note of Triumph* was scheduled for coast-to-coast broadcast that very evening.

Corwin immediately alerted Charles Lewin and they assembled the cast, rounded up a crew, and arranged a late-morning rehearsal. Soundmen, under the direction of Berne Surrey, devised and tried out an assortment of effects—one was a thunderous splash of dunking at high speed to represent the narrator's dive beneath the sea. They used a manual splash tank with a huge paddle wheel, with supplementary sounds from records and a film soundtrack.[9] Lud Gluskin, who only a week before had conducted forty musicians for Corwin's *Word from the People*, quickly summoned an orchestra to rehearse Herrmann's score.

In Studio A of KNX—the very same studio where Corwin had produced *We Hold These Truths*—the cast gathered for the first read through. If Corwin had doubts about his script, he put them aside. Gabel remembered him as being "supremely confident."[10] The playwright-producer prescribed the script's objective and patiently led his players through the show, calling for anger here, insolence there, contriteness, courage, simplicity, sadness, sometimes exultation, expansive declaration—a myriad of moods marking the beginning and the end of the war.

At cast breaks, Corwin conferred with his soundmen. They were having trouble with the splash. At first, it was too light; then it did not sound right. The positioning of the microphones over the tank, for an adequate pickup and to avoid wetting the instruments, proved critical. As for other effects, timing and perspectives had to be mapped out in meticulous detail.

A little after three in the afternoon, with a rehearsal of *Triumph* in progress, the control room telephone rang. It was CBS in New York. Washington had denied the Kennedy report of peace as false, and the AP story was apparently premature. CBS canceled the evening broadcast.

For Corwin, the news was both a disappointment and a deliverance. He realized, for the first time, the intense pressure he had faced. He did not notify his cast immediately; instead, he continued the rehearsal as if the program were going on as scheduled. He recorded a dress rehearsal, then dismissed the actors with news of the postponement, and summoned them back the following afternoon.

After the participants had left the stage of the empty studio-theatre, Corwin and several assistants listened to the playback. He seemed pleased, but he made notes for several production changes.

The official announcement of VE Day was delayed twenty-four hours. CBS rescheduled the victory special for the following evening, May 8, in prime time. On that day, after an additional rehearsal, Corwin and his cast stood ready by air time, 7:00 p.m. PWT.

On a Note of Triumph opened with a brassy orchestral statement, which gave way for the narrator's brittle, almost arrogant observation:

So they've given up!
They're finally done in, and the rat is dead in an alley back of the Wilhelmstrasse.
Take a bow, G.I.,
Take a bow, little guy.
The superman of tomorrow lies at the feet of you common men of this afternoon.
This is it, kid, this is The Day, all the way from Newburyport to Vladivostok.

You had what it took and you gave it, and each of you has a hunk of
   rainbow around your helmet.
Seems like free men have done it again![11]

Martin Gabel moved through Corwin's crisp, cutting phrases with
steadfast assurance, exulting at the achievement. And then the program offered a unique aural surprise—a "folk song," with humorous
and pointed lyrics:

SOLOIST: We're gonna tell the postman,
           Next time he comes 'round,
           That Mr. Hitler's new address
           Is the Berlin burying ground.

CHORUS: Round and round Hitler's grave,
          Round and round we go.
          We're gonna lay that feller down
          So he won't get up no mo'.[12]

The song, which appeared with various lyrics at points throughout
the program, had been composed *ad libitum* by a group of folksingers
and musicians, including Millard Lampell, Woody Guthrie, and Pete
Seeger—best known, perhaps, as the Almanac Singers. It was first
used for another Corwin program, the initial show of *This Is War!*
Now, for *Triumph*, new verses added a sardonic commentary on the
enemy's plight. Corwin himself contributed a stanza. The song was
performed by Johnny Bond and a trio.
   Then:

Now we are ready.
The voice you hear will be that of the conqueror—
The man of the hour, the man of the year, of the past ten years and
   the next twenty.

With these words, Gabel advanced Corwin's alter ego, the Common
Man—in this instance, a soldier of the Allied forces. The simplicity of
his voice, a mere private first class, offered a striking contrast to the
gravity and implied greatness of the introduction. Other soldiers, as
the program progressed, would modestly step forward to quietly introduce a concern, each posing a pertinent question. Corwin, through
narration and dramatic analogy, would define the answer.
   "Who did we beat?"

Look at our German now:
Fat and sassy, swastika on his arm band, cobblestone in hand,
    ready to advance the cause . . .

Last week, pillage; this week, murder; next week, burn the books,
    and don't forget the Bible . . .

Eastward, look, the land is bright!
You can read an occupational order by the flare of the burning
    church . . .[13]

Newsweek later would praise the program as powerful, frequently poetic, yet emphasized that "as a contribution to literature it is better propaganda than art."[14] Its writing, direction, performance—true enough—exposed unreined hatred for fascism and the Nazi stratagem. It candidly dramatized German brutality, boldly recounted conquests of the Reich, and personified the callous mentality of Hitler's storm troopers. The incidents were based on fact, and included the words of William L. Shirer telling of the fall of France.

Corwin had remembered Shirer's moving report of the surrender in the Compiegne railway car. He could not utilize the actual broadcast, for network policy forbade the use of recordings. So, rather than have an actor impersonate Shirer, Corwin contacted the CBS correspondent and requested him to repeat live his commentary on the program. Shirer was in San Francisco at the announcement of VE Day, and Corwin dispatched the following network teletype:

FOLLOWING IS TEXT OF SPOT CONCERNING YOU. ANNOUNCER SAYS— QUOTE—SHIRER, THE REPORTER, STANDS AT THE EDGE OF THE CLEARING, WATCHING THE PARTY ADVANCE TO THE ARMISTICE CAR. HIS EYES ARE ON THE FACE OF THE FUHRER, WHO THE OTHER DAY DID A LITTLE DANCE FOR THE NEWSREEL CAMERAS WHEN HE LEARNED THE GOOD NEWS OF THE DEATH OF FRANCE—UNQUOTE. IMMEDIATELY UPON THE CUE GOOD NEWS OF THE DEATH OF FRANCE YOU COME IN WITH THE FOLLOWING—QUOTE— HE GLANCES SLOWLY AROUND THE CLEARING, AND NOW, AS HIS EYES MEET OURS, YOU GRASP THE DEPTH OF HIS HATRED—REVENGEFUL, TRIUMPHANT HATE. SUDDENLY, AS THOUGH HIS FACE WERE NOT GIVING QUITE COMPLETE EXPRESSION TO HIS FEELINGS, HE THROWS HIS WHOLE BODY INTO HARMONY WITH HIS MOOD. HE SWIFTLY SNAPS HIS HANDS ON HIS HIPS, ARCHES HIS SHOULDERS, PLANTS HIS FEET WIDE APART. IT IS A MAGNIFICENT GESTURE OF BURNING CONTEMPT OF THIS PLACE—UNQUOTE. WE WILL BE ON THE PHONE WITH YOU LATER CONCERNING EXACT TIME OF SHOW AND APPROXIMATE TIME YOUR SPOT COMES IN. MILLION THANKS AND GREETINGS APPROPRIATE TO THE DAY. BEST, CORWIN.[15]

Corwin's favorite part of *On a Note of Triumph* occurred shortly after Shirer's commentary. To contrast life in London with that in Berlin, Corwin cross-faded an air raid siren with the strains of a Strauss waltz and introduced a contralto singing Grieg *lieder* in a rathskeller in occupied Norway. And over this:

> And war was glorious!
> And the best champagnes of France were poured on the tables of the Schutzstaffel,
> The finest grade of Danish bacon sputtered in the skillets of loyal party workers,
> Paintings from the Louvre hung tastefully on the walls of Berchtesgaden,
> And the iron ore of Sweden alloyed well with the bauxite of Spain . . .[16]

After this portrait of the enemy ("the man you have beaten"), another question was posed: "How much did it cost?"

> Well, the gun, the halftrack, and the fuselage come to a figure resembling mileages between two stars—
> Impressive, but not to be grasped by any single imagination.
> High octane is high, and K rations in the aggregate mount up; also mosquito netting and battleships.
> But these costs are calculable, and have no nerve endings,
> And will eventually be taken care of by the federal taxes on antiques, cigarettes, and excess profits.
> However, in the matter of the kid who used to deliver folded newspapers to your doorstep, flipping them sideways from his bicycle,
> And who died on a jeep in the Ruhr,
> There is no fixed price, and no amount of taxes can restore him to his mother . . .[17]

One listener wrote:

> Three of us listened in our darkened living room as the program came with clarity over our FM station. I was glad the lights were out, for tears were there—and I don't think I was the only person who shed them. After the broadcast had been on for about ten minutes, I had switched the lights out for fear some friend would knock on the door and break the spell.
>
> I can recall no other occasion when radio has been able to sustain a mood for such a length of time.[18]

To Martin Gabel, the hour-long program was a relentless performance. It called for tempo and intensity that were at times trying, and in rehearsals Gabel appealed for cuts to ease the pace. Corwin complied in some instances, but was adamant in his persuasion that the narration should have force and momentum. Gabel knew, of course, that Corwin had an infallible feel for pace and structure.[19]

Now, as the live program progressed, Gabel returned the listener to the "conqueror," a soldier who asked: "But what do we know now that we didn't know before? What have we *learned* out of this war?"

> What have we learned?
> For one thing, Evil is not always as insidious as advertised,
> But will, upon occasion, give fair warning, just as smoke announces
>   the intention of flame to follow . . .

The script spoke of warnings ignored, of the impracticality of isolation, of failures and deceit at home, of the nature of human resistance. Actor Peter Witt impersonated Haile Selassie in a speech before the Geneva Conference, in which the Ethiopian Emperor pleaded the cause of "international morality."

> SELASSIE: Je suis venu pour avertir l'Europe de la catastrophe qui l'attend.
> INTERPRETER: I came to give Europe warning of the doom that awaits it.
> SELASSIE: Je suis venu pour défendre la cause de toutes les petites nations menacées d'agression.
> INTERPRETER: I came defending the cause of all small peoples who are threatened with aggression.[20]

(For years after the program, whenever Gabel and Witt met on the streets of New York, they greeted each other with the salutation, "*Je suis venu!*")[21]

Corwin capped his catalogue of lessons learned with a voice montage, which concluded with the commonsense observation of an upstate Vermonter:

> We've learned that freedom isn't something to be won and then forgotten. It must be renewed, like soil after yielding good crops; must be rewound, like a faithful clock; exercised, like a healthy muscle.[22]

Again, the voice of the G.I. Triumphant: "What do we do now?" It was clear. The war continued; peace was only partially fulfilled.

Corwin pointed to the task ahead—"unfinished business in Asia, killing to be done among the archipelagoes." To enact cautious, restrained jubilation, with sober realization of a job yet to be done, Corwin used the imagery of a mobile mike—overtaking a bomber in flight, to speak to the pilot, then lowering to the depths of a warship's engine room, to query an engineer on duty, then up and overboard, to dive beneath the sea, where, finally—many fathoms below—the news of victory is declared to a sunken submarine. The narrator hammers on its hull, but there is no answer.

Gabel was impressed by this sequence. In his narrative, he spoke feelingly to the dead:

> Over your heads and above the sea, victory has risen like the sun
> And moves west as we tell these things to you . . .

Then another question—no doubt the concern of every soldier, every citizen: "Is it gonna happen again?" The answer:

> Peace is never granted outright; it is lent and leased.
> You can win a war today and lose a peace tomorrow,
> Win in the field and lose in the forum . . .

But:

> Soldier—don't you feel in your bones that it doesn't have to happen
> again?[23]

As the soldier pondered fate and the future, the program's finale voiced its prayer of hope and challenge. The prayer, as solemnly intoned by Gabel, was backed by a quiet, reverential, orchestral mood. Bernard Herrmann, the composer, later complained that conductor Lud Gluskin had misinterpreted the passage "by playing it too slowly"; but Corwin disagreed. Indeed, as it built slowly beneath, it reinforced the powerful significance of the script's final words, sweeping ultimately into a triumphant conclusion.

Of Gabel's reading of the prayer, Corwin thought his narrator "stood up when addressing the God of Victory. His hat was in his hand, but his heart was not in his mouth."[24]

> Lord God of test tube and blueprint,
> Who jointed molecules of dust and shook them till their name was
> Adam,

Who taught worms and stars how they could live together,
Appear now among the parliaments of conquerors and give
  instruction to their schemes:
Measure out new liberties so none shall suffer for his father's color
  or the credo of his choice:
Post proofs that brotherhood is not so wild a dream[25] as those who
  profit by postponing it pretend:
Sit at the treaty table and convoy the hopes of little peoples through
  expected straits,
And press into the final seal a sign that peace will come for longer
  than posterities can see ahead,
That man unto his fellow man shall be a friend forever![26]

Unlike the traumatic minutes following *We Hold These Truths,* the
control room telephone began ringing long before the system cue
signaled an end to the show. The first caller was Frank Stanton, the
network's next president. Other calls followed in fast succession, and
Corwin found it difficult to break away to thank his cast. A thousand
calls were received by CBS in New York, and more than 1,600 calls at
KNX, the point of origination.

The next day further confirmed the success of *On a Note of Triumph.*
A delivery of 4,278 letters, cards, and telegrams arrived in sacks and
cartons—and this was only the initial response to the VE Day broadcast. Press response was widespread and at times ecstatic.

Billboard:

Once in a decade something comes down the pike that is so good it
deserves to belong not to its creator or its sponsor but to the people.
Last week, radio had just such a something . . . *Triumph:* . . . the single
greatest—and we use greatest in its full meaning—radio program we
ever heard.[27]

Variety:

Without equivocation, chalk this up as one of the high-water marks in
radio listening, a fitting, joyous climax to a memorable day in history.[28]

Among many newspapers which applauded the program were:[29]
the *Toledo Blade:*

. . . a literary gem . . . as stately and magnificent as an ode, as ide-
alistically disturbing as a bomb

the *Little Rock Gazette:*

> *Triumph* impresses one as an enduring and historic work of art, befitting the epic event it commemorates.

the *Cleveland Plain Dealer:*

> Will stand as a monument to those who gave all for the cause of freedom . . . amazing force and intensity

the *Akron Beacon Journal:*

> Stirring, biting, at times beautiful . . . something for all of us to hear at frequent intervals, for our own good and for the good of the country

the *Des Moines Tribune:*

> Play of plays . . . a poetic, dynamic conception

In New York, where the program caused great excitement at CBS headquarters, an interdepartmental memo, issued the next day, invited employees of CBS to hear a replay of *On a Note of Triumph.* At four o'clock, scores of secretaries, producers, and staff workers left their jobs early to assemble in designated studios to listen to what was universally acclaimed as the broadcast of the year.

A rebroadcast of the VE Day show was scheduled for coast-to-coast airing the following Sunday. Corwin, in Hollywood, again assembled his cast and prepared to repeat history. "Radio's second nights are never as exciting as their openings, and I very much dislike to produce repeats. But this one, thanks to Gabel's consistency and the solid virtues of my cast and music, was a pleasure to do."[30]

In the second broadcast, Gabel stumbled slightly on the line ". . . big contributions from a couple of big industrialists"—a minor and the only fluff in some 120 minutes of air time. A remarkable achievement, it was later cited by schools of drama as an exemplar of dynamic acting. Gabel, in fact, improved his performance, projecting even greater intensity and involvement in the repeat broadcast.

The second program was recorded for public release as a commercial 78 rpm album by the Columbia Recording Company.[31] Its sales were brisk, requiring additional pressings. Likewise, the Simon and Schuster book edition of *On a Note of Triumph* proved popular. Within a week, the publication sold out and a second printing of 25,000 copies was rushed to bookstores throughout the country. For two weeks, the book remained on the national best-seller list.

Neither William Paley, who at the time was attached to the armed services in England, nor Paul Kesten, Paley's appointed *pro tem* president of CBS, had heard the VE Day broadcast of *On a Note of Triumph*. Kesten, who had been abroad briefly, returned to confront a critical decision. Should he authorize a repeat production of the celebrated broadcast? As significant as the program appeared to be, its rebroadcast would involve interrupted schedules and commercial rebates.

On May 14, 1945, the day after the second broadcast of *Triumph*, Kesten explained his dilemma, and his delight, in a telegram to Corwin:

THE BLINDEST DECISION I EVER MADE PROVED PERFECT VISION, INCLUDING FORESIGHT, HINDSIGHT, AND SECOND SIGHT. I REFER TO THE QUICK 'YES' I GAVE TO THE PROPOSAL FOR REPEATING YOUR TREMENDOUS *ON A NOTE OF TRIUMPH* TEN MINUTES AFTER I RETURNED FROM ABSENCE ABROAD, WITHOUT HAVING HEARD BROADCAST OR SEEN SCRIPT. I DEEPLY BELIEVE BOTH CORWIN AND RADIO TOUCHED AND MAINTAINED A NEW DIMENSION IN YOUR INCREDIBLE MASTERPIECE. YET, YOUR TOUCH WAS SO FIRM AND YOUR HAND SO STEADY THAT I KNOW THIS WAS NO SINGLE TRANSCENDENT CREATIVE PEAK, BUT MERELY AN AUGURY OF THE PLANE TO WHICH YOU HAVE CLIMBED BY VISIBLE AND AUDIBLE STEPS OVER THE YEARS. THAT PLANE IS AS WIDE AS IT IS HIGH, AND I ENVY YOUR MASTERY OF IT. I AM CABLING PALEY HE CAN BE DOUBLY PROUD OF CORWIN, OF CBS, AND OF RADIO.[32]

The trade shared Columbia's enthusiasm, and acknowledged the show's success. The president of the Mutual Broadcasting System, Edgar Kobak, wired William Paley:

WHENEVER ANY PROGRAM OF THIS GREATNESS IS ACHIEVED, IT REFLECTS TO THE BENEFIT OF ALL RADIO AND I WANT TO THANK CBS.[33]

But it was not *all* orchids. Despite overwhelming acclamation, there were dissenters, notably a *New York Times* column by Jack Gould, titled "A Minority Report," and, most acrimonious of all, a review by Bernard De Voto for *Harper's* magazine. Gould felt *Triumph* "woefully lacking in one element—heart." He conceded that Corwin was for the people, "passionately, vigorously, and articulately, but *Triumph* was not of the people."³⁴ De Voto conceded nothing but distaste, denouncing the effort as "dull, windy, opaque, pretentious, false . . . saccharine . . . essentially cheap . . . commonplace . . . vulgar." He likened the program to Pare Lorentz's film *The River,* which he despised, and concluded that *Triumph* was "a mistake from the first line" and "a failure."³⁵

De Voto's venom attracted some attention and was countered in the columns of several newspapers. Stanley Anderson, of the *Cleveland Press,* wrote:

> De Voto is alone in his attack . . . [It is] remarkable that one lone-wolf critic has taken it upon himself to slug.³⁶

John Mason Brown, who had written a full and flattering review of *On a Note of Triumph* as a cover story for the *Saturday Review of Literature,*³⁷ seemed puzzled by De Voto's opinion. Over lunch in the Oak Room of the Plaza Hotel, he reassured Corwin that De Voto's attack was not unusual. Brown pointed out that it was De Voto's nature to ignite literary feuds, as he had done previously with Sinclair Lewis and others, and Brown surmised that Corwin's failure to take issue had probably disappointed him.³⁸

The Provost Marshal General of the U.S. Army ordered transcriptions of the VE Day special to be distributed on OWI discs and played for mass assemblies of former Nazi soldiers incarcerated in camps around the country. The response was often docile or dubious, and occasionally defensive. A report from the Assistant Executive Officer of the POW camp in Blanding, Florida, was typical:

> All [of the prisoners] listened silently throughout the playing. There was no audible reaction displayed during the playing, or immediately after. There was, however, some laughter when the "Heil Hitler" oath was uttered, and at the singing of "Round and Round Hitler's Grave." . . . All of them took issue with the broadcast where it condemns the entire German people for supporting the ascendancy of Hitlerism and the brutal acts of the Nazi regime. Even our good anti-Nazis (from way back) felt that this blanket indictment was unfair.³⁹

Praise for *On a Note of Triumph* exceeded even the unprecedented plaudits accorded *We Hold These Truths.* Carl Sandburg called the VE show "a vast announcement, a terrific interrogatory, and certainly one of the all-time great American poems." In November 1945 the National Council of Teachers of English gave a first award to the program, commending it as "the most notable contribution in the field of radio." The play was also cited by the Association of Teachers of Social Studies of New York City. Then, on March 9, 1946, *Billboard* announced that *Triumph* had been voted "the most outstanding broadcast of 1945" by a national poll of radio editors, edging out the broadcast of the Japanese surrender aboard the U.S.S. *Missouri*. Editorials and sermons and countless letters from people all over, especially servicemen, lauded the work and its thesis of hope. And there were to be instances, years later, when churches and synagogues would include the closing prayer of *On a Note of Triumph* as part of their printed program.

Letters continued to trickle in and as late as 1971 a teacher in San Francisco wrote to Corwin:

> I would like you to know that *On a Note of Triumph* has helped close the generation gap for many of my students in promoting understanding by them of what the war and the ending of the war meant.[40]

On a Note of Triumph, at the moment of its broadcast, caught the mood of the people. But more than that, it evidenced dramatic significance and transcended its timely impact. In the minds of many, it had enduring prophecy, as well as the emotional fervor and the skill of technique to make it, like MacLeish's *The Fall of the City,* a classic in American radio.

ON A NOTE OF TRIUMPH. "So they've given up; they're finally done in . . ." Martin Gabel narrates Corwin's classic VE Day broadcast. (CBS)

14 AUGUST. Orson Welles, after an all-night news vigil awaiting word of the Japanese surrender, listens as Corwin explains his special VJ program. (CBS)

ONE WORLD FLIGHT. Lee Bland joins Norman Corwin, the first recipient of the Wendell Willkie One World Award, in waving from a Pan Am ramp before embarking on their fact-finding global journey. (Corwin Collection)

ONE WORLD FLIGHT. Corwin stands amid the rubble of the famed Warsaw Ghetto, one of the many sites of mixed disillusionment and hope witnessed on his postwar tour of the world. (Corwin Collection)

NEWLYWEDS. Norman and Kate, after their marriage and en route to the West coast, are pictured together by a newspaper photographer. (Milwaukee Journal)

CORWIN OBSERVED. The author confers with Norman Corwin during a seminar visit to Indiana University. (Photo by Mel Miller)

THE TEACHER. Norman Corwin conducts a class in creative writing at the Idyllwild School of Music and the Arts in California during the summer of 1983. (Photo by A. Blanco)

11. The World: Flight of Unity

> The distances between
> continent and continent are shorter,
> but what should this mean if
> the distance between man and man
> were not likewise shorter?
>
> —*Program to Be Opened in a Hundred Years*

With the war in Europe over and momentum toward victory in the South Pacific gaining impetus with each conquered island, the impending direction of a world at peace was of more than passing interest. Delegates from fifty nations assembled in San Francisco in late June to sign the United Nations charter.

CBS, meanwhile, decided to resume Corwin's interrupted summer series of a year ago. The first broadcast of the newly activated *Columbia Presents Corwin,* on July 3, 1945, dealt in a most unusual way with society's prevailing concern. By it, Corwin wanted to express optimism for world unity; no heavy discourse—rather, a light, entertaining half-hour musical. He collaborated with composers Earl Robinson and Burton Lane, and lyricist E. Y. Harburg, in creating what he called "a carnival for your living room."

Unity Fair starred Alfred Drake as a carnival barker who proclaimed the virtues of cooperation and the nobility of the Common Man. It offered some bright and funny moments, with Groucho Marx and Keenan Wynn (Groucho did a hilarious impersonation of H. V. Kaltenborn).

The new series next saw a revival of *Daybreak,* a geographic mood piece originally written and produced for *26 by Corwin;* this time, the star was Ronald Colman. Although Corwin found Colman a consummate actor, he felt that the new effort did not measure up to the original.

He completed, meanwhile, what proved to be one of his all-time favorites, a rhymed fantasy, *The Undecided Molecule*. Not since *The Plot to Overthrow Christmas* had he attempted a verse play of this type, and he found it a particular delight. Robert Benchley opened the program with this greeting:

> Lucky you! You have happened to dial
> This program in time to attend a trial
> Stranger than any since we first learned the knack
> Of breathing—and that was a long time back.
> The poor folks listening to other stations
> Will lose all this. But congratulations
> To you for being no such fool
> As to miss *The Undecided Molecule!*

The cast included Groucho Marx, Elliott Lewis, Vincent Price, Norman Lloyd, Keenan Wynn, and Sylvia Sidney. It was, in effect, a trial—to decide the fate of a rebellious molecule. Groucho gave the role of the judge the same lilting, leering humor that typified his Marx Brothers movies.

> CLERK: The court will rise and face
> The justice who will adjust the case.
> See that your concentration centers
> On His Honor the Justice just as he enters—
> Which he is doing even now.
> Everybody bow. Everybody bow.
>
> JUDGE: (COMING ON) Arrumph . . . garrumph . . . ahem . . . to wit . . .
> Contrary notwithstanding . . . you may sit.

Benchley served as interpreter for the molecule, Vincent Price was the prosecutor, and Keenan Wynn performed no fewer than four roles. As the trial progressed, representatives of the vegetable and mineral kingdoms recounted the advantages of their classifications, but the wayward molecule remained undecided. At length, "Anima" (played by Sylvia Sidney) spoke for the animal kingdom and, despite her candid appraisal of mankind, swayed the molecule. The defendant, speaking as an oscillating tone, was interpreted by Benchley to acknowledge:

> The common guy
> Both thinks and feels.
> Nothing's too high
> For his ideals.
>
> Though it cost him sadly
> To put down jerks,
> He's not done badly—
> Look at his works!
> For all his pains
> We owe him thanks.
> And I do gladly
> Join his ranks.

The judge, meanwhile, was attracted to the spokeswoman of the animal kingdom, and flirtatiously advanced:

> As for you, Miss Anima, you were great.
> It's slightly extralegal—but have you a date
> For later in the evening? Do you like to dance?
> Have you any marked tendency toward romance?

A place for the molecule is found when Anima agrees to marry the judge and, together, they decide to adopt friend X (the molecule) as their offspring. The molecule oscillates a happy yes and the clerk of the court heralds the ending:

> Will the court musicians kindly advance
> To the mike and play a wedding dance;
> And then, after that, please segue and sally
> into a sort of a kind of finale?

MUSIC: A SORT OF A KIND OF FINALE.[1]

On July 24, 1945, Orson Welles narrated *New York: A Tapestry for Radio,* another program resurrected from the series *Twenty-Six.* The original had starred Martin Gabel, and Corwin compared the two performances:

Both interpretations were affirmative and challenging. Gabel gave it a youthful impetuousness; Welles, a mature and philosophic quality.

Gabel shaped scenes, Welles concentrated on lines. From a standpoint of virtuosity it would be like comparing Horowitz and Rubenstein— each of them a master, each going his own way, each eminently listenable.[2]

A Walk with Nick, program five of the reinstated *Columbia Presents Corwin,* was not the tribute to an English setter Corwin had dreamed of creating during the "dog days" of his Palisades retreat. Rather, it was a very human story of a girl and the two men in her life—a returning veteran and a liberal congressman at home. It starred John Hodiak, Joan Lorring, and Elliott Lewis.

Glenn Ford once had mentioned to Corwin how much he had enjoyed *Savage Encounter,* and how much he would have liked playing the part of the pilot. So, upon deciding to repeat the drama, Corwin cast Ford in the role. At the instant that the actor was rehearsing its story of a flight into utopia, an American B-29 hovered over Hiroshima. Its mission, as a stunned world would soon learn, was to drop the first atomic bomb. The irony of the two events—what might be hoped for and what existed—held frightening dimensions.

The following evening, from CBS in Hollywood, *Savage Encounter* portrayed its exotic concept of peaceful coexistence. In Nagasaki, some 6,000 miles away, there occurred the savage encounter of the second atomic bomb. Three days later, there was a premature report of the surrender of Japan.

The next day, August 13, 1945, William Fineshriber called from New York and asked Corwin if he had anything in mind for a victory broadcast. Corwin, of course, explained that he was busy preparing the next program of his series, a comedy to star Charles Laughton, called *L'Affaire Gumpert.* Fineshriber insisted that he drop all plans and immediately develop something to represent CBS upon official confirmation of the Japanese surrender. The network executive emphasized immediacy, for an announcement was expected at any moment.

Corwin sat up all night to create what he called "a fistful of lines" which attempted, like *Triumph,* to take a cautious, considered view of victory. He made the piece simple: a single voice, one sound effect, several music cues.

As the new day dawned, he called Orson Welles. Welles had kept vigil throughout the night as a newscaster for KFWB, Los Angeles, awaiting word of Hirohito's reply to the Allied ultimatum. He had been thirty-six hours without sleep and was exhausted; nevertheless, he rushed to KNX to rehearse Corwin's VJ Day special. Lud Gluskin, meanwhile, had organized a group of arrangers, copyists, and musicians. By air time—in the usual slot for *Columbia Presents Corwin*—Corwin stood ready to produce *14 August*. It began:

> Congratulations for being alive and listening.
> Millions didn't make it.
> They died before their time, and they are gone and gone, for the
>   Fascists got them.
> They are not here, but their acts are here.
> And they are to be saluted from the lips and from the heart before
>   the conversation drifts around to conversion.
> Fire a cannon to their memory!
>
> CANNON.

The narrative, in its poetic sweep, rejoiced briefly, then pondered the price paid. Finally, it reminded the living to remember:

> The turtle is young at sixty-one, but the flier is dead at eighteen.
>
> Remember them when July comes around
> And the shimmer of noon excites the locusts,
> When the pretty girls bounce as they walk in the park,
> And the moth is in love with the fifty-watt bulb
> And the tar on the road is blistered.
>
> They've given their noons to their country,
> They've trusted their girls to you.
> They are face to face with an ally's earth
> For a bunch of tomorrows.[3]

14 August received more than a thousand letters, all favorable. The program actually proved a runnerup to *On a Note of Triumph* and *Untitled* in listener response, even though George Rosen expressed a feeling, in *Variety*, that the broadcast may have been "ill-timed," that "no one was as yet ready to control sheer emotion or to harness joy to a narration, no matter how simple its exposition or sincere its content."[4]

Five days later, on Sunday, Corwin produced an expanded version of the narrative under the title *God and Uranium*. The broadcast commemorated the National Day of Prayer proclaimed by President Truman. For the occasion, Corwin asked Olivia de Havilland to assist Orson Welles. He was unaware that, at the time, the two were not speaking.

With *L'Affaire Gumpert* two nights later, CBS rang down the curtain on *Columbia Presents Corwin*. Once again, the series was abbreviated by a demand for Corwin's time and talent. The final show featured Charles Laughton and Elsa Lanchester, and was jogged a bit by Corwin's jocosity. Two characters in the play were named after people involved in the series: "Dr. Mishkin" for Leo Mishkin, and "Dr. Ashworth" for Lou Ashworth, Corwin's assistant. And Corwin gave as Gumpert's address 261 Fineshriber Avenue in Philadelphia—an allusion to the CBS vice president, who hailed from Philadelphia.

Revenue for network radio continued to rise in 1945 (3.2 percent over 1944's record income of $121,757,135),[5] and competition for clients and listeners became a stratagem of guile, of bold promotion and creative prowess. CBS decided to herald its new fall schedule with two big variety extravaganzas, and asked Corwin to conceive and direct one from New York, William N. Robson the other from Hollywood. Douglas Coulter detailed network expectations in a lengthy telegram to Corwin:

THE DATE WILL BE SEPTEMBER 16 IN NEW YORK AND WILL BE 90 MINUTES LONG. WE HAD A MEETING WITH PRINCIPAL AGENCIES YESTERDAY AND THEY ASSURE US OF COMPLETE COOPERATION FROM TALENT. BUT WHAT THEY WOULD LIKE TO HAVE FIRST IS SOME SORT OF GENERAL OUTLINE OF THE SHOW, SO THEY CAN INDICATE TO TALENT HOW MUCH TIME EACH PERSON WILL HAVE. THIS I REALIZE, YOU CANNOT GIVE IN MORE THAN SKELETON FORM, BUT I WISH YOU WOULD THINK ABOUT IT OVER THE WEEKEND AND WIRE ME MONDAY AS TO WHAT YOU THINK MIGHT BE DONE WITH THE FOLLOWING PEOPLE, WHICH AGENCIES ASSURE US THEY CAN DELIVER: KATE SMITH, *THE ALDRICH FAMILY, INNER SANCTUM, WE THE PEOPLE,* JAN PEARCE OF *GREAT MOMENTS IN MUSIC,* LILY PONS AND KOSTELANETZ, BOB HAWK, *ADVENTURE OF THE THIN MAN,* PATRICE MUNSEL, *FAMILY HOUR, HIT PARADE* ORCHESTRA, MELTON OF *TEXACO STAR THEATRE,* PHIL BAKER OF *TAKE IT OR LEAVE IT, IT PAYS TO BE IGNORANT* WITH HOWARD AND SHELTON, LULU MCCONNELL AND HARRY MCNAUGHTON; HELEN HAYES; RODZINSKY OF THE PHILHARMONIC, *REPORT TO THE NATION,* PROBABLY ONE OVERSEAS PICK-UP AND DANNY KAYE. AS YOU CAN SEE, WHAT WE ARE TRYING TO DO IS TO GET AS BROAD REPRESENTATION AS POSSIBLE, BUT THE EXTENT TO WHICH WE WILL USE EACH REPRESENTATIVE WILL BE

PRETTY MUCH UP TO US, OR RATHER NORMAN CORWIN WITHIN REASON. OBVIOUSLY, WE WANT ALL THESE PEOPLE TO BE KEPT WITHIN CHARACTER OF THEIR PROGRAMS. A GOOD SUGGESTION MIGHT BE TO HAVE ONE OF THESE INDIVIDUALS ON YOUR LIST AS EMCEE. WE HAVE NO TITLE FOR THE SHOW AND FEW PRECONCEIVED NOTIONS. WE WILL SUPPLY, THROUGH THE AGENCIES, THE MATERIALS FOR ANY OR ALL THESE ACTS, ON YOUR SUGGESTION AND UNDER YOUR DIRECTION. OBVIOUSLY, THE OVERALL CONCEPT—LINKING TOGETHER AND EDITING—WILL BE YOURS.

REGARDS, COULTER.[6]

In a reply, Corwin complained of the limited time for developing a program of such dimension, and insisted on help from Chuck Lewin (then on KNX assignment) and Lou Ashworth.

On Sunday afternoon, September 16, 1945, from 3:00 until 4:30— time normally filled by the New York Philharmonic Orchestra on CBS—Corwin showcased most of the featured headliners mentioned in Coulter's wire. The program, appropriately, was titled *Stars in the Afternoon*.

Corwin organized his script to use the home setting of *The Aldrich Family*, wherein its characters received an array of radio personalities and guests who were to be featured in Columbia's new fall schedule. The show began with youthful Henry Aldrich, his cracked, adolescent voice familiar to most listeners, answering the telephone:

HENRY: Hello?
CBS: (FILTER) May I speak to Sam Aldrich, please?
HENRY: Who's calling, please?
CBS: (FILTER) C.B.S.
HENRY: Who?
CBS: (FILTER) C.B.S. This is C.B.S.
HENRY: Father . . .
FATHER: (OFF) Who is it?
HENRY: There's a navy man on the phone for you.
FATHER: (CLOSER) A navy man?
HENRY: Yes, he's a Seabee.[7]

Henry's father, Sam Aldrich, was then told that the network wanted to parade through his living room outstanding stars who were to visit similar living rooms all over America in the months to come. In what *Variety* termed "the promotion stunt of the year,"[8] there followed excerpts from upcoming CBS programs—comedy, drama, music, commentary—with guest appearances by Helen Hayes, reading the prayer from *On a Note of Triumph,* by Bess Myerson, exhibiting her musical talent as the reigning Miss America, and by Edward R. Murrow, philosophizing about radio, which he likened to a mirror which reflects the good and bad of society. Bernard Herrmann coordinated the music, which featured Al Goodman, Archie Blyer, and André Kostelanetz. *Variety* reported:

> CBS shook up a giant cocktail last Sunday afternoon. It took $100,000 worth of star-dusted talent, added a thick 90-minute slice of top time, and spiced with the brains of a half dozen writers and almost that many musical conductors in charge of a 75-piece orchestra. Sensibly letting Norman Corwin shake this colossal concoction . . . it reflected a good deal of what's good in radio, CBS or any other net.[9]

Corwin seemed captivated by almost any challenge offered by the medium. By an obvious enthusiasm for radio, he was in every sense a "workaholic"; he never wearied of deadlines, production pressures, or the inevitable abnormality of show business. He accepted his developing fame with characteristic modesty, intent always on the next hurdle.

His next project was presented by Mrs. Ogden Reid, the publisher of the *New York Herald-Tribune,* in a visit to Corwin's office. She asked if he would join a number of eminent personalities in contributing to the fourteenth annual Herald-Tribune Forum, which was to be held at the Waldorf-Astoria on October 29, 1945. Specifically, she wanted him to dramatize the Forum's theme, "The Responsibility of Victory," as the keynote feature of the program. Corwin agreed, but decided against a formal dramatization and wrote a single-voice narration instead, which he titled *Set Your Clock at U235.*

Mrs. Reid read it, liked it, and quickly decided that it should be appropriately performed by a war veteran. Moreover, as she envisioned it, it should be a *wounded* veteran. And suddenly, enthusiastically, she concluded it had to be a *black* wounded veteran. Tactfully, Corwin cautioned her that a combination of such qualities, plus an ability to act, might be difficult to come by. But Mrs. Reid seemed not to listen. "Paul Robeson!" she cried, completely dismissing her previous specifications.[10]

For the first time since *Ballad for Americans,* Corwin and the great singer-actor had occasion to collaborate, and from this event emerged deep-toned words of prophecy and scruple:

> . . . Beneath the loud and glooming auguries of doom are modest noises of beginning, keenly awaited as the cry of the newborn, or the first cuckoo of spring.
> It can well be an entrance, not an exit, that we made between pillars of flame arising from bombs one and two . . .
>
> The choice rests in the trusteeship of victory;
> One or nothing; wealth, or laying waste . . .[11]

The year of victory, 1945, came to an end as America entered a postwar period of unleashed extravagance and uneasy optimism. The boys were coming home and blessings unobtainable, until now, were embraced by all with eagerness and thanksgiving. Despite the nation-wide spending spree and an obvious obsession with the present, there was nonetheless an abiding concern for the future. The atom bomb had blasted dreams of a secure tomorrow.

Corwin, radio's eloquent spokesman for national purpose in time of war, now became an advocate of world unity under peace. He had expressed the ideal often, as in *14 August:*

> Are we agreed that all is one?
> That the world's a single continent?[12]

The vision undertook added dimension the day Jacques Ferrand, executive secretary of the Common Council for American Unity, visited Corwin. Ferrand, a former member of the Nobel Committee, was also associated with the Willkie Memorial of Freedom House. He informed Corwin that friends of Wendell Willkie had established the One World Award in honor of the great liberal Republican and statesman. It was to be a subsidized around-the-world trip, patterned after Willkie's historic flight of 1942. The noted radio writer had been named its first recipient, and Ferrand wanted to know if Corwin would accept.

Corwin wanted it to be a "working" trip, if he accepted: an opportunity to record people in the various countries he visited for the possible development of a series of documentaries. It was up to CBS, he said. "If Paley declines to let me go or has urgent work for me, I must respect my contract and pass up the award. I will not try to persuade him."[13]

Paley needed no persuading. Davidson Taylor immediately forwarded a letter to Freedom House, stating that "CBS is proud" and informing the sponsors that the network "will cooperate." In approving the working-trip plan, Paley also authorized the network to underwrite an aide to accompany Corwin. The writer-producer had the pick of the lot and chose Lee Bland, a production man who had been most efficient with the logistics and planning of *Stars in the Afternoon.*

On February 18, 1946, the fifty-fourth anniversary of Wendell Willkie's birth, the One World Award was announced at a banquet on the Starlight Roof of the Waldorf-Astoria. There were present, in one of the last stands of undismayed liberalism before McCarthyism enveloped the land, the ranking Willkie-minded people of the day. Former mayor of New York City, Fiorello LaGuardia, made the official presentation. On the dais with him was Philip Willkie (son of the memorialized political leader), Charles Evans Hughes Jr., Walter Lippmann, Spiros Skouros, Helen Hayes, Marquis Childs, Dr. Harry Gideonse, and Walter White.

Later, on the West Coast, some 500 Hollywood celebrities assembled in the Florentine Room of the Beverly Wilshire Hotel to honor Norman Corwin. Hosted by Robert Young, the program included excerpts from Corwin's award-winning works as read by Edward G. Robinson, Ona Munson, Dane Clark, Alfred Drake, Keenan Wynn, Joan Lorring, Martin Gabel, and Charles Laughton. After Paul Robeson paid tribute to Corwin and introduced the guest of honor, Corwin spoke:

> In a few weeks, I shall be setting out on the Willkie Memorial trip. I know I shall find turmoil and trouble, hunger, poverty and restiveness in many places—too many places. But I know also that I shall find hope intermingled everywhere, and the ageless and unquenchable passion to be free, and I know I will find people who are eager to join with you in the making of a better day.[14]

The next day, he returned East to be the master of ceremonies for a dinner honoring five delegates to the Security Council of the United

Nations. The date was April 25, the first anniversary of the founding of the UN in San Francisco.

The official farewell dinner for Norman Corwin followed in a few days, sponsored jointly by the Willkie Memorial, the Common Council for American Unity, and the Columbia Broadcasting System. In the Jade Room of the Waldorf-Astoria, Corwin addressed an audience of outstanding personages—leading businessmen, politicians, scientists, and Nobel laureates, among whom were Dr. Joliot-Curie and Dr. Otto Loewi. Corwin spoke of the journey as no pleasure trip; rather, as an odyssey of inquiry, he said—a search for common ties and yearnings for world unity.

On June 15, 1946, a cluster of friends gathered for Corwin's departure at LaGuardia Municipal Airport. His parents were there, along with Katherine Locke, a few relatives, and several colleagues. Corwin was not told that his mother was to undergo serious surgery soon. He little realized that her tearful embrace was more poignant than a mere goodbye.

Hours later, after their plane skidded to a stop at Heathrow Airport in London, Corwin and Bland shared a taxi with Mrs. Ernest Hemingway, Martha Gellhorn. Later, in his hotel suite at the Claridge, Corwin interviewed several members of the government, but his most significant recording was to occur at Number 10 Downing Street.

Prime Minister Clement Attlee was both cordial and casual, as he seated himself across from Corwin at a long, bare table in the cabinet room. Wearing a cardigan sweater, he puffed at his pipe as he spoke of "positive peace." He suggested that "the first thing is to realize that there's something quite different in peace from 'no more war.' If you continually think of the prevention of war you don't get very far. You've got to think of positive peace, and that really depends on a greater understanding, not just between governments but between peoples—not just about politics, but about ways of life."[15]

The next stop was France. Premier Bidault was busily forming his cabinet and unavailable for an interview, but Corwin managed to corner an official spokesman for each of the three major parties.

Bland, meanwhile, flew to Frankfurt, in hopes that American technicians might fix his wire recorder. They were not entirely successful, and the machine's malfunctioning would plague the pair from country to country. "It was a monstrous device," Corwin recalled. "It was bulky and heavy and its quality was miserable. The wire would sometimes spill off the spool and become entangled. Splicing was tedious and was done by tying a knot in the two ends of the wire and fusing it with a lighted cigarette."[16]

In Denmark, the next country of call, the Corwin mission received a lavish welcome. Corwin had intended only a twenty-four-hour layover and no interviews, but he found the Danes eager to participate. To accommodate their concern and cordiality, the One World emissaries delayed their departure.

From Copenhagen they flew to Oslo, and when Bland again encountered difficulties with the wire recorder, Norwegian engineers tried in vain to repair it. Resorting to acetate discs, Corwin recorded the harrowing experiences of Paul Lycke, head of Norway's radio, who vividly recalled the Nazi occupation. Sigurd Evensmo, a writer, told Corwin of being the only survivor in the escape of eighteen underground fighters from Nazi execution.

Corwin observed a country that, in spite of its perilous past and uncertain future, held fast to pride and hope with rare insight. When Corwin complimented Foreign Minister Halvard Lange on the wisdom of an observation, the Norwegian smiled and said, "It is easy to be wise in a small country. Nobody has any reason to fear us."[17]

As Corwin stepped off the plane in Stockholm, he was met by an attaché from the U.S. embassy and was handed a letter from President Truman, extending congratulations for being named the first recipient of the One World Award. He was further accorded treatment befitting a dignitary by Sweden's foreign office and by Radiotjanst, the government radio system. But the ultimate gesture of friendship was extended by radio officials, who offered their newly acquired General Electric wire recorder, which they said the Americans could use for the remainder of their trip. Corwin and Bland gladly accepted.

In Warsaw, personnel of Polish Radio provided Corwin with a sound truck and a complement of technicians to facilitate his mission. At the Belvedere Palace, Corwin spent more than two and a half hours recording an interview with President Boleslaw Bierut. The Polish leader insisted on talking out his answers before committing them to wire. In his discussion, he propounded a dramatic plan for the rebuilding of Warsaw.

Later, Corwin walked through the rubble and ruins of the Warsaw Ghetto. With the emotion of the experience still fresh, he returned to his hotel, to learn the shocking news of a pogrom in Kielce, a town less than 200 miles away. He took his microphone around Warsaw to test, at random, the reaction of Polish workers and officials.

Although the war had seemingly ended fascism, there was evidence of fear in the world that some political force might again assert itself to threaten world peace. Uppermost in the minds of many was the rising tension between the United States and Russia. The polarization was reflected in viewpoints from Scandinavia to the Philippines.

On a bright July morning in 1946, Corwin left Warsaw in a Red Army plane for Moscow. His diary details:

> It was a lend-lease DC3, and stenciled on a motor cowling in perfectly good American was the legend, "Use Filler-Neck Type Oil Heater." The Russians fly their planes well, but informally: no safety belts, no food aboard, nothing resembling a steward. Thanks to a mystery of currency exchange which baffles me, the fare for Bland, myself, and 350 pounds of luggage, from Warsaw to Moscow, a distance of almost 900 miles came to $17.66. I understand this was the result of an occluded front between the zloty and the ruble.

Upon his arrival in Russia, Corwin submitted a "request" list of thirty items, of which twenty-seven would be accommodated. The others were not denied, but never arranged. Among the latter were meetings with Stalin, Shostakovich, and the chairman of the Soviet Committee on Religions. Corwin was denied seeing two people he had looked forward to meeting, not by official action but due to personal illness. On the eve of arranged interviews with Sergei Eisenstein and Prokofiev, he developed a strep throat. Russian and American doctors ordered Corwin to bed, where, reluctantly, he compiled a list of questions for Lee Bland to ask in his absence.

Bland found Eisenstein in pajamas, recovering from a recent heart attack. In the garden of his two-story dacha, a seven-room house situated among tall pine trees, they talked of films and art, of the

United States and Russia.[18] Asked to rate what he believed to be the greatest of motion pictures, Eisenstein admitted there were many, but, without hesitation, his first choice was D. W. Griffith's *Birth of a Nation*. As second, he ranked all the films of his friend Charlie Chaplin. And third? Mickey Mouse cartoons.

Lee Bland interviewed Sergei Prokofiev at his home, also set among pine trees some 40 miles outside Moscow. The composer gave a strong endorsement of cultural exchange. He said, "Even the exchange between countries of a single sheet of music is important. For culture is the best meeting ground for the people."[19]

The One World flight continued on to Czechoslovakia, where, in Prague, Corwin's microphone probed for opinions in all quarters of public and private life—students, lawyers, doctors, Minister Plenipotentiary Jan Papanek, President Beneš from his office in Hradchany Palace. He talked with miners, and found them decidedly oriented toward Russia (they spoke of their "Soviet brothers").

They doglegged to Rome via Paris and Marseilles, where, in a brief stopover, Corwin filed for CBS some impressions of a current Peace Conference. Italy appeared to be in great turmoil following its recent elections, overrun by hunger and unemployment and filled with confused emotions.

In the Vatican, Corwin had a private audience with the Pope. He also interviewed Premier De Gasperi, in the Presidential Palace, and later visited Roberto Rossellini, the film director. Rossellini arranged a special showing of his *Open City*, and they sat in the projection room with the film's writer (Sergio Amadei) and discussed filmmaking. Rossellini said that he had received a number of offers from Hollywood, which Corwin urged him not to accept.

Seven hours out of Rome, Corwin and Bland arrived in Cairo, where they were met by George Polk,[20] Middle East correspondent for CBS. They were whisked through customs without delay, a courtesy made possible by Polk, who had the officials believing that the two visitors had arrived by special invitation of King Farouk. There, on August 9, Corwin witnessed the official celebration of Egyptian independence. From a nearby rooftop, he saw the country's flag raised over the Citadel, for the first time in sixty-five years.

As a passenger in a Beechcraft, piloted by a U.S. military attaché, Corwin was flown over the Suez Canal, the Bitter lakes, and the apex of the Red Sea. He saw explosive flashes below in the desert, where ammunition dumps were being blown up in preparation for the British departure from Egypt.

Corwin and Bland then flew a converted York bomber to India via Syria, Iraq, Iran, the Persian Gulf, and Trucial Oman. They encountered a monsoon en route and the plane had difficulty in landing at New Delhi. It was an arduous trip and Corwin arrived totally exhausted. Immediately after lunch, to Corwin's dismay, his American host insisted on reading a three-act play he had written.

At the Viceregal Palace, Corwin had an off-the-record interview with the Viceroy, Viscount Archibald Wavell, who spoke of the hopelessness of India's problems. Amid the country's angry political tumult, Pandit Nehru provided rare sanity in a forty-five-minute interview. He said:

> We have tried all along to think that India cannot and should not live an isolated existence, but must cooperate with the rest of the world. We try to cooperate with our neighbors; but really, the ideal we have before us is world cooperation. And that can only be based on world freedom.[21]

Leaving the capital, the CBS pair flew much of the way over the flooded Ganges to Calcutta. Fires were burning in the city as their plane circled overhead. The atmosphere was tense and dangerous, and a strict curfew was enforced during their brief stay.

Because of the threatening situation, they departed for China early in the morning the next day. It was 3:30 a.m. when Corwin and Bland boarded a battered transport with bucket seats, no toilet, no water, no heating system, no insulation, and several of its eight windows without panes. It lumbered to a takeoff, and for the next twenty-four hours subjected its passengers to freezing cold, as it climbed above the Lesser Himalayas, then sweltering heat as it set down at several stops. They flew over the Yangtze Gorge, stopped at Hankow at dusk, and arrived in Shanghai late at night.

In a brief trip to Peiping to visit General Marshall's "Executive Headquarters," Corwin was met by a large delegation of Chinese. From the group stepped forth the Minister of Information, who said: "I am very happy that you arrived at our capital on the birthday of Confucius, who is the forerunner of the One World idea."[22]

Flying from Shanghai to Tokyo—directly over Fuji's crater on the first cloudless day in months—the One World flight arrived in Japan. Corwin obtained an off-the-record interview with General Douglas MacArthur and met informally with U.S. Ambassador George Acheson. The future of Japan, Corwin found, was a subject of international concern. Yet most of his interviews tended to be a triangulation of hearsay. He was puzzled at the official attitude and policy toward the Emperor, and he could not understand the renewed glorification of Hirohito.

In a long flight via Okinawa, the One World emissaries arrived in Manila at 5:50 in the morning. They hitched a ride into town on a truck, the only transportation available at that hour. This was not their only inconvenience during the visit. Corwin's interviews, which included talks with President Roxas and Ambassador Paul V. McNutt, found little sentiment for One World and divided feelings about Philippine independence. Fighting and general unrest were in evidence.

Attempting to leave Manila at 3:30 in the morning, Corwin and Bland unexpectedly found themselves "offloaded" from their Australia-bound military airplane. Due in Sydney in two days, where his hosts awaited with an extensive program, Corwin was dismayed. He was emphatic in stating his case, but the Manila ATC personnel, long hostile to edicts from headquarters and apparently annoyed at General MacArthur's VIP endorsement of the CBS missioners, were not accommodating. When Corwin insisted that if they were to be denied passage, their luggage must be removed from the plane, an arrogant captain replied that to remove the luggage would take at least an hour, and they did not have the time. The waiting room was now emptied of passengers and personnel, and it was 4:30 a.m. Corwin picked up a telephone and, without identifying himself, coolly called the tower and ordered: "Hold that ship on the ground until further notice."

The ruse worked. Without question, the order was observed. The captain fumed. Corwin, meanwhile, telephoned to awaken McNutt's naval aide, who made several calls, but in vain. Corwin and Bland were left to watch helplessly as the heavy transport, loaded with their luggage and recording equipment, received the green light and taxied down the runway, lifting off at dawn in the direction of Australia.

The affair became an incident. The plane was ordered to land at Maritius, where their luggage was taken off and placed on a northbound plane. Until their luggage could be returned, Corwin and Bland were lent clothes to wear, and a special flight was arranged. They were practically the only persons aboard the huge American troopcarrier. Later, there would be a court-martial for the servicemen involved.

Corwin was impressed with Australia and Australians were similarly impressed with Corwin, since many of his radio plays had been produced in that country and were quite popular. He was received graciously for an extensive program of social and professional affairs, given vast press coverage, and invited to make a national radio address.

They then flew across the Tasman Sea, in a converted Sunderland flying boat, and landed in Auckland, the crowded, humming, first city of New Zealand—and into a controversy caused by a former attaché to the U.S. Information Service. Corwin, in a satiric, national radio address, countered the controversial views of the former official, who had written slanderously of the country and published his article in the States. The Prime Minister was so pleased that he invited Corwin to sit beside him in a cabinet meeting, and later requested permission to repeat the broadcast.

The final leg of the journey touched down at New Caledonia, the Fijis, Canton Island, Hawaii, and ultimately Los Angeles. A CBS contingent, headed by William N. Robson, met Corwin's plane at the Los Angeles International Airport. In spite of repeated cautions, before and during the trip, to "secure" equipment and expensive possessions while visiting depressed, poverty-stricken areas of the world, no item was stolen until the pair returned to American territory. In Honolulu, the final stop before home, Corwin discovered his Hermes typewriter was missing.

The mission had taken four months and covered 37,000 miles, over which he had traveled by nineteen different commercial and military carriers. More than a hundred hours of voices, of people of all ranks, were recorded on magnetic wire or acetate discs and returned to the States by diplomatic pouches of the U.S. State Department. It had been an exhausting, exhilarating, and instructive project. Of Corwin's mission, playwright Jerome Lawrence observed, "It was good to send a poet around the world. He has a way of listening to the rhythms of tomorrow."[23]

The global odyssey formed for Corwin—and for the nation, through his later broadcasts—a personal view of a battle-weary, post-war world and the conclusion that, despite promising, gallant hopes for the future, the One World dream of Wendell Willkie was still as remote as ever.

12. The Art: Beginning of the End

Sing a song of unsung heroes
Whose Crossley rating is down to zeroes

—*A Man with a Platform*

American radio had emerged from World War II greatly admired, with an enviable record of involvement, of service, of exceptional achievement. Its importance as an intimate, abiding source of information and entertainment was undeniable. But it was big business too. And so existed the dichotomy—profit versus public service—that created a telling issue which, among other influences, signaled an inevitable transformation of the medium.

Variety viewed the trend toward excessive commercialism as unfortunate, and in January 1947 described the difference between intent and action:

> True, there is some lofty talk from the direction of CBS aimed at exposing multi-millions of listeners to vital documentaries by knocking off on occasion cream time commercial shows, but when a Norman Corwin series growing out of his 'One World' tour winds up 'Behind the Hope Ball' at 10 o'clock Tuesday night it obviously raises the question of how serious is the intent of the network to assume its public obligation.[1]

When the Federal Communications Commission became aware that the affluent medium was forsaking its public service commitment to fatten its profit margin, it began to scrutinize license renewals more carefully and to contrast promise with performance. In March 1946 the Commission shocked the industry with the issuance of its "blue book," *Public Service Responsibility of Broadcast Licensees*.

Broadcasters rebelled; NAB President Justin Miller even decried the Communications Act concept, which decreed that people own the air, as "hooey and nonsense," while *Broadcasting* magazine likened the governmental interference to Nazism and cautioned that "there is more at stake than the ultimate pattern of American broadcasting."[2] In time, the FCC would give in, and by 1947 the matter of public service seemed up to the stations and, paradoxically, up to the public.

There seemed, however, another threat to the independent dominance of radio: television. Events like the opening of the UN Security Council and the Joe Louis–Billy Conn heavyweight title match, televised to a limited audience, proved the reality of the new medium. The public clamored for sets when they first became available, in the closing months of 1946, and an estimated 6,000 television receivers were purchased. The very next year, thirty times that figure were sold.[3]

The sudden impact of television had been impressive. Obviously, with both sight and sound (and eventually color), the medium was seen early as an effective means of advertising. To hasten video's development, therefore, network officials decided that TV should be financed by the returns from radio—for NBC alone, an $8 million investment. The strategy proved good business, since such sums could be considered business losses and partially absorbed as a tax writeoff.

All this, of course, disheartened Corwin. He saw in radio's inexorable trend a dilution of art, of importance—a complete suspension of efforts to advance the medium. Sustaining programs had become passé. Public service had regressed to simple spot announcements or, at best, programs consigned to unsalable times. He saw his talent, his function, his position slowly fading into the oblivion of broadcasting's commercial obsession.

When the One World flight ended in Los Angeles, October 18, 1946, Corwin was very weary. The four-month mission had been a strain, so he relaxed a few days before flying East. On October 27 he arrived in New York, where he was met by Emil, Freda, Katherine Locke, and some twenty reporters and photographers who wanted his opinions of conditions abroad.

On November 8 he provided a full report of his trip at a meeting of the two sponsoring agencies, which convened in the Willkie Memorial

Building in Manhattan. It included what he termed "an even dozen conclusions":

1. We seem to be farther from Willkie's One World today than we were when his thesis became the best-selling book of America. . . . None of us will get far in any direction if the leading powers of the world fail to set an example.
2. The reservoir of good will toward the United States about which Willkie spoke enthusiastically in 1942 had drained to a dangerously low level.
3. A powerful and elemental sense of fairness, as well as an overwhelming will and anxiety for peace, pervades all of the peoples of the earth.
4. It seemed to me that the greatest peril today is a sort of Frankensteinian phobia created by factions who would have people everywhere believe there is no room in one world for more than one economic and social system. In view of the existing facts, such a world obviously could not be achieved without a war in which one crushes the other. . . . And the most important contribution to be made toward this goal is to convince the peoples of the world that a war is not inevitable.
5. In view of the existing tendency to diplomatic impasse, the principle of mutual compromise must replace the Gibraltar complex in international politics.
6. I believe the democracies of the West should watch with neighborly interest and good will, rather than with distrust, the social experimentation of countries like Czechoslovakia, Australia and New Zealand, all of whom are trying to reconcile extremes of socialism and private enterprise.
7. One of the most frequently and strongly reiterated impressions of the entire trip was that the United States, in the eyes of the rest of the world, is a colossus without precedent and without peer . . . that peace lies not in the stars, but in us.
8. I believe all nations should acknowledge more readily the principle of cultural exchange, especially as it applies between countries whose political relations are strained.
9. I believe freedom of information is an international must, but to establish it, we must abrogate freedom of misinformation. Let the radio, press and cinema of the world . . . regulate themselves so that misinformation becomes a punishable violation of their own laws.
10. I believe the world would benefit greatly if two pieces of modern writing were made compulsory reading in every classroom of the

countries of the United Nations: Willkie's *One World* and Hersey's *Hiroshima.*

11. I believe from what I've seen, that to despair of the world is to resign from it. I believe that to assume human nature is committed to another war is to assume that suicide is the only solution to our problems.

12. I have lost no hope. I believe that ultimately we will find unity and brotherhood in this world, but that the quest will go on through terrible trials and agonies, until a true democracy, not merely a lip-service democracy, is achieved for the entire world. I believe each of us can assist in this mammoth task.[4]

Corwin busied himself, in the days to follow, sorting out the many hours of actuality (on-the-scene recordings) obtained on his global journey. The advent of audio tape had rendered wire recording obsolete, so CBS engineers transferred Corwin's interview material to magnetic tape to facilitate editing. From typed transcripts, Corwin then proceeded to write the thirteen programs of the proposed documentary series. He titled it *One World Flight.*

Possibly because of the inconsistency of early tape recorders, the actuality excerpts were dubbed in sequential tracks on acetate discs for insertion at the time of production. The programs were produced live, with live music—a score by Lyn Murray. Corwin narrated, and direction was assisted by Guy Della Cioppa.

One World Flight proved to be a forerunner of a new trend in radio documentary. It was historically significant, too, in that it contributed to an elimination of the antirecording ban long held by CBS and the other networks. Another historical footnote was the eventual revelation that, aside from several network commissions, *One World Flight* would be Corwin's final major work for CBS.

The year 1947 was to be eventful for Corwin, and it began the afternoon of January 11, three days prior to the premiere broadcast of *One World Flight.* He escorted Katherine Locke to the Metropolitan Opera to see the first production of *The Warrior,* a one-act opera which credited Corwin as the librettist. It had come about when the composer, Bernard Rogers, asked Corwin if he could base a short opera on one of his radio plays. Because of his interest in classical and biblical themes, it was not unexpected that Rogers should choose *Samson,* from the series *26 by Corwin.*

Rogers, an established American composer and member of the faculty at Rochester's Eastman School of Music, had for the last fifteen years authored a variety of orchestral suites and vocal works; significantly, *The Passion*, an oratorio in six scenes, which was introduced in Cincinnati in 1944. Prior to that, he had earned a Pulitzer Traveling Scholarship to study abroad, and was also the recipient of a Guggenheim Fellowship.

The one-act opera bore the title of Corwin's play, and the League of Modern Composers offered to feature it on a program of the organization's regular CBS series, *Invitation to Music*, under the baton of Bernard Herrmann. Corwin, invited to sit in on a piano rehearsal, found the music "surprisingly atonal," but "despite its modern sound, nevertheless had an Old Testament quality about it."[5]

Later, they broke for lunch. Over a table at Louis and Armands' Restaurant, around the corner from CBS, Corwin witnessed a startling attack by Herrmann, who ruthlessly criticized Rogers' work as he sat across from the composer. Herrmann categorically hated the work, he said; he called it a failure. Corwin was embarrassed, for Rogers—a gentle, talented man—was obviously crushed. Later, Herrmann would withdraw the operatic work from his broadcast schedule.

This incident, which occurred in June of 1945, did not mark the end of the opera. Rogers decided to submit it in a competition sponsored by the Alice M. Ditson Fund of Columbia University. All entries were to be anonymous, and the winner was to receive full production at the Metropolitan Opera. Because of the recent furor over the opera, Rogers suggested that the title be changed to *The Warrior*. Corwin felt that the composer had been perhaps too faithful to the play, and he agreed to the change.

In February 1946, while visiting his parents in Boston, Corwin received word that the opera had been awarded first prize. Al, who was on army leave, had been occupying Norman's apartment when the telegram arrived from Edward Johnson, head of the Met. Corwin had forgotten the opera and told Al on the phone that the telegram had probably been missent—that perhaps it was intended for Norman *Cordon*, a noted opera singer of the day. It was no mistake, and one year later the creators, Bernard Rogers and Norman Corwin, were honored at a reception by the American Society of Composers, Authors, and Publishers (ASCAP) at the Lotus Club, West 57th Street, on the eve of the operatic event.

The Warrior featured Mack Harrell, singing the role of Samson, and Regina Resnik as Delilah. The short opera by Rogers shared the bill with *Hansel and Gretel*—hardly a compatible pairing because of the dark, macabre mood that dominates Samson's downfall. Critics concluded that *The Warrior* did not attain "unequivocal success." Rogers' score, it was said, attempted to convey (in tone) a psychological conception, and possessed a feeling for drama in musical sound; still, it failed to achieve effective continuity for the stage and was, in the opinion of *Variety*, "pedestrian."[6] Although Corwin's original radio play had been applauded, the conversion to operatic form was received with mixed feelings. The *Musical Courier* considered the opera's language "a hybrid neither epic nor realistic."[7]

The opera was but a footnote to a busy routine, as Corwin concentrated on writing, producing, and narrating *One World Flight*. He was grateful for high-level support, for William Paley, in particular, appeared enthusiastic about the documentary endeavor. Paley, who often visited Corwin's control room during production of the series, seemed certain that *One World Flight* met the tenets of his programming philosophy, which he had espoused only a few weeks earlier at the NAB convention.[8]

There was obvious pressure, nevertheless, for postwar radio to seek "something new, something interesting, something cheap." Beyond that, pragmatism dictated programming for mass appeal. Still, both CBS executives, Paley and Frank Stanton, seemed convinced that broadcasting needed adventurous efforts as advanced by the likes of a Corwin. Indeed, Stanton even asked Corwin to join him one day in an affiliates meeting. After Corwin had spoken to the group, a radio station manager from Buffalo expressed hope that *One World Flight*, which he considered a pathfinder in radio programming, might be the way of the future; but he was not optimistic. He had taken a poll of his listeners, he said, which revealed "not what you're thinking, gentlemen. They want more disc jockeys." He asked, sadly, "What's radio coming to?"[9]

One evening, suddenly, Norman Corwin proposed marriage to Katherine Locke. It was, most certainly, an impetuous act—as much a surprise to him as to her—and the effect on both of their lives had to be considered. It was ten years since her first Broadway success—since the thrill of that morning (February 21, 1937) when critic Burns Mantle announced in the *New York Daily News:*

> I give you . . . a little girl named Katherine Locke. She is playing the girl who meets the boy in *Having a Wonderful Time.* She gives a characterization not a jot short of magnificent. I shall classify them as a joint hit this morning . . .[10]

Born in Russia and brought to the States as a small child, Katherine Locke had grown up in the cultural emphasis of an erudite New England home. Her father, a Hebrew scholar and teacher, was also a cantor, whose voice many compared to Caruso. She pursued her natural interest in music and enrolled at the Damrosch Conservatory of Music in New York, with the ambition to become a pianist. Her love for the theatre, however, prompted her, after a brief matriculation at New York University, to leave academe for the stage at the age of seventeen.

Her ascendancy to Broadway stardom was precise and promising, as she won plaudits for a series of sensitive portrayals. After *Having Wonderful Time,* which ran for 372 performances, she was acclaimed for her Ophelia in Maurice Evans' production of *Hamlet.* In March of 1940, she appeared opposite Franchot Tone in Ernest Hemingway's *The Fifth Column.* A year later, she joined Tallulah Bankhead, Lee J. Cobb, and Robert Ryan in Clifford Odets' *Clash by Night.*

She was married briefly to Maurice Helprin, an assistant to the noted film director Alexander Korda, and they lived on a 117-acre farm in New Jersey. Her divorce had been final only a few weeks when she was introduced to Corwin by a mutual friend, Giuliana Taberna, at a busy Madison Avenue intersection near CBS. Both were preoccupied by the pressures of their careers, so that theirs was a casual friendship, with only occasional social encounters.

Although it seemed unlikely that anyone could end Corwin's thirty-seven-year-long bachelorhood, there were contrary indications—and a prophetic incident. During rehearsal of a *This Is War!* program, Corwin, noticing Kate alone, studying her script during a break, asked her facetiously, "Will you marry me?" "Of course," she replied, lightly. The pleasantry passed as it was intended—a frivolous moment. Marriage, at the time, was far from the mind of either.

The wedding was as sudden as their engagement. They left by train on Monday morning, March 17, to be married shortly before noon by a justice of the peace in Elkton, Maryland. The trip to another state was necessitated by Corwin's neglect to obtain a New York marriage license. He had been too busy to cope with the essential forms, and he refused to wait the one week required. Maryland waived such formalities.

On the train to Elkton, Norman and Kate were accompanied by a friend, Mabel Schirmer, who went along to serve as a witness. En route to Maryland, Mabel and Kate sat together, chatting, while Corwin worked alone in a small compartment, writing his next *One World Flight* program. After the brief ceremony, the trio had lunch, then returned by train to New York that same day, in time for Corwin's rehearsal and broadcast.

Kate knew then that she was irrevocably married to Corwin's career. Even though newlyweds, they sat separately on the return journey, in order that Norman would have privacy to complete his script.

The series ended in April. On June 5, 1947, Kate and Norman left by car on a leisurely cross-country trip to Hollywood. Again, they were accompanied by Mabel Schirmer, and Kate remembered "sitting between the two worst drivers in New York."[11] They visited Kate's parents in Milwaukee, her uncle's farm near Mapleton, Wisconsin, and arrived in Los Angeles on the 19th of June.

By fall, an uneasy edge had crept into cocktail conversations of the movie colony. Concern centered on an investigation into the film industry which was being conducted by the House Committee on Un-American Activities. In a letter dated October 18, 1947, Corwin wrote a friend:

> Seems Hollywood has roused itself over the House Un-American Activities committee and a great many people not hithertofore associated with liberal causes or the fight against thought-control have come out swinging. William Wyler, John Huston, Burgess Meredith, Marsha Hunt, George Stevens, Gregory Peck, even David O. Selznick. We had a big meeting at the Shrine Auditorium last Wednesday in which the nineteen 'unfriendly' witnesses were guests of honor. I was one of the speakers for the evening.[12]

Two days later, climaxing weeks of closed-door testimony, public hearings opened in Washington under the chairmanship of Representative J. Parnell Thomas of New Jersey. Motion picture executives were torn between loyalty to their art and anxiety over charges their industry had been undermined by Communistic influences. The indictment gathered momentum as the congressional probe took on a vindictive mood.

On the West Coast, Corwin read daily headlines of the developing confrontation and, like his colleagues of the film world, anticipated its threat to free expression. He joined Hollywood notables to organize resistance. They called themselves the Committee for the First Amendment, and they turned to radio for their platform.

On October 26, 1947—one week after the public hearings had opened in Washington—*Hollywood Fights Back,* a bristling rebuttal, was aired by the ABC network (1:30–2:00 p.m., EST). The broadcast originated from both coasts, with Corwin producing the principal segment from Hollywood and William N. Robson directing in New York. The show featured a parade of movie stars and others who stated in unstinting terms their apprehension. The program began with a disclaimer:

The following program is sponsored by the Committee for the First Amendment, and the views expressed on the program are those of the committee members.

The stars introduced themselves:

This is Judy Garland. Have you been to a movie this week? Are you going to a movie tonight, or maybe tomorrow? Look around the room. Are there any newspapers lying on the floor, any magazines on your table, any books on your shelves? It has always been your right to read or see anything you wanted to. But now it seems to be getting kind of complicated.

For the past week in Washington, the Thomas-Rankin House Committee on Un-American Activities has been investigating the film industry. I have never been a member of a political organization, but have been following this investigation—and I don't like it.

There are a lot of stars here to speak to you. We're show business, yes, but we're also American citizens. It's one thing if someone says we're not good actors; that hurts, but we can take it. Something else again to say we're not good Americans.

Jane Wyatt appeared:

> Have you seen *Crossfire*[13] yet? Good picture? It's against religious dis-
> crimination. It is one of the biggest hits in years. The American people
> have awarded it four stars, but the Un-American Committee gave the
> men who made it three subpoenas . . .

Others followed, including Joseph Cotten, James Gleason, Peter
Lorre, and John Huston. Huston said:

> The House Committee has been in existence for nine years. It has spent
> millions of dollars of taxpayers' money investigating what it calls subver-
> sive activities. The idea was that the Committee would come up with
> legislation to counteract anything subversive. Well, in nine years it has
> proposed exactly one piece of legislation—and that was rejected as
> unconstitutional, along with a scathing denunciation by the United
> States Supreme Court.

Danny Kaye, Margaret Sullavan, Walter Wanger, Paul Henreid,
Charles Boyer, and Richard Conte also made statements. Evelyn
Keyes said:

> James Colescott said 'The Un-American Committee program so closely
> parallels the program of the Klan, there is no distinguishable difference
> between them.' And who is James Colescott? The Imperial Wizard of
> the Ku Klux Klan.

The program continued with Burt Lancaster, Vincent Price, Ava
Gardner, Gene Kelly, and Florence Eldridge—each expressing personal feelings about what was deemed a trial of terror. Marsha Hunt
quoted John Rankin, member of the House committee, as having said
on the floor of Congress that Walter Winchell was "a communistic
kike." Robert Young appeared, as did Eddie Cantor; but Sylvia Sidney,
for reasons unknown, left the studio. Humphrey Bogart, in his typical, uncompromising manner, asked:

> Is Democracy so feeble that it can be subverted merely by a look, or a
> line, an inflection, a gesture?[14]

Fredric March followed, to ask:

> Who do you think they're really after? Who comes after us? Is it your
> minister who will be told what he can say in his pulpit? Is it your

children's schoolteacher who will be told what she can say in a classroom? Is it your children who will be told what they can write in their
school newspaper? Is it you who will have to look around nervously
before you say what is on your mind? Who are they after? They are
after more than Hollywood. This reaches into every American city—
and we take you to New York.

At this cue, the program switched from Hollywood to New York,
where John Garfield stepped to the microphone and warned that
there was no guarantee the Un-American Committee would stop with
the movies. "Already, the American theatre—which I love—has been
attacked." Garfield revealed that, in the view of the Committee, 44
percent of the plays on Broadway had been subversive. He added,
"That's news to Broadway."

Frank Sinatra suggested that the inquisition would soon involve
radio:

> Once they get the movies throttled, how long will it be before the
> Committee goes to work on the freedom of the air? How long will it be
> before we will be told what we can or cannot say into a radio micro-
> phone? If you make a pitch on nationwide network for a square deal for
> the underdog, will they call you a commie? Will we have to think Mr.
> Rankin's way to get into the elevator at Radio City? Are they going to
> scare us into silence? I wonder. If this Committee gets a green light
> from the American people now, will it be possible to make a broadcast
> like this a year from today?

Similar concerns were expressed by Deems Taylor and Artie Shaw,
by Dr. Harlow Shapley, director of the Harvard Observatory, and by
Senators Elbert D. Thomas of Utah, Wayne Morse of Oregon, and
Glen Taylor of Idaho.[15]

The broadcast was credited as having some impact, for a lull in
committee activity followed. But only briefly. The witchhunting hysteria would soon resume, to engulf all media.

The immediate concern was *then*, October 1947, and the focus was
Hollywood. The Washington investigation, fed by rumor and innuendo, moved on relentlessly. Helplessly, famed motion picture personalities watched the proceedings from the rear of a House Office
Building caucus room. Danny Kaye typified the gathering gloom
when, at a press conference of the Committee for the First Amendment, he introduced a colleague, and himself, with the quip, "Gene

Kelly is a hoofer with a broken leg, and I'm a comedian with no jokes today."[16]

Corwin expressed his pessimism in a letter to Bill Fineshriber, dated November 11, 1947:

> Of course, a man does not live by gold alone, and our spirits have been weighted down by the way things have been going in the world. There seems to be a new atrocity everyday. The latest item in this direction, the report that 33 of 35 people cashiered from our State Department since the recent purge turn out to be Jews. If this is correct, it is just something too close to official anti-Semitism to be merely coincidental. And if the Rankins and Peglers have finally convinced the government that communism and Judaism are synonymous, I can just see the expanded fields of inquisition awaiting Messrs. Thomas and Stripling.[17]

Corwin began work November 17, 1947, on the scenario for a significant motion picture. It was a screenplay based on Robert Penn Warren's novel *All the King's Men*, about a Southern demagogue. CBS had granted an extension to his six-month privilege to do "outside" projects, which gave rise to the speculation that Corwin might be leaving radio for films. *Variety* even headlined the possibility:

CORWIN TAKING A LONG WALK?[18]

In truth, Corwin was never much impressed by Hollywood procedure, and even with the challenge of this important picture he deeply felt the strain of movieland's bureaucracy. In March of 1948, in a letter to Mrs. Gerald M. Maulsby, wife of a CBS executive, he complained:

> I have just finished a screenplay after grappling with its problems for four months, and I am glad to be rid of it. I find film processes so pitted with assembly line psychology and commercial considerations that the joy of creation is reduced to a quality of routine.[19]

Disenchantment with *All the King's Men* became an issue when the film's producer, Robert Rossen, decided he should collaborate with Corwin on the final script. Corwin's attorney, Arnold Grant, objected. He felt his client's established status deserved lone credit as to authorship. Corwin acceded to this legal advice and withdrew from the project, which probably was a mistake. In retrospect, he felt he might have learned much by working with Rossen.

The film garnered instant praise upon release, and became a box office hit. *All the King's Men* won three Academy Awards, including one for its star, Broderick Crawford, and another naming it Best Picture of 1948.

In midsummer 1948, Corwin was invited to join seven outstanding individuals in New York to serve as a special One World Commission, honoring the memory of the late Fiorello H. LaGuardia. The former mayor of New York had succeeded Corwin as the second recipient of the Wendell Willkie Award (announced publicly on the final broadcast of Corwin's *One World Flight*); however, he had died in September of 1947. A special commission was therefore named to make the global journey in his honor.

The delegation included Mrs. LaGuardia; Dr. Emily Greene Balch, co-winner of the Nobel Prize for Peace in 1946; Morris S. Novik, former director of WNYC; Fritz von Unruh, author; James H. Sheldon, administrative secretary of the Non-Sectarian Anti-Nazi League; Mona May Karff and Iris Gabriel, both associated with the One World Movement; and of course Corwin.

Corwin was low in spirits as he boarded the Santa Fe *Chief*. He did not like leaving Kate behind, and he was still disturbed by the implications of the Communist probe. He was perturbed, too, by the current direction of radio, bothered by his relative inactivity, and he longed for some challenging project. Of concern, of course, were contract negotiations with CBS. Difficult discussions seemed inevitable. By co-incidence, William S. Paley and his wife boarded the same train in Pasadena. The CBS president was pleased to see Corwin, but, being very tired, said all he wanted to do the first day was sleep. They agreed to have lunch together later.

Paley and Corwin sat across from each other in the diner the next day, as the *Chief* hurtled through the sunlight of America's scenic West. They discussed topics pertaining to the future of the network, to radio specifically, and to Norman's career.

Weighing especially heavy on Paley's mind was the Shirer controversy. William L. Shirer, a notable wartime voice on CBS, had been dropped by his sponsor and subsequently shifted to a time which the correspondent considered inferior. As a result, he had resigned. The network was criticized for cancelling liberal commentators. Some quarters, however, applauded Paley for having disposed of Shirer. Paley, caught in the middle, found his position awkward and untenable. He had no wish to penalize Shirer, he told Corwin.

Paley felt other pressures as well. To him, radio was more competitive than ever, and "getting tougher." And although he viewed the current trend with considerable misgivings, he understood and accepted the good business maxim of mass audience appeal. "If we do not reach as many people as possible, then we're not making the best use of our talent, our time, and our equipment."

To Corwin, the thrust of his meaning was clear. But Paley was specific. He and "a special audience" were appreciative of Corwin's work, he told the writer-producer, but he hoped that such talent might be directed to a broader audience. "We've simply got to face up to the fact that we're a commercial business."[20]

The *Chief* rumbled on. Outside, a confusion of countryside slipped by; inside, the clarity of an inevitable future confronted Corwin. He was being called upon to adopt the dogma of popular, commonplace radio, to deny his fundamental philosophy, to pander to commercial practicality. He was saddened—not so much for himself as for the medium he served.

Paley talked on about a worsening political climate, the appearance of television, the advent of the LP (long-playing record). His monologue moved through areas of pessimism and promise. And while much of what he said seemed undermined by uncertainty and anxiety, Paley was not dismayed. Things might even be looking up for Columbia. For one thing, he announced, Jack Benny was coming over from NBC.[21]

The end of an era was all too evident, and the fact would be emphasized with sober finality within the next few months. Corwin would then realize, with the receipt of a new contract, that CBS was ambivalent about his return. No previous contract had been so restrictive. In a letter dated October 1, 1948, Corwin stated his surprise to Frank Stanton:

> Many thanks for your letter of the 25th. It was wonderful to have a good talk with you again.

I naturally look forward to the prospect you suggest of resuming talks, either on your next trip west or my next east. Only, I hope by that time there is a basis of association between myself and CBS.

I say this because I have lately received from Becker [I. S. Becker, known as "Zac"] proposals for a new contract so shocking that I had to blink six times before reading them again. I am not going to inflict you with the details since the matter is a typhoon in Zac's teapot, except to mention that the new proposals, advanced over the dead body of an agreement made between us last November, are strikingly inferior to my last two Columbia contracts in every last respect.

I have not yet replied with counter proposals, but I just want you to know, Frank, that if this 'contractitus' should result in my ending the long and happy relationship between Columbia and myself, the act would in no way lessen the affection and esteem which I hold for you and which has grown steadily through the years.[22]

The objectionable clause in Corwin's new contract would grant CBS rights to 50 percent of his subsidiary earnings derived from plays or programs created for the network, such as anthologies or screen adaptations. The document, an implied threat to Corwin's future, was unacceptable.

This concern, however, was yet to come. At the moment, the cold reality of Bill Paley's frank analysis consumed Corwin. He had said goodbye to Paley, and returned to his compartment to rest. As he lay there, thinking, his career passed quickly before him. Somehow, he felt he had fallen short, that his work had been of fleeting value. Feeling quite vulnerable, Corwin believed that his writing days had probably ended.

In New York, he took a cab to Mabel Schirmer's apartment. She happened to be visiting Hollywood at that time, so they had arranged to exchange accommodations. Disconsolate as he perused the empty apartment, he wandered to a bookcase, idly surveyed the titles, and at random took down a large volume about Joseph Conrad. The book fell open to a diary account that expressed Conrad's heavyheartedness at a particular time, when he doubted he would ever write again. For a 500-page book to unexpectedly open to an observation so closely allied to Corwin's frame of mind seemed almost psychic.

Immediately, he felt better.

13. The Blacklist:
Cast of Concern

Signs and portents!
It was no furtive tapping on the window sill at night,
But clamorous pounding in the public square.

—On a Note of Triumph

As soon as Kate Corwin put the receiver down, she informed her houseguest, Mabel Schirmer, of the news. Norman had telephoned to tell her that it was possible for her to join him for the LaGuardia Memorial Commission trip to Europe. She therefore joined a select group which now included Jo Davidson, sculptor; Freda Kerchway, magazine publisher; Clifford Durr, former chairman of the Federal Communications Commission; and Dr. Otto Nathan, later to become the executor of the estate of Albert Einstein.

The Corwins and members of the commission boarded the Polish ship *Batory* on the 14th of August 1948,[1] and one week later docked at Gdynia. Because Fiorello LaGuardia had earned the love and admiration of many countries through his service as United Nations Relief and Rehabilitation Administration chairman, the mission of the One World group was to dedicate, in his name, schools, hospitals, streets, and municipal squares in five European countries.

For Corwin, it was a brief, nostalgic return to similar scenes of his previous odyssey abroad. In Rome, however, he was felled by a flu virus, and though some commission members continued on to Israel, Norman and Kate, with a few others, returned to New York on a nonscheduled flight of Alaska Airlines. The skies over the Atlantic were stormy, and the flight was forced to describe a wide circle via Iceland, Greenland, and the wastes of northern Canada. Thus, years before polar routes became routine, Corwin remembered the flight as "unexpectedly arctic and exhausting."

A few days' stopover in New York, prior to a return to the West Coast, gave rise to speculation that CBS might have plans for Corwin, that he might be asked to divide his time between radio and television. In truth, he was still at loggerheads with the network over conditions for continued employment. As for Corwin's future, a luncheon meeting with an old friend at the United Nations building was to be of consequence.

W. Gibson-Parker had been with BBC at the time Corwin was producing *An American in England,* and since had joined the UN as a member of the secretariat in communications. At the luncheon, to which Parker had invited Corwin, was also the head of UN Radio, Peter Aylen, a Canadian. It was Aylen who, when Corwin mentioned his contractual problems with CBS, suggested that he join the United Nations as a producer of special projects.

The offer was enticing. Corwin's career had been characterized by eloquent expressions of international brotherhood, and never so much as now. His programs had promoted ideals of good will and peace; he had, obviously, dedicated his art to realization of the goals advocated by the UN organization. He said he would think about it seriously.

Norman and Kate returned to Hollywood September 29, 1948, and in December he received a letter from Werner Michel of the CBS Documentary Unit.[2] It concerned a Corwin proposal to develop for the Unit a special program, perhaps a cantata, about Palestine. Michel mentioned that the project might be considered controversial and concluded with the facetious plea, "If my information concerning the cantata is correct, please don't give me away to the House Un-American Committee."[3]

It was no joke. Radio, as many had warned, found itself more and more involved in the broadening dimensions of a national obsession against communism. Private vigilantes extended even the Attorney General's list of subversive groups, and action was urged against the networks, sponsors, and agents. Most, at the moment, refused to take such accusations seriously. In time, they would.

Despite the deepening concern, several promising options opened for Corwin with the coming of the new year. Joseph Losey, producing a new play by Howard Koch, wanted Norman and Kate to accept acting roles in New York. They were intrigued by the prospect of appearing on stage together and considered it. Also, Corwin was anxious to arrange the production of his own play, a stage interpretation of *Mary and the Fairy*, which had been optioned by Irene Selznick, wife of the movie mogul. Neither project materialized—nor, for that matter, a third alternative, headlined in a January 1949 issue of *Variety:*

NBC EXTENDS ITS WELCOME MAT TO NORMAN CORWIN, COLUMBIA'S GEM[4]

The show business journal concluded that NBC would "make every effort" to land Corwin, especially in view of its talent losses. It conceded, nevertheless, that it was a "toss-up whether Corwin switches allegiance to NBC or signs up again with CBS."

He did neither. He chose to remain independent. And ultimately he decided to join UN Radio, part-time. Aylen happily welcomed Corwin by creating for him a unique post: Chief of Special Projects. It would be his responsibility to produce radio specials promoting UN activities and aims, involving the best of world talent. The appointment was officially announced on March 8, 1949.

Spring 1949 in Manhattan was a season of industry and apprehension for Corwin. He wrote to his parents:

> I am in one of the worst pressure jams for some time, and it is reminiscent of the old days when I was riding three horses in six different directions, and juggling Indian clubs at the same time.[5]

In May, he was interviewed by Eleanor Roosevelt on her daily talk program over ABC. He read Whitman from the Green Room, at the intermission of a CBS Symphony concert. For various reasons, he met with prominent personalities, including Marlene Dietrich, Archibald MacLeish, and Admiral Nimitz. He urged Irene Selznick to do something about his play. He worked at a draft of the CBS documentary, scheduled for airing in July as a Unit production, and he began planning a fall series for United Nations Radio.

In June, Corwin was jarred by a disclosure that the FBI had included his name on a list of notables accused of being Communist sympathizers and "fellow travelers." The fact was made known in the public reading of the list at the espionage trial of Judith Coplon, a twenty-eight-year-old former analyst in the Department of Justice who had been accused of stealing government secrets with the intent to aid a foreign power. Although irrelevant to the trial, the FBI list named as principals Fredric March and his wife, Florence Eldridge. It also included Edward G. Robinson, Paul Robeson, Dorothy Parker, Donald Ogden Stuart, Ruth McKenney, Albert Maltz, Alvah Bessie, Dalton Trumbo, Millen Brand, and Michael Blankfort—as well as the president of Boston University, many actors and writers, and, of course, Corwin.[6]

No longer was it a distant, impersonal headline, a hearing, a vague witchhunt. The threat was real. The finger had been pointed. He had been named.

By whom? By "confidential informants," the report stated. As reported by the *New York Times,* each charge was accompanied by a coded accuser, cited anonymously as "Confidential Informant ND 402," or, with reference to Corwin, "Confidential Informant ND 336." No other identification was given, no indication of how reliable the informants were, no evidence of how much credence the FBI placed in the reports.

The absurdity of the charge lay in the simplicity of the indictment. Corwin was supposed to be "connected" with communism because he had written *Set Your Clock at U235* (originally for the Herald-Tribune Forum, October 1945), which was read by Fredric March on December 5, 1945, at a Madison Square Garden meeting, the topic of which was "Crisis Coming, Atom Bomb—for Peace or War?" Other participants at this meeting included Dr. Harley Shapley, Julian Huxley, Senator Charles W. Tobey, R. J. Thomas, Colonel Evans Carlson, Dr. Harold C. Urey, Helen Keller, Danny Kaye, Jo Davidson, and Henry A. Wallace.

At the revelation, the Columbia Broadcasting System immediately issued a statement which pointed out that Mr. Corwin had not been on its staff for more than a year. It added, obligingly, "We do not believe he is a Communist or a fellow traveler."[7]

Corwin, of course, was incensed by the FBI report. He told the press:

I am not a Communist. I am not a fellow traveler. But I do have contempt for irresponsible smear lists, whether issued by career crackpots or 'chicken-little' agents.[8]

All who were affected by the report emphatically denied Communist affiliations. March decried it as "absurd." Brand sardonically observed that he was in "distinguished company." President Daniel L. Marsh, of Boston University, felt it was all "very idiotic." Dorothy Parker declared:

> This makes me very sick. I'm damned glad to be an American and always have been.
> I regret to say I know no Russians, but I wish I did. Maybe it would help understanding if we all knew some Russians.
> I have no desire to sell any secrets, because I don't know any.
> Overthrow the Government?

She laughed:

> I want to overthrow prejudice and injustice.[9]

It was difficult to work under the weight of suspicion and public distrust. The fear of Communist infiltration and influence had induced such anxiety and fanaticism that one wondered if the cure might be more injurious than the malady. Merely to mention communism seemed to make it exist, and many innocent victims, caught in this web of paranoia, would suffer great personal harm. Corwin, on the other hand, tried to shake off the onus and apply himself with the same zeal and idealism as before. His topics of world order and peaceful coexistence, however, invited the scrutiny of self-appointed watchdogs.

His commissioned script for the CBS Documentary Unit was readied for production July 10, 1949. Advancing a UN theme, it was titled *Citizen of the World*, and Lee J. Cobb narrated. It began with a complex pattern of sound, with music and voices:

PLANE
One of them took a fast plane to Kashmir to stop a war.
TRAIN
One of them took a night train to Poland to fight beetles and Bang's disease.
BOAT WHISTLE
One of them took a slow boat to China, trailing a dope smuggler.
And one fed a million children.
And one got shot in an ambush.

And one stopped an epidemic.
And one was a poet.
And one was an emperor.
And one was a prophet.
And one was a businessman.

And at first there were only a few of them scattered around the
   world.
But now there are many and growing,
And they are around you.

And for all you know, you may be one yourself.[10]

Citizen of the World was described by the *New York Times* as "a generally restrained plea for the individual's active interest in solving the
problems of the world."[11] It was later made available on disc for the
broadcasting systems of Sweden, Australia, and England. A critic for
the *London Daily Express* wrote:

> About Corwin, there is a brazen simplicity about his writing that is
> unchallengeable. His pen cuts like a surgeon's knife to the bone of his
> subject matter, and the red light is barely warm before you are en-
> trapped in his story-telling.[12]

In August, Corwin's character and reputation came under attack
again, this time from the floor of Congress. Senator Pat McCarran, a
Democrat from Nevada, stood up in the Senate and bitterly denounced persons who had gone, in his words, "directly from fields of
subversive activity" to positions of authority in the United Nations. He
singled out Dr. Ludwig Rajchman, executive director of the United
Nations International Emergency Children's Fund, and Norman Corwin of UN Radio.

The Senator said, "If the case of Norman Corwin were an isolated
instance, it would not be greatly disturbing. It is, unfortunately, characteristic of a number of people who have been selected to serve in the
Secretariat of the United Nations." He continued: "Mr. Corwin is
cited as communist and subversive by the Attorney General of the
United States. Mr. Corwin is or has been a member of a long list of
Communist front organizations."[13]

At Lake Success, Corwin countered with the contention that Mc-
Carran was "a political mad dog." Angrily, he suggested that Senator

McCarran's "public outcry for war and his generally hydrophobic attacks on personnel of the United Nations are typical of his contribution to the hysteria which has already done so much damage to the lives and reputations of innocent people and encouraged an undermining of respect for constitutional guarantees." Corwin called himself a "vastly better patriot" than the Senator, and wearily concluded that the routine of restating one's denial of Communistic tendencies was "getting to be daily exercise for anybody who ever entertained a liberal idea."[14]

Corwin, as McCarran accused, had been named by a number of "citations." Most of them, however, seemed innocent, innocuous, even false. He had, for instance, been erroneously linked to a school for writers on King's Road in Hollywood, a supposed Communist front, as a guest lecturer. He had been among a list of eminent people published in the *New York Times* as having been *asked* to help in behalf of Russian War Relief. A subversive publication had compared Corwin to Walt Whitman. He was recorded as having read a Stephen Vincent Benét poem, *This for Russia,* at a Russian War Relief benefit at the Hotel Commodore in New York City on May 27, 1942. In 1943, Corwin was guest at a reception honoring the Soviet novelist and movie director, Mikhail Kalatozov, at the Mocambo in Hollywood. Corwin was even listed for having written a piece for the President's Birthday Ball Committee, broadcast on all major networks in 1943.

It was so easy. In all his works concerning the war, in his world travels, in his contacts with international literary figures, in his efforts to encourage his art, it was so easy to associate Corwin with people and efforts which had since passed from favor. He was accused of belonging to more than 150 Communist front organizations.

It concerned him, of course, but his sympathy was with a multitude of media practitioners—many personal friends—who were feeling the pressure of this unrelenting probe. Its obvious unfairness of indictment by rumor, by innuendo, was incredible to him in a free, democratic society. Only a short while before, he had chronicled the rise and fall of a Fascist regime which had displaced individual rights in the demands of authoritarian rule. Now, about him, he saw the same fear rekindled in a confused atmosphere of suspicion and inquisition. Reputations of respected citizens were being suspended on the tenuous judgment of amateur informants.

By the fall of '49 the phobia had reached frightening dimensions and the future looked bleak. The lists were growing. And there were more to come.

Corwin inaugurated his new job with a six-program documentary series for UN Radio, which was broadcast over the NBC radio network. It began with his original, *Could Be,* followed by contributions from Millard Lampell, Allen Sloane, W. Gibson-Parker, Len Peterson, and the writing team of Jerome Lawrence and Robert E. Lee. The project offered the directorial talents of Gerald Kean and Canada's Andrew Allen.

Corwin's show, *Could Be,* enthralled millions of listeners in the United States and abroad by its expansive imagination. It possessed the flavor of documentary and fantasy, a "wish-day-come" concept, as Corwin described it, a future-time approach to peaceful coexistence and concerns enacted by the same stratagem and cooperation with which countries of the world wage war. The hypothesis was stated in a simple introduction:

> This comes to you, in a sense, with the compliments of the future. It is based on what could be, in the lifetime of most of us; based on what is now known and scientifically possible. It is a dream view, a storyboard, a synopsis of what could happen if the nations of the world got together and attacked common problems with the same vigor, determination, and resources with which, from time to time, they have attacked each other.
>
> Suspend your belief for long enough to belong to a time that could conceivably arrive—a future whose distance from now need be only as long as we make it.
>
> Come in, year X . . . come in . . . come in . . .

Then followed a broadcast report from the roof of the Secretariat Building at the permanent headquarters of the United Nations, overlooking the East River in New York City. There was talk of "zero hour," of a "Peace Blitz"; and with the calling in of correspondents at various vantage points in key centers around the world, a story was told of an unprecedented international movement to improve the condition of Man. There were doubters, dissenters, but the "invasion" against disease and hunger and poverty continued on a broad front. Participants reported the action:

... I can't hear myself above the roar of these motors all around us here! The whole force, the whole army is moving east, uprising ground . . .

. . . I'm flying this plane alone. There's a hopper under my seat holding a half ton of rice seed, and all I have to do is push a button . . .

All we're out to exterminate is rats, bugs, lice, vermin, and locusts. We're the ground force of a crew that . . .

Success seemed at hand:

This is Observer 1 on the roof of UN Headquarters in New York. A cheering, shouting throng is voicing its appreciation of the dramatic efficiency with which the first gunless, bloodless, and creative Blitz in the history of the world is taking place without impediment . . .

The observer's voice and the cheering then faded away to silence, and reality returned with the narrator's cold conclusion:

A dream, a dream, a dream!
We awaken rudely, we leave the future behind, we return to the
    present, and nobody is cheering.

Finally, there was optimism, in an ending of speculation:

But there is also a hope, and more than a hope, and what could be may one day break through and become. At least one part of the dream is true—all those dams, wind towers, seeding planes, heat pumps, atomic piles, the radar on the fishing boats, the techniques, the manpower, the international agencies, the funds—they're all here *now;* and in some instances cooperation has already begun among nations, through the UN itself.

Could it be, then? Could this fantasy in which peace and cooperation are more exciting to the world than war—could this possibly be?[15]

It was a brisk, sunny afternoon as Fleet Admiral Chester W. Nimitz started for a Sunday stroll. He had just put on his coat when he heard the opening to Corwin's broadcast over the radio. The next day, September 12, 1949, he wrote:

... the program had to be good to keep me indoors for the full hour, but I stayed in until *It Could Be* [*sic*] was finished.

I wish to congratulate you on one of the best radio dramatizations that has ever been my good fortune to hear, and I wish not only every American but all foreigners could hear it. In this connection, I have a criticism which is not directed against the program but at the lack of publicity it received before I heard it.[16]

Could Be, which *Variety* termed "Orson Welles' Martian scare in reverse,"[17] was repeated by NBC and later heard in Britain, Canada, and Australia. It was appreciated by the foreign press. London's *Radio Times* lauded Corwin, concluding:

The important thing about *Could Be,* apart from its technical brilliance, is that it is no speculative dream, but a dramatized statement of the facts and findings of a recent United Nations conference on world resources. Dream-print? Blueprint? Could be![18]

The year was to end with an exceptional event, planned for the stage of Carnegie Hall, to celebrate the Universal Declaration of Human Rights. Peter Aylen had approved Corwin's idea to have Aaron Copland write a musical setting for a narrative of the preamble to the UN document. It was arranged that the composer would receive $500 for one-time rights. And to perform it, Corwin hoped to acquire Serge Koussevitzky and the Boston Symphony Orchestra.

At the time, Corwin happened to be discussing with film star Jean Arthur the possibility of her playing the lead in the stage production of *Mary and the Fairy.* And while he was her houseguest in Williamstown, Massachusetts, he decided to drive south to Tanglewood to see Koussevitzky. The old man listened intently to Corwin's plan, but shook his head. His doctor had adjured him against doing anything beyond his normal schedule.[19] Still, no worry, he said; he had in mind a bright young man in whom he had much interest and who, he was certain, could capably conduct in his place. His name was Leonard Bernstein.

Now Corwin needed a narrator. Someone suggested Laurence Olivier, but it seemed improbable that the noted actor, knighted in 1947 and a recent Academy Award winner (for *Hamlet*), would consent to come all the way from England to appear *gratis* in a minute-and-a-half performance. But boldly, Corwin asked; surprisingly, Olivier accepted.

NBC television covered the occasion, on December 10, 1949—the first program ever televised from Carnegie Hall. Copland's music soared and Sir Laurence delivered the preamble with lilt and force. Everything went well, except for one oversight. At the conclusion of the program, conductor Leonard Bernstein forgot to call upon Aaron Copland for a bow, a prearranged gesture of respect. Afterward, in a cab, Bernstein acknowledged his error, but he told Copland not to mind. "The music is the important thing," he said.[20]

It was a strange, unpredictable time. On one hand, Corwin was commended for touting the prerogatives of peace and unanimity among nations; on the other, he was distrusted and looked upon with suspicion for his liberal views. With the arrival of the new decade, the same disquieting concerns clouded the field of communications and the arts. New lists involved new people daily. Most broadcast executives despised the witchhunt, then accepted it, and later participated.

The One World concept was no longer in vogue—a fact reflected in disinterest for programs produced by the United Nations. The Mutual Broadcasting System, however, consented to collaborate with UN Radio for the broadcast of six special documentaries in the spring of 1950. Corwin was to supervise the programs, which were presented under the series title *The Pursuit of Peace*.

In March, a month before the inaugural broadcast, a spokesman for Baltimore's Mutual affiliate, WCBM, announced:

> WCBM is pleased to state that it is a pleasure not to accept these programs. We reject the offer on one point only—we object to any association with Norman Corwin, a self-admitted leftist. It would be like having Fulton Lewis cover the Russian activities of the UN.

In the WCBM letter to Mutual, the spokesman expressed surprise and "deep regret" that the network had "seen fit to employ this man." In New York, Mutual countered with the fact that Corwin was doing only two of the programs, and said that the station's point was "far-fetched" with respect to a series that had "nothing to do with leftists or rightists, but the straight story of the UN."[21] John Elmer, the owner of WCBM, soon intervened and said that his station would carry the UN-MBS series.[22]

Undeterred, Corwin set about to prepare the first broadcast, an hour-long documentary depicting the significance of the Universal

Declaration of Human Rights. Featuring an all-star, international cast, *Document A/777* was broadcast on March 26, 1950.

The voting which marked the adoption of the Human Rights Bill had been fully recorded at the UN General Assembly in Paris in December 1948. Corwin therefore listened to the tapes of the conference, heard the discussion—the delegates voicing their approval or disapproval—and the final decision. He hit upon the idea of using the actual roll call as the unifying thread:

PRESIDENT: Guatemala?[23]
DELEGATE: Si!
PRESIDENT: Haiti?
DELEGATE: Oui.
PRESIDENT: Honduras? Honduras . . .?
VOICE: Absent.
PRESIDENT: Iceland?
DELEGATE: Yes!
PRESIDENT: India?
NARRATOR: Hold it. Look below there. Do you see the little white-haired woman sitting among the Indian representatives at this General Assembly here at the Palais de Chaillot in Paris? That is Mrs. Vijaya Lakshmi Pandit, chairman of her nation's delegation. A woman. Bear this in mind, because—
PRESIDENT: India?
NARRATOR: Please, hold it. History has been long enough at the job in India to permit a few moments of reminiscence here.

The roll call was interrupted at particular countries as Corwin dramatized incidents peculiar to each, illustrating the basis of the various articles accepted by the United Nations Commission on Human Rights. Van Heflin narrated, and the cast included such stars of stage and screen as Richard Basehart, Charles Boyer, Ronald Colman, Joan Crawford, Maurice Evans, José Ferrer, Reginald Gardner, Jean Hersholt, Lena Horne, Marsha Hunt, Charles Laughton, Vincent Price, Edward G. Robinson, Hilda Vaughn, and Emlyn Williams.

By the facility of audio tape, Corwin recorded separate scenes to be inserted among the actuality. In this way, no more than several actors ever had to be present at a time. Sir Laurence Olivier was added when Corwin decided to use recordings of the actor reading the preamble and articles as originally performed four months before at Carnegie Hall.

Document A/777 opened on a suspenseful note: an ominous musical mood, over which actor Robert Ryan cautioned:

> Ladies and gentlemen: There is a man-made force thousands of times greater than the hydrogen bomb. It's an instrument of many parts— small—can fit into a handbag; yet it has the power to penetrate in every area of human life. Details can be found in *Document A/777*.

Following introductory credits, the setting of mystery is enhanced by the suggestion of "a rendezvous near a huge plant next to a bomb-sight factory."[24] There, the narrator meets a contact man (played by Alexander Knox) and the listener is led down a long corridor to confront a young girl. Heflin, the narrator, reports: "Her face betrays no emotion. She could be a clerk in any bookstore."

Ironically, she *is* a bookstore clerk, and her transaction for 10¢ is *Document A/777, Universal Declaration of Human Rights.* As the amazed narrator begins to peruse the preamble, the listener is tweaked by a sprightly cue, part of an excellent score by Lyn Murray. Out of it emerges the laughter of Van Heflin:

> (CHUCKLING) Sure, that's the way it is in radio. Catch the listener on a fishhook dangled in the air, a bright spinner of music, an angle of urgency in the voice, a promise of bombs and secret rendezvous. But it is true, that bulletin cast in the stream . . .[25]

By its scope, its skill, its poetry of sound and movement, its purpose, *Document A/777* approached a pinnacle achieved in Corwin's established classics, *We Hold These Truths* and *On a Note of Triumph. Variety* pointed out that it possessed "almost epic quality."[26] Critic Jack Gould of the *New York Times:* "The radio documentary was restored to its place of honor last week by Norman Corwin and the United Nations radio staff."[27] *Billboard* called the program "outstanding . . . a potent expression of the needs and aspirations of the world's population."[28] In her column, Harriet Van Horne wrote:

> It was a beautiful program. Yes, beautiful—in concept, in production, in the force and clarity of its message. The cast was worthy of the noble spirit implicit in the program.[29]

Overseas reaction was equally flattering. The *London Evening Express:* "A magnificent presentation."[30] The *Glasgow Herald:* "Another of his triumphs over difficult material."[31]

Variety offered two viewpoints:

> . . . For some time now there has been a growing awareness that some of our best and most exciting radio is emanating from the United Nations.
>
> . . . Corwin is still championing the cause of good writing for radio by his own example, and proving conclusively that fine radio is on par with fine works in all the other arts.[32]

Three weeks later the combination—Corwin and UN Radio— scored again. He masterminded the third program of the series *The Pursuit of Peace.* The show, *Fear Itself,* was written by Allen Sloane and narrated by Martin Gabel. But it was Corwin who juggled an array of actuality excerpts which told in striking historical perspective the fast-deteriorating relations between nations, especially former allies.

Broadcast over Mutual on May 7, 1950 (the fifth anniversary of VE Day), it depicted the camaraderie among the victorious Allies only five years before, and contrasted that atmosphere of accord with the existing crisis of "cold war" confrontation. The program featured the recorded voices of Winston Churchill, Harry Truman, Douglas Mac-Arthur, Joseph Stalin, King George, Bernard Baruch, Fiorello La-Guardia, Trygve Lie, and others.

Listeners heard two thousand guns roaring a VE Day salute in Moscow, heard Mrs. Churchill toasting the Russians, heard released prisoners in the Belsen concentration camp sing "God Save the King." Then, as time soured the euphoria of final conquest, countries polarized—Churchill denounced the Iron Curtain before an audience in Fulton, Missouri; Russian radio assailed the Truman Doctrine, its work in Turkey and Greece; charges and countercharges were issued by the Americans, British, and the Russians. The program dared to suggest that the resulting tension and fear had created hysteria, and witchhunts, and offered as its thesis a conclusion that only the UN could find a way out of the morass.

On May 19, Corwin arrived at the UN building at Lake Success in time to witness a playback of *Document A/777* for members of the Human Rights Commission. He wrote of the experience in his diary:

I chanced on the scene just as the narration touched on the allusion to the thirty-second President, and there was a bright smile on the face of Mrs. Roosevelt. She beamed and even chuckled throughout the Jefferson section. And throughout the credits, she spoke to the packed conference room about freedom and other ideals advanced by the group.

For that moment, listening to her, Corwin could almost believe in a future of fairness for all mankind.

The Communist hunt had its Cassandras—on both sides. Many predicted a dire posture for American ideals if the suspected subversion by organized Red interests was not soon discovered and exposed. Most agreed, for with the deterioration of U.S.-Russian relations, the expanding cult of Soviet ideology, the assumed threat of Communist infiltration, the nation was stricken by fear that the country could be undermined by foreign agents. There were those, however, who saw in the frantic investigations and accusations a reckless impetuosity which endangered prized democratic principles. And they spoke out to warn against the diminution of vital liberties.

The hint of purge had surfaced along the corridors of network radio. Attention had been focused by former FBI agents Kenneth M. Bierly, John G. Keenan, and Theodore C. Kirkpatrick, who quite early joined the crusade with their publication of *Counterattack: The Newsletter of Facts on Communism*. In a lengthy issue devoted to radio, it was observed:

> Exact degree of infiltration by Communist party members and other Communists in CBS or any other network is hard to determine. But it's plain that NBC and Mutual are least satisfactory to Communists . . . that American Broadcasting Company is about at halfway between most satisfactory and least satisfactory . . . and that CBS is tops as far as Communists are concerned.

By midsummer 1949, the talent unions in radio had met to express alarm at the revelation of a "blacklist" designed to remove many of their members from employment. The first casualty had already been reported. William Sweets, longtime director of *Gangbusters* and *Counterspy*, had been forced to resign because of sponsorship pressure on the program packager, Phillips Lord.[33]

It became a touchy, tentative existence for all creative participants in radio. Many who had been "listed" feared for their jobs and cowered before Kirkpatrick and the editors of *Counterattack,* often in a vain attempt to clear themselves.

In June 1950 the publishers of *Counterattack* produced their most damaging indictment yet—a 215-page book exposing an alleged conspiracy. Titled *Red Channels: The Report of Communist Influence in Radio and Television,* it listed 151 people with "citations." It was alphabetically arranged for easy reference.

The integrity of those on its tally sheet made the revelation a shock to the industry. It proved to be a virtual honor roll of highly talented and respected persons in broadcasting. Among those accused were Luther Adler, Leonard Bernstein, Himan Brown, Abe Burrows, Lee J. Cobb, Aaron Copland, Howard Da Silva, Alfred Drake, Howard Duff, Clifford J. Durr, José Ferrer, Martin Gabel, John Garfield, Will Geer, Ruth Gordon, Dashiell Hammett, E. Y. Harburg, Lillian Hellman, Judy Holliday, Lena Horne, Langston Hughes, Burl Ives, Howard Koch, Millard Lampell, Gypsy Rose Lee, Burgess Meredith, Zero Mostel, William N. Robson, Pete Seeger, Artie Shaw, Robert Lewis Shayon, William L. Shirer, Howard K. Smith, Gale and Hester Sondergaard, Paul Stewart, Orson Welles, and Josh White.[34] Prominent among the *C*'s was the name Norman Corwin.

The cast and the scene were seemingly set for one of the great traumatic dramas in American history, to be played before the microphone and the television and motion picture camera, and its theatrics would encompass a variety of forms: sometimes comic, at times farcical, too often tragic. And waiting in the wings was the junior senator from Wisconsin, Joseph McCarthy.

14. The Future: Of Film,
Footlights, and Philosophy

My poor child, don't you know that the only wishes that really matter
are those you make come true yourself?

—*Mary and the Fairy*

Good evening, Mr. and Mrs. North and South America, and all the
ships at sea—let's go to press!

In his typical rapid-fire delivery, Walter Winchell opened his popular
Sunday evening broadcast of news and gossip. Suddenly, among the
torrent of stories which tumbled to the clatter of a telegraph key,
Corwin's name was mentioned. Winchell said that Corwin, wanted for
questioning by the McCarran Committee, was hiding out in the High
Sierras. An unbelieving aunt in New England immediately telephoned
Kate in Hollywood.

Corwin, en route to New York on a plane, did not hear the Winchell
report and learned of it for the first time after calling Kate upon
landing. He was furious. He telephoned Winchell to tell him that he
happened to be in New York and that he was upset at such irresponsible reporting. Winchell apologized, and later broadcast a retraction.

The incident was typical of the erratic, edgy behavior which characterized the growing disquietude over communism. The concern was
given credence by the actions of Senators Joseph McCarthy and Pat
McCarran. McCarran, in fact, was so convinced that Communists had
infiltrated the UN that he brought his Senate committee to New York
for a full-fledged investigation. Corwin, of course, was called to testify.
But after fifteen minutes, the session adjourned and Corwin was never recalled.

It was a time of uncertainty and suspicion, and this made decisions difficult and tenuous. Plans to produce a film version of Corwin's UN radio program, *Document A/777*, were suspended in the summer of 1950 by MGM production chief Dore Schary. Schary sensed a waning interest in the ideals represented by the UN document on human rights, and he was convinced the studio could not recoup the $2 million budgeted for the picture.

During the dark days of blacklisting, Corwin was never denied gainful employment, but its effect followed him closely. He frequently faced unexpected and inexplicable stalemates in negotiations for work. He would be summoned, and favorably evaluated, but the next, logical step was never taken.

A case in point: Corwin one day was requested by Dore Schary to write, *gratis,* a special script for a charity event. After Corwin consented, a period of delay followed. Corwin then heard the program had been cancelled. Then he heard, later, that the show was to go forward as planned—with another writer. It was obvious. Someone had interceded to warn the charity against using a blacklisted author.

Such repudiations were demeaning, to be sure, but not inconsistent with the time. Corwin experienced it early, immediately upon publication of *Red Channels*. Prior to its appearance, a promoter with cultural pretensions had spent weeks trying to entice a reluctant Corwin to serve as one of five judges to determine the recipient of a newly created award for dramatic writing. As soon as Corwin's name appeared on the blacklist, the man panicked, called a press conference, and quickly announced that he had dropped Corwin's name.

As the Red Scare became formidable and pervasive in the arts and the media, friends urged Corwin to confront the self-appointed monitors of patriotism in Hollywood—Adolphe Menjou, Ward Bond, George Sokolsky, *et al.*—to plead his innocence. He refused. The most he would do, he said, would be to make a statement which might strengthen the position—and defense, if necessary—of any employer who might hire him.

The resulting paper, an eloquent statement of his liberal views and beliefs, emphasized his advocacy of the American government:

I have been explicit as to what I mean by liberalism, and the United States government had been lately most explicit as to what it meant by communism. There can be no question that, in official circles of the government, communists and their fellow travelers were commonly understood to advocate and represent certain definite things . . .

He named them, and then:

> In my case, it was not a matter of being in a position to sneak a sentence into a speech. If I were a communist or fellow traveler, I had one of the best platforms in the world. I had the ear of millions of Americans—63 million in one night on one occasion. I had no interference in the form of censorship and none of the usual checks of supervision. I could say what I wanted, and in the dozen or so years that I enjoyed that opportunity—years in which I did hundreds of programs—I would defy anyone to find anything advocating a foreign system of any kind superior to ours. I defy anyone to show that in whatever allusions I ever made to the forms and ideals of our government, as apart from the occasional abuses of those ideals, I had done anything but strengthen our respect and deepen our appreciation for the United States, its laws, its people, its constitution. Each of these advocacies and beliefs has been expressed, not once but many times, in many different forms—in my broadcasts, writings, speeches, letters, and interviews.[1]

Corwin's former colleague, Bill Robson, had been among those blacklisted and besieged by inquiries, accusations, and professional indifference. He appeared before the Hollywood vigilantes to argue his case, and he overheard Corwin's name mentioned derogatorily. Robson was emphatic in his contention that Corwin was *not* a Communist or Communist sympathizer. Robson later recalled that Ward Bond, the movie actor, seemed to agree, but answered with dispassionate coolness, "He'll do until one comes along."[2]

This constant threat to Corwin's reputation and career was not his only concern. He deprecated the erosion of art and program experimentation in radio. In the February 1951 issue of *The Writer,* Corwin bared his cynicism in a tongue-in-cheek article which advised writers to "be mediocre" if they wanted to be successful. He wrote that if the radio writer was "willing to curb his imagination" and look to the medium as "a trade outlet, not an art, it's a living." He suggested that broadcasters wanted "the safe, routine, unspectacular, competent, journeyman script . . . with maybe a fresh twist no bigger than what you give to a lemon peel in a Martini."[3]

Although Corwin's dismay might be understood, radio of the early fifties remained in form and fundamental programming much the same as before. There were at least forty-four well-established dramas on radio in 1950. But the creative sheen that had graced the airwaves in previous years was now being tarnished by a trend which made supreme the giveaway show—programs that awarded consumer products, all-expense-paid vacations, even money, to participating listeners or studio contestants. Symptomatic of the time, too, was a paranoia over program ratings, intensified by the threat of television.

In fact, it was only because the Federal Communications Commission ceased to issue further TV allocations—a temporary suspension to unravel interference problems—that radio was able to maintain its facade of former years. With fewer than a hundred TV stations in operation, most national sponsors preferred to stay with radio.

The handwriting was on the wall, nevertheless. Radio network sales were dropping and TV income was rising. And though the 1950 revenue for CBS-TV was only 18 percent of the network's radio gross, CBS President Frank Stanton predicted that TV earnings would escalate to 50 percent by the following year. In April 1951, Stanton announced that CBS, for the first time in network history, would cut its prime-time radio rates.[4] Other networks followed suit. It had become obvious that advertisers, aware of television's tremendous impact, awaited the waking of a sleeping giant—a forced slumber they felt would soon end.[5]

The corporate concerns of radio no longer involved Corwin. He was now devoting full time to film writing. He completed three commissioned screenplays, but all three were aborted by a lack of funds. Then, for producers Jerry Wald and Norman Krasna, he adapted a French scenario, *The Blue Veil*. Released in October 1951 and starring Charles Laughton and Jane Wyman (for which she was nominated for an Academy Award), it concerned a woman who, unable to have children of her own, took the "veil" of nurse and governess to lavish her love on other people's offspring.

Being childless was a sensitive situation, close to the personal dilemma of the Corwins. Kate's two pregnancies had ended in miscarriage, and they had thought seriously of adopting a baby. Ironically, the very next screenplay by Norman Corwin was about an adopted child.

Scandal for Scourie, based on a story by Mary McSherry, depicted the fight of a Protestant couple against the bigotry of their small Ontario town when they took into their home a little Catholic girl. Although it starred Greer Garson and Walter Pidgeon, the film did not do well, due to a lack of promotion. The MGM picture had an inauspicious opening in a small Manhattan moviehouse in June 1953.

In between the two films, Corwin produced for UN Radio an hour-long documentary which celebrated both the anniversary of the United Nations and the opening of the sixth session of the General Assembly in Paris. Titled *Windows on the World,* the program utilized the new Secretariat Building on New York's East Side as a symbol of responsible world citizenship. The roving microphone moved floor by floor through the UN building, from the third subbasement to the top-level domain of Secretary General Trygve Lie, sampling opinions of UN personnel—everyone from truck drivers to diplomats. Douglas Fairbanks Jr. narrated.

Windows on the World was broadcast in prime time on November 4, 1951, over the Mutual Broadcasting System. As soon as the broadcast was over, Corwin immediately left the studio for a flight back to Hollywood. Word had reached him that Kate was again expecting.

They had decided, given Kate's history, to go forward with plans for adoption and had received an infant son, Anthony. But fortunately, Kate gave birth to a daughter, Diane. Like twins, Tony and Diane grew to possess strikingly similar attributes; each was quiet, even tempered, artistic in nature.

Corwin's post as Chief of Special Projects for United Nations Radio had become increasingly difficult. Distribution of UN programs, for one thing, was harder to effect in the face of radio's diminished role. Besides, Corwin found shuttling back and forth between Hollywood and New York a tiresome, costly, time-consuming routine. He wanted to resign. Departing the UN—and, in effect, radio—was not easy for Corwin, but it was the only practical decision, he concluded, for his West Coast interests now took precedence.

He still had cause to visit New York on occasion, and he happened to be in the city at the time of Edward R. Murrow's exposé of Senator Joseph R. McCarthy. Corwin had called the day after he arrived to compliment Murrow on the *See It Now* program he had seen the night before. It had portrayed a rehearsal of the New York Philharmonic in particularly endearing, human terms; Corwin thought it quite charming. Ed was pleased, and he asked Corwin if he planned to be in town the following week. "I've a helluva program and I hope you can catch it."[6]

By 1953, the age of McCarthyism had reached its zenith. The junior senator from Wisconsin, having gained surprising acceptance by a public duped into believing his tirades against communism in high places, had reached the height of demagoguery. No one seemed capable, willing, or interested in a showdown with this feared maverick—least of all, the U.S. Senate. The evening of March 9, 1954, therefore, marked an important event in American journalism. The Murrow-Friendly telecast of *See It Now* boldly examined the senator in a simple but devastating indictment that was revealed principally through McCarthy's own words and actions.

Corwin, having arranged to have lunch with Murrow the next day, wondered if the furor and acclaim accompanying the telecast might cause a cancellation of their plans. Murrow said no, of course not; they would meet at his office and take a cab to the Century Club.

It was noontime and the elevator was crowded. Corwin remembered: "It was as if Jesus Christ had got on at the 22nd floor. People just wanted to touch him." And the aura of admiration followed them into the street; strangers came up to thank Murrow. At the Century Club, waiters and members alike surrounded him with praise.[7]

Corwin, with Murrow, was witness to what seemed a rebirth of hope and faith in human nature—factors seriously diminished in the evil vindictiveness of McCarthyism.

Corwin "concluded" his radio career October 4, 1955, with a play aired by BBC for United Nations Radio. He had written it by invitation of radio officials at the UN, knowing that the American networks (due to drastic cutbacks in public service programming) would not likely be interested. UN sponsors thus turned to the British Broadcasting Corporation. The production, *A Charter in the Saucer,* featured an all-English cast and starred Laurence Olivier.

The intent of the program was to promulgate the UN charter as an instrument of survival. Corwin took a light approach, and satirized a science fiction convention which holds that all visitors from outer space must possess superior powers. By contrast, "Vuz," whose flying saucer lands by mistake on earth, turns out to be a mild, meek, and apparently inferior being. He is particularly perplexed by a radio message which has garbled the reading of the UN charter with various slogans and claims of certain radio commercials. Olivier, who plays a UN investigator, acts as a liaison between Vuz and the UN organization.

It would be some time before Corwin would again venture into radio, and only to answer special requests as the "elder statesman" of the art. For now, it was film, and a meeting with John Houseman marked a significant occasion in Corwin's career. Houseman seemed concerned. MGM's option on Irving Stone's best-selling biography of Van Gogh, *Lust for Life,* was nearing an end, and two attempts to develop a suitable screenplay had failed. Houseman wanted Corwin to try.

After reading the book, Corwin could see the difficulties. He had reservations about its cinematic qualities. But as he researched the subject, he found fascinating material in Van Gogh's letters. Using these as a basis of his scenario, while retaining the title of Stone's book, Corwin conceived a viable shooting script.

Houseman had quite early cast Kirk Douglas in the lead, and determined that Vincent Minnelli should direct, but it was Corwin who proposed Anthony Quinn for the role of Paul Gauguin. When Quinn showed reluctance, hefting the script to demonstrate that the part was perhaps too small, Corwin countered, "For God's sake, Tony, it's not a side of ham."[8]

For his role, Anthony Quinn was to receive an Oscar as the best supporting actor, while *Lust for Life* was named among the ten best pictures of the year (1956). The film was honored for its color, its authenticity. Kirk Douglas was lauded for his portrayal of Van Gogh, and Corwin received both an Academy Award nomination and the Film Critics Circle Award for the best screenplay of 1956 adapted from another medium.

The stage was still an alluring medium for Corwin, and though he had been frustrated by his first effort (*Mary and the Fairy*), he worked with new zeal on a plot based on the Lincoln–Douglas debates. *The Rivalry,* once completed, went into rehearsal under the author's direction and took to the road for its first national tour in September 1957. Martin Gabel, the very personification of "the Little Giant," played the part of Stephen Douglas with fire and conviction. Raymond Massey appeared as Lincoln, and Agnes Moorehead was Mrs. Douglas.

The tour completed (ninety-one cities in four months), Massey and Moorehead left the company because of film commitments and Richard Boone and Nancy Kelly took over as Lincoln and Mrs. Douglas. With these new principals and Martin Gabel, *The Rivalry* opened on Broadway in February 1959. It ran for eighty-one performances at the Bijou Theatre.

In his review for the *New Yorker,* Kenneth Tynan wrote:

> By conventional Broadway standards, Norman Corwin's *The Rivalry* is not a play at all. Yet, it is unquestionably theatre. To see it is to realize, with a shock of disquiet, how many theatrical weapons our authors have lately allowed to rust . . .
> He [Corwin] has directed his own play superbly.[9]

An aging but active Carl Sandburg was Corwin's houseguest for a month in 1959. He had come to Hollywood to accept a tribute in his honor, which was also an occasion to raise funds for the Braille Institute and several UCLA scholarships. Corwin had agreed to arrange and produce the affair without fee.

In what movie director George Stevens considered "the finest evening of theatre I've ever witnessed,"[10] the Sandburg presentation at UCLA's Royce Hall utilized simplicity and contrast to project the character and quality of this venerable man of letters. Corwin set an otherwise bare stage with a simple podium and a semicircle of high-backed, upholstered chairs (from the 20th Century–Fox prop department). One by one, such Hollywood personalities as Burt Lancaster, Anthony Quinn, Jack Lemmon, Glenn Ford, Francis X. Bushman, and Eva Marie Saint stepped from the wings, each to read a Sandburg selection and then take a seat onstage. Dr. Frank Baxter, educator, Shakespearean authority, and at the time a recognized TV personality, was host for the evening.

The climax followed the showing of an Edward R. Murrow interview with Carl Sandburg, in a kinescope loaned by CBS and projected on a giant screen in the auditorium. As the film ended, the spotlight picked out Sandburg as he walked on stage—a minute figure after the magnificent closeups seen on the two-story-high screen only a moment before. The magical moment was greeted by a thunderous ovation.

The success of the Royce Hall event aroused the interest of a producer, Armand Deutsch, who approached Corwin with an idea to develop a similar evening for nationwide tour. With this inducement, Corwin devised *The World of Carl Sandburg*, which portrayed the poet's literary life through selected works adapted for the stage. He cast Bette Davis and her husband, Gary Merrill, as the featured performers, and also directed. The production went on tour, reaching Broadway September 14, 1960. Bette Davis remained as star, but Merrill, who was engaged to do a film in Hollywood, relinquished his role to Barry Sullivan. For the same reason, Sullivan would turn over the part to Leif Erickson before the play opened at the Henry Miller Theatre in New York. The Broadway run closed in October, after twenty-nine performances.

Corwin flew to Boston after the final curtain to visit his parents, and on his first evening home, his mother had an accident. Corwin intended to take his parents out for the evening, when Sam, rushing to get ready, suddenly entered the bedroom, unaware that Rose was standing behind the door. Her fall resulted in a broken hip, and months of recuperation in Massachusetts General Hospital.

During her confinement, the doctors were deeply troubled. An aneurysm of the aorta, discovered fifteen years before during a routine examination, was the basis of their concern. No remedy had been sought at the time, due to limitations in cardiovascular surgery; so she had resigned herself to a Damoclean existence. But now, physicians felt, surgery should no longer be postponed. Rose, nevertheless, was reluctant. The family—Emil, Al, Beulah, and Norman—agreed with the doctors, but they also felt their mother's wish should be respected, especially in view of her recent ordeal and protracted stay in the hospital. So she was released—then upon reconsideration, readmitted. Corwin made a special trip from California to be with his mother, but Dr. Sam Levine, a heart specialist, advised against the operation.

Rose was happy in the home of Beulah and her husband, Irving Belkowitz, and she insisted on doing her share of the cooking and cleaning. Months later, having returned home to Sam, she was preparing a few things in the kitchen in anticipation of a visit by Freda and Emil. She had returned to the living room to rest and, while seated on the couch, collapsed. An ambulance was quickly summoned, but she was dead on arrival at the hospital.

Her passing was a shock, for despite her eighty-one years, her shyness, and her physical infirmities, Rose had been a source of family strength. Sam lived on, to become a minor celebrity for his remarkable longevity, remaining active and alert even after his age had passed the century mark. Until Beulah and Irving persuaded him to join them in 1980, he had lived alone in a senior-citizen apartment, cooked his own meals, and corresponded with countless friends and relatives in a firm handwriting which belied his age. Of him, Corwin wrote:

> My father defies every rule and maxim of longevity. He is small, has looked frail for the past 60 years, eats like a sparrow and used to smoke malevolently odoriferous cigars (the aroma even clung to his letters). To this day he puts away nearly a pint of sherry daily.[11]

Corwin continued apace with his writing, as his postradio career explored various media with his customary enthusiasm, energy, and expectation. An old passion of his, the Bible, motivated his next movie, *The Story of Ruth,* which was made with a virtually unknown cast and released in 1961.

In the early sixties, Corwin turned to television. He wrote the first and final programs of a twenty-six-part portrait of President Roosevelt, titled *FDR* and aired by ABC in 1963. A year later, for NBC, he scripted a ninety-minute examination of Hollywood and its industry, *Inside the Movie Kingdom.* Then, for oceanographer Bruno Vailati, Corwin annotated and narrated a series of hour-long documentaries, *Seven Seas,* which was released in 1970 for TV syndication. In the fall of that year the senior vice president in charge of programming and production for Westinghouse Broadcasting offered Corwin the opportunity to write, produce, direct, and even host, an anthology drama series for television. Reminiscent of his days of preeminence in radio, the series bore his name: *Norman Corwin Presents.*[12]

Four years later, he was called on to contribute to another significant television event. Stanley Kramer, the noted film director (*The Defiant Ones, Inherit the Wind, On the Beach*), asked Corwin to write a ninety-minute special for his ABC-TV series, *Judgment.* Corwin studied 4,100 pages of transcript and the testimony of 286 witnesses to script *The Court Martial of the Tiger of Malaya,* a story about General Yamashita, who was sentenced and hanged—unjustly, in the view of some historians—by a U.S. military tribunal.

Corwin collaborated in the writing of several cantatas. His first, *The Golden Door* (1955), he produced himself for the Jewish community in Cleveland. With music by Maurice Goldman, the program was presented in the city's vast Music Hall and starred Luther Adler and Joseph Wiseman, with a large cast, chorus, and orchestra. It was applauded by page-one reviews, and even by an editorial in the *Cleveland Plain Dealer.*

At UCLA in 1962, he narrated a cantata composed by Franz Waxman, titled *Joshua;* and in 1968 he wrote for the United Nations, in collaboration with Spanish composer Cristobal Halffter, *Yes Speak Out Yes,* a cantata commemorating the twentieth anniversary of the Universal Declaration of Human Rights.

For the stage, he resurrected with relish a favorite radio play, *The Odyssey of Runyon Jones,* adapted as a musical for two-week run in Los Angeles (1972). With Richard Kiley in the lead, Corwin directed *Cervantes,* his original play about the author of *Don Quixote.* It opened in Washington, D.C., in September 1973. Then, to celebrate the nation's bicentennial, he wrote and directed a historical perspective for the stage, *Together Tonight! Jefferson, Hamilton, and Burr,* which premiered at Indiana University in January 1976, before starting a national tour.

Not all Corwin endeavors were unqualified successes. Some, for various reasons, proved disappointing. His play *Cervantes,* for instance, opened to hostile reviews, the result of perplexing technical and aesthetic problems. It also invited an unfair comparison with the hit musical *Man of La Mancha.* But perhaps Corwin's most agonizing experience occurred in the mid-sixties. He had traveled to Rome to research and write a film biography of Francisco Goya, the great Spanish artist, only to have the subsequent production marred by dissension between the stars (Anthony Franciosa and Ava Gardner) and the director. It resulted in a picture so poor that Corwin tried, in vain, to have his name removed from the credits.[13]

Corwin's undeniable dominance during the golden moments of radio's yesteryear seemed to make his latter-day excursions into other media, aside from several extraordinary triumphs, pale by comparison. And yet, always, there was in each an incomparable style, a standard of quality and concern that touched a responsive chord in humankind. At will, and not always by assignment, he spoke to the moment with timely imagery and emotion.

He ushered in the new decade with *Prayer for the 70s* (1969), a poetic narrative performed by Eddie Albert on the *Ed Sullivan Show*. He created one of his finest pieces in 1974—an ode to open the Jerusalem Fair in Los Angeles. He read the work, *Jerusalem Printout*, before an audience of 3,000, among whom was a number of dignitaries, including the mayor of Jerusalem, Teddy Kollek. The poem exploited the modern idiom of the computer:

Feed to the computer the name Jerusalem and behold the printout:

Click: The burnishing sun latitude 32 Tropic Cancer
The solar wind blowing old gold on the hills . . .

And touched on apocalyptic events of the city, ending:

If in the toils of war, the holy places be spared
Then make all places holy.

If from the stones of a hallowed parapet, repose and joy and
    heartbreak-yearning of long ages be consummated,
Then extend the Western Wall across the planet.

If on the prayer rugs and at the arks and altars of Jerusalem the
    name of Peace is chanted every day
And in the streets, the commonest coins of courtesy say *Salaam* on
    one side, *Shalom* on the other.
Then let the fame of Peace accumulate until it stands in honor
    everywhere,
Observed, preserved, attended, minded,
Public as God himself. Selah.

End of printout.

Reload for next millennium.[14]

In resonant tones, magnified by a microphone, Corwin spoke of "the austere, the beautiful, the vexed city"; of massacre, of mercy, of the marauding Crusaders. And when he had finished and stepped down from the platform, Kollek arose from his seat and embraced him with great emotion.

America's bicentennial brought forth a Corwin of old, as once again he enunciated the spirit of his nation by characterizing in words an image of its people. The poem was printed full page, July 4, 1976, in the *Los Angeles Times*. It began:

> Some seeds transport on the wind, or are water-borne; others travel
> by their own device:
> Each of us bears in his genes some memoir of wandering.
> Even the moccasined hunter, a flicker of bronze among the ferns
> when the first pale man beached
> Was himself as migratory as a bird cruising the lordly flyways down
> from the Asian straits . . .

Then, at its conclusion:

> American perfection, or as close to it as anyone can come,
> Is in the seeking of our imperfections
> And the tending to them.
>
> Our names are fixed to that.
> And they are good names.
>
> Good names tested in the grand retorts of time and circumstance.
>
> We.
>
> We.
>
> The People.[15]

The trend of American broadcasting made distant, obsolete, the practices and priorities of radio's remembered epoch. The entrepreneurs were now young, aggressive practitioners who knew not, nor needed, the inspiration of radio's golden era. Simplicity, sales, service, were keys to success. As one observer acknowledged, to adapt to the cursory, community-oriented concept of contemporary radio, "they had nothing to unlearn."[16]

But, as from all experiences of historical value, radio's great versatile age offered important precepts: a sense of artistic purpose, an aura of style and importance, a concern for substance, an accountability to more than the sponsoring agent. These were important lessons, even for modern radio.

Still, aside from archival interests or the pursuit of trivia, the Golden Age of Radio had faded from memory and its people were obscured by time and circumstance. Even CBS, obsessed with the future, had been casual about its past. In 1955, a callous executive at Columbia decided to clear the shelves of old "air checks" for the expediency of space. Corwin, in New York at the time, learned from a friend that the discs were being hauled away to the dump. Fortunately, he managed to salvage his *Columbia Workshop* programs.

CBS, nevertheless, recognized the significance of Corwin when it celebrated its golden anniversary. Corwin was asked to provide a concluding feature for Columbia's week-long remembrance of network events and achievements. On television, Walter Cronkite read Corwin's *Network at Fifty:*

> . . . Years of the electric ear!
> The heavens crackling with report: far-flung nearby, idle,
>   consequential
> The worst of bad news and the best of good,
> Seizures and frenzies of opinion
> The massive respirations of government and commerce
> Sofa-sitters taken by kilocycle to the ball park, the concert hall, the
>   scene of the crime
> Dramas that let us dress the sets themselves
> Preachments and prizefights,
> The time at the tone, the weather will be, and now for a word,
> The coming of wars and freeways
> Outcroppings of fragmented peace
> Singing commercials and the Messiah.
> And then the eye.

> Cyclops the one-eyed giant put to work
> As picture-maker to uncountable galleries:
> No longer the imagined but the living face in the glowing mosaic,
> Not only the tap of the dancing foot but the swirl of the twirling
>   skirt,
> Not only the bounding arpeggio but the dazzle of running fingers . . .[17]

Corwin, the *beau ideal* among radio dramatists, was indeed the person who could best describe the excitement, emotion, the power, and public good that were a part of broadcasting. He had been frequently consulted on matters of the media and the arts. And in addition to his books (*Overkill and Megalove, Holes in a Stained Glass Window, Trivializing America*), in which he commented on society, life, and the media, he had written numerous articles about the arts, aesthetics, and creativity.

Often he was asked about radio's glory days and its implications for the future. Can radio drama, for instance, ever make a comeback? "It can exist as a viable form only if given the atmosphere and cultural configurations that once made it a practical commodity." But he cautions: "If it is to truly exist, it must be worthy of its existence."

Poetry? "Poets and teachers often thanked me 'for contributing to public awareness and appreciation of poetry'—a sort of midwifery, I suppose. But broadcasting can do a great deal for poetry, and vice versa. Too bad the telephone oracle and the singing commercial have preempted Frost, Benét, and others, including myself."

Are the goals of commercialism and art incompatible in broadcasting? "No. And while instances of compatibility are not high, neither are they impossible."

Do you miss anything of the old days? "The camaraderie. The pride CBS took in its cultural accomplishments, the sense of eagerness to do good work, to expand artistic frontiers, to rush in where fools and NBC feared to tread."[18]

A camaraderie of old *does* exist occasionally, when former colleagues assemble to enjoy nostalgia sweetened by time. And at meetings, dinners, he may be hailed by a constituency of veterans who were witness to his works and who appreciated his influence.

But closer than even the accolades of his peers are the lingering echoes of audiences the world over who have cheered his achievements. Corwin made an impression on a medium which once bore classic dimensions. And if, in its evolution, radio has since lost its ability to reach aesthetic heights, there remains a benchmark in the memory of a man who rose through the ranks of broadcasting to establish radio's efficacy as an art form.

In the words of Norman Corwin himself: "I was lucky enough to be part of a breaking wave at the full tide of radio's creativity. I like to think that I ran up the shore a little way in helping the medium reach its high water mark."

Appendix:
A Chronology of
Norman Corwin's Radio Programs

1938

WORDS WITHOUT MUSIC
December 25—*The Plot to Overthrow Christmas*
Cast: Will Geer played the role of the Devil, House Jameson was Santa Claus, and Eric Burroughs was Nero; others.

1939

WORDS WITHOUT MUSIC
February 19—*They Fly through the Air with the Greatest of Ease*
Cast: House Jameson narrated; with Luis Van Rooten, Karl Swenson, Don Costello, Arnold Moss, Adelaide Klein, and Gladys Thornton.

COLUMBIA WORKSHOP
April 14—*Seems Radio Is Here to Stay*
Cast: Narrated by House Jameson; with Kermit Murdock, Robert Dryden, Paul Mann, John Griggs, Horace Braham, Edwin Lewin, Adelaide Klein, Gladys Thornton, Shirley Grayson, Hester Sondergaard, Mert Koplin, Joan Lorring, Elaine Kent, and Sydney Berry.
Music: Bernard Herrmann.

SO THIS IS RADIO
July 24—*Putting Programs on the Air*
Cast: House Jameson narrated; with Everett Sloane and the author.
Music: Bernard Herrmann.
July 31—*Twenty Years, the Career of Broadcasting*
Cast list unavailable.
August 14—*Radio Special Events Department*
Cast list unavailable.
August 21—*Education via Radio*
Cast: Everett Sloane and others.
Music: Bernard Herrmann.

September 7—*Arrangement and Production of Musical Programs*
Cast: Martin Gabel narrated; with Everett Sloane, Frank Gallop, John Gibson, Karl Swenson, and Sydney Smith.
Music: Bernard Herrmann.
September 29—*National Association of Broadcasters*
Cast: House Jameson narrated; with John Gibson, Arnold Moss, Minerva Pious, Adelaide Klein, Bernard Zanville (Dane Clark), John M. James, Gladys Thornton, Rosaline Gould, Lou Babien, and Sam Raskyn.
Music: Raymond Scott and Perry Lafferty.

1940

COLUMBIA WORKSHOP
March 7—*My Client Curley* (adapted from story by Lucille Fletcher)
Cast: Everett Sloane as the Agent, Kingsley Colton as Stinky; also, Jeanette Nolan, Karl Swenson, Byron McCormick, Joseph Julian, Luis Van Rooten, Hester Sondergaard, and John Brown.
Music: Composed by Raymond Scott; Howard Barlow conducted.

PURSUIT OF HAPPINESS
April 21—*The Oracle of Philadelphi*
Cast: Gale Sondergaard was the Oracle; Burgess Meredith narrated.
Music: Composed by Ralph Wilkinson; Mark Warnow conducted.

FORECAST
August 19—*To Tim at Twenty*
Cast: Charles Laughton and Elsa Lanchester.
Music: Wilbur Hatch.

CAVALCADE OF AMERICA
October 23—*Ann Rutledge* (directed by Homer Fickett)
Cast: Jeanette Nolan as Ann, Agnes Moorehead, the mother; also, Karl Swenson, Kenneth Delmar, Clayton Collyer.
Music: Donald Voorhees.

1941

26 BY CORWIN
May 4—*Radio Primer*
Cast: Everett Sloane, Beatrice Kay, John Brown, Ted de Corsia, Hester Sondergaard, Frank Gallop, Frank Lovejoy, Jack Smart, Peter Donald, and Luis Van Rooten.
Music: Lyn Murray.
May 11—*Log of the R-77*
Cast: House Jameson, Frank Lovejoy, John Gibson, Burl Ives, Luis Van Rooten, Everett Sloane, Peter Donald, Paul Stewart, Norman Ober, Martin Wolfson, Lucille Meredith, Edward Juris.

Music: Lyn Murray.

May 18—*The People, Yes*

Cast: Everett Sloane, Burl Ives, others.

Music: Composed by Earl Robinson; Lyn Murray Chorus conducted by Mark Warnow.

May 25—*Lip Service*

Cast: Larry Adler, Ted de Corsia, Minerva Pious, Joan Alexander, Luis Van Rooten, Mildred Natwick, Don Morrison, John James, and Frank Lovejoy.

Music: Larry Adler.

June 1—*Appointment*

Cast: Everett Sloane played Peter, Paul Stewart was Mark, Arthur Vinton the Commandant; with Ed Mayehoff, Tom Tully, House Jameson, Norman Lloyd, Bartlett Robinson, Ruth Gilbert, and the author.

Music: Lyn Murray.

June 8—*The Odyssey of Runyon Jones*

Cast: Larry Robinson was Runyon, Roy Fant was Father Time, Mother Nature was played by Hester Sondergaard, the Giant by Arthur Vinton.

Music: Alexander Semmler.

June 15—*A Soliloquy to Balance the Budget*

Cast: House Jameson was the soliloquist.

June 22—*Daybreak*

Cast: Frank Gallop as the pilot; with Joan Banks, Clifford Carpenter, Frank Lovejoy, Gilbert Mack, Ed Mayehoff, Don Morrison, Hester Sondergaard, Paul Stewart, Rosaline Greene, Martin Wolfson, and La Coehlo.

Music: Lyn Murray.

June 29—*Old Salt*

Cast: Everett Sloane played Gramp, Larry Robinson was Billy, June Havoc the main siren (assisted by the Symphonettes).

Music: Lyn Murray.

July 6—*Between Americans*

Cast: Ray Collins narrated, Frank Lovejoy was the orator, Peter Donald the maestro; and others.

Music: Alexander Semmler.

July 13—*Ann Rutledge*

Cast: Florence Robinson as Ann; with Agnes Moorehead, John McIntyre, House Jameson, Frank Lovejoy.

Music: Alexander Semmler.

July 20—*Double Concerto*

Cast: Zaragoza was played by Paul Stewart, Poganyi by Peter Donald, Twombly by Morgan Farley, Mrs. Twombly by Rosaline Greene; also, Ed Mayehoff, Phillips Werner, Bill Watts, Jerry Macy, Kenneth Hayden, John Dickens, and the Koralites.

Music: Paul Belanger, Carol Marsh, Vera Brodsky.

August 3—*Descent of the Gods*

Cast: Henry Morgan played Nick, the God of Trivia, Eileen Burns was Venus,

Winfield Hoeny was Mars, and House Jameson was Apollo; also, Winston O'Keefe, Frank Lovejoy, Hester Sondergaard, Henry Jones, Ed Mayehoff, Lucille Meredith, Norman Ober, Giuliana Taberna, and Everett Ripley.

Music: Clavichord (only instrument) played by Edith Weissman.

August 10—*Samson*

Cast: Martin Gabel performed the role of Samson, Mady Christians played Delilah.

Music: Bernard Herrmann.

August 17—*Esther*

Cast: Martin Gabel, Arnold Moss, Everett Sloane, Joan Vitez, Winston O'Keefe, Genevieve Rowe, Harrison Knox, Eugene Lowenthal, and Kenneth Jones.

Music: Lyn Murray.

August 24—*Job*

Cast: Charles Laughton as Job; with Ray Collins and Hans Conreid.

Music: Deems Taylor.

August 31—*Mary and the Fairy*

Cast: Elsa Lanchester played Mary, Ruth Gordon the fairy; with Hans Conreid, Thurl Ravenscroft, Earl Ross, Frank Graham, and The Sportsmen (singers).

Music: Lud Gluskin.

September 7—*Anatomy of Sound*

Cast: Gale Sondergaard.

September 14—*Fragments from a Lost Cause*

Cast: Everett Sloane, House Jameson, others.

Music: Alexander Semmler.

September 21—*The Human Angle*

Cast: Frank Lovejoy, Martin Wolfson, Jerry Macy, Everett Sloane, Horace Braham, Ed Mayehoff, Norman Ober, James Van Dyke, and Eric Burroughs.

September 28—*Good Heavens*

Cast: Bartlett Robinson narrated, Henry Morgan was the prosecutor for the *Columbia Workshop,* Martin Wolfson played the harassed volunteer; also, Luis Van Rooten, Ed Mayehoff, Ann Boley, Norman Ober, Bill Watts, Kenneth Delmar, John Brewster.

Music: Lyn Murray.

October 5—*Wolfiana*

Cast: The author narrated; with Arnold Moss, Giuliana Taberna, Ed Mayehoff, Blanche Gladstone, Roger DeKoven, Ann Hollahan, Martin Wolfson, Norman Ober, Rosaline Gould.

Music: Alexander Semmler.

October 12—*Murder in Studio One*

Cast: Ruth Gordon as Cameo Klopf, a woman detective; with Minerva Pious, Eddie Mayehoff, Frank Lovejoy, Alan Drake, Kenneth Delmar, Hester Sondergaard, Ann Shepherd, Norman Ober, Peter Goo Chong, The Symphonettes and The Four Clubmen.

Music: Alexander Semmler.
October 19—*Descent of the Gods* (special repeat)
Cast: Same cast as in August 3rd production.
Music: Clavichord by Edith Weissman.
November 2—*A Man with a Platform*
Cast: Budd Hulick was the Man, with Arlene Francis as Miss Depew, Henry
Morgan as Timkins, Hester Sondergaard as Marylou Susabelle Bettymae
Brown, Ed Mayehoff as Hutchins; also, The Symphonettes and The Four
Clubmen.
Music: Lyn Murray.
November 9—*Psalm for a Dark Year*
Cast: Author served as the Principal Voice; with Frank Lovejoy, Martin Gabel,
Parker Fennelly, Anne Boley, Hester Sondergaard, Sidney Smith, Jean
Ellyn, Ian Martin, and Charles Carroll.
Music: Alexander Semmler.

BILL OF RIGHTS SPECIAL
December 15—*We Hold These Truths*
Cast: James Stewart narrated; with Edward Arnold, Lionel Barrymore, Wal-
ter Brennan, Bob Burns, Walter Huston, Elliott Lewis, Marjorie Main,
Edward G. Robinson, Rudy Vallee, Orson Welles, and others.
Music: Bernard Herrmann.
NOTE: Commissioned to commemorate 150th anniversary of the American
Bill of Rights, this hour-long program was aired over the combined na-
tional networks (CBS, NBC–Red, NBC–Blue, MBS) eight days after Pearl
Harbor.

1942

THIS IS WAR!
February 14—*America at War*
Cast: Lt. Robert Montgomery narrated; with Berry Kroeger, House Jameson,
Ted Jewitt, Theodore Goetz, Stefan Schnabel, Joseph DeSantis, Edward
Racquello, Lilli Valenti, Gerald Kean, Ed Mayehoff, Almanac Singers; also,
Archibald MacLeish.
Music: Lyn Murray.
March 24—*It's in the Works*
Cast: John Garfield, Katherine Locke, Henry Hull, Paul Stewart, Hester Son-
dergaard, Frank Lovejoy, Norman Ober, Peter Goo Chong, Jack Smart, Ed
Mayehoff, Martin Wolfson, and Joan Banks.
Music: Lyn Murray.
April 11—*The Enemy*
Cast: Clifton Fadiman was narrator; others.
Music: Donald Voorhees.
April 18—*Concerning Axis Propaganda*
Cast: Donald Crisp; others.
Music: Alexander Semmler.

May 2—*To the Young*
Cast: Joseph Julian; others.
Music: Johnny Green.
May 9—*Yours Received and Contents Noted*
Cast: Raymond Massey; others.
Music: Tom Bennett; conducted by Frank Black.
NOTE: Norman Corwin directed twelve of the thirteen programs in this series, which included scripts written by William N. Robson, Maxwell Anderson, Stephen Vincent Benét, George Faulkner, Philip Wylie, and Ranald MacDougall. The series was broadcast on the combined national network.

AN AMERICAN IN ENGLAND

August 3—*London by Clipper* (rebroadcast after shortwave interference interrupted transmission of premiere performance, July 27)
Cast: Joseph Julian narrated; with MacDonald Parke, Betty Hardy, Julian Somers, Arthur Young, John Snagge, Angela Glynne, Leslie Bradley, Thorley Walters, and Phillip Cunningham.
Music: Benjamin Britten; conducted by Wing Commander R. P. O'Donnell.
August 10—*London to Dover*
Cast: Joseph Julian, narrator, with Gerald Cooper, Leslie Bradley, Harry Ross, David Baxter, John Bryning, Terence de Marney, Julian Somers, Betty Hardy, Dorothy Smith, Arthur Young, Frank Cochrane, Clifford Buckton, and John Snagge.
Music: Benjamin Britten; conducted by Wing Commander R. P. O'Donnell.
August 17—*Ration Island*
Cast: Joseph Julian, narrator, with Edward R. Murrow, Belle Chrystall, Gladys Young, Laidman Browne, Arthur Young, Betty Hardy, Terrence de Marney, James McKechnie, Gwen Day Burrows, Julian Somers, and John Snagge.
Music: Benjamin Britten; conducted by Wing Commander R. P. O'Donnell.
August 24—*Women of Britain*
Cast: Joseph Julian, narrator, with Clifford Buckton, Olga Edwards, Julian Somers, Dorothy Greene, Curigwen Lewis, Laidman Browne, Betty Hardy, Dorothy Smith, Joan Miller, Arthur Young, Gladys Young, and John Snagge.
Music: Benjamin Britten; conducted by Wing Commander R. P. O'Donnell.
August 31—*The Yanks Are Here*
Cast: Joseph Julian, narrator, with Richard George, Lyn Evans, Edward R. Murrow, MacDonald Parke, Betty Hardy, Julian Somers, Leslie Bradley, Harry Ross, Tommy Duggan, Paul Fierro, Tommy Palmer, Laidman Browne, and John Snagge.
Music: Benjamin Britten; conducted by Wing Commander R. P. O'Donnell.
September 7—*An Anglo-American Angle*
Cast: Joseph Julian, narrator, with Lyn Evans, Julian Somers, MacDonald Parke, John Bryning, Laidman Browne, Betty Hardy, Clifford Buckton,

Dorothy Smith, Arthur Young, Robert Marsden, Edward R. Murrow, and John Snagge.

Music: Benjamin Britten; conducted by Wing Commander R. P. O'Donnell.

NOTE: Shortwave interference made reception in the U.S. impossible and prompted network decision to complete the series in the Stateside studios of CBS. This program was rebroadcast December 15, 1942.

December 1—*Cromer*

Cast: Joseph Julian; with Frank Lovejoy and others.

Music: Lyn Murray.

December 8—*Home Is Where You Hang Your Helmet*

Cast: Joseph Julian; with Everett Sloane and others.

Music: Lyn Murray.

December 15—*An Anglo-American Angle*

Cast: Joseph Julian; with Edna Best, Nicholas Joy, and Alfred Shirley.

Music: Lyn Murray.

December 22—*Clipper Home*

Cast: Joseph Julian and others.

Music: Lyn Murray.

1943

CRESTA BLANCA CARNIVAL

January 13—*A Program to Be Opened in a Hundred Years*

Cast: House Jameson played the presiding speaker, with Berry Kroeger the Chinese, Katherine Locke the Russian, and Stefan Schnabel the German.

Music: Morton Gould.

NOTE: This short Corwin script was commissioned for the Cresta Blanca commercial variety program and was directed by Arthur Daly for broadcast over the Mutual Broadcasting System.

AMERICA SALUTES THE PRESIDENT'S BIRTHDAY PARTY

January 30—*A Moment of the Nation's Time*

Cast: David Gothard, narrator.

Music: Bernard Herrmann.

TRANSATLANTIC CALL (An Anglo-American informational series produced alternately by CBS and BBC. Corwin wrote and directed the following U.S. broadcasts.)

February 14—*New England*

Cast: Author narrated, with Gerald Keene, Will Geer, Roy Fant, Berry Kroeger, Karl Swenson, Jerry Macy, Arnold Moss, Charme Allen, Parker Fennelly, and Hester Sondergaard.

Music: Bernard Herrmann.

February 18—*Washington, D.C.*

Cast: Author narrated, with Art Carney, Joseph Julian, Karl Swenson, Jackson Beck, Arnold Moss, Berry Kroeger, Maurice Tarplin, Olive Deering, Kermit Murdock, and Elspeth Eric.

Music: Bernard Herrmann.

March 14—*Midwest: Breadbasket and Arsenal*

Cast: Miller was narrator,* with guests Wendell Willkie and Carl Sandburg; CBS correspondents George Cushing (Detroit), Lambert Kaiman (St. Louis), Lawson Deming (Cleveland); professional citizenry, such as a steward in an automotive union and the president of Inland Steel Corp. Guy Della Cioppa, Ted Robertson associate producers.

Music: Bernard Herrmann.

PASSPORT FOR ADAMS

August 24—*Introduction* (pilot program)

Cast: Robert Young starred as Douglas Adams, a young country editor, and Dane Clark played Perry Quisinbury, a veteran photographer; with Paul Stewart, Ray Collins, and Harry Davenport.

Music: Bernard Herrmann.

September 21—*Tel Aviv*

Cast: Robert Young, Dane Clark, Joan Lorring, Hans Conreid, Robert Harris, and Max Lipen.

Music: Lud Gluskin and Lucien Moraweck.

September 28—*Moscow*

Cast: Robert Young, Dane Clark, Ludwig Donath, and others.

October 12—*Stalingrad*

Cast: Robert Young, Dane Clark, others.

1944

COLUMBIA PRESENTS CORWIN

March 7—*Movie Primer*

Cast: Everett Sloane, Frank Gallop, Minerva Pious, Ted de Corsia, Peter Donald, Tony Marvin, Hester Sondergaard, Ralph Bell, Donna Keath, Alex Englander, Yung Ying Hsu.

Music: Lyn Murray.

March 14—*The Long Name None Could Spell*

Cast: Martin Gabel narrated, with William L. Shirer, Joseph Julian, Kermit Murdock, Carl Frank, Giuliana Taberna, and Michael Ingram.

Music: Lyn Murray.

NOTE: This program was originally written as a stage event and presented at Carnegie Hall (May 28, 1943) and directed by Joseph Losey, for American Friends of Czechoslovakia. The next program in *Columbia Presents Corwin* was *The Lonesome Train*, by Millard Lampell and Earl Robinson (broadcast March 21, 1944)

*Because of Corwin's illness, a Chicago actor (first name unknown) was quickly substituted as narrator.

March 28—*Savage Encounter*
Cast: Carl Frank performed the role of the pilot, Joan Alexander was Ara, Arnold Moss was the Native, and the author appeared as the Prosecutor.
Music: Bernard Herrmann.

April 4—*The Odyssey of Runyon Jones*
Cast: Michael Artist starred; with Roy Fant, Arthur Vinton, Hester Sondergaard, and others.
Music: Alexander Semmler.

April 11—*You Can Dream, Inc.*
Cast: John Griggs was the vice president in charge of sales, Ralph Bell was the Esthete, Minerva Pious was Minnie, Samuel Raskyn appeared as Dad (the Keats fancier) and Joseph Julian and Ruth Gilbert did the elevator scene; Robert Trout and Harry Marble played themselves. Also, Lon Clark, Eleanor Sherman, and Kermit Murdock.
Music: Alexander Semmler.

April 18—*Untitled*
Cast: Fredric March appeared as Hank Peters, Charmé Allen as the mother, Donna Keith as the girlfriend, Hester Sondergaard the music teacher, Kermit Murdock the editor; with Joseph Julian, Paul Mann, Allen Drake, and Michael Ingram.
Music: Bernard Herrmann.

April 25—*Dorie Got a Medal*
Cast: Canada Lee as Dorie Miller, with Josh White, Mary Lou Williams, Jim Bachus, Laura Duncan, Earl Hyman, Ken Renard, Rosetta Lenoir, and the Golden Gate Quartet.
Music: Jeff Alexander, Josh White, Langston Hughes, and Mary Lou Williams.

May 2—*The Cliché Expert*
Cast: Narrated by Robert Trout and starring Roland Young, with Betty Comden, Adolph Green, Jackson Beck, Ralph Bell, John McGovern, Kermit Murdock, Paul Mann, Robert Dryden, Allen Drake, and Gene Leonard.
Music: Adolph Green and Betty Comden.

May 9—*Cromer*
Cast: Narrated by Joseph Julian, with Frank Lovejoy, Nicholas Joy, Minerva Pious, Bertram Tanswell, Nora Howard, Jay Malcolm Dunn, John Moore, Kermit Murdock, Berford Hamden, and Roland Bottomley.
Music: Lyn Murray.

May 16—*New York: A Tapestry for Radio*
Cast: Narrated by Martin Gabel, with Minerva Pious, Tana de Gamez, Hester Sondergaard, Paul Mann, Richard Huey, Donna Keith, Kermit Murdock, Sam Raskyn, Sid Kassell, Walter Burke, and Ed Cullen.
Music: Frederick Steiner; conducted by Lyn Murray.

May 23—*Tel Aviv*
Cast: Myron McCormick as Adams, Paul Mann as Quiz, with Joan Alexander, Joseph Julian, Olive Deering, Margaret Foster, Maurice Franklin, Robert Harris, Mordecai Kossover, and Martin Wolfson.

Music: Bernard Herrmann.

May 30—*Untitled* (repeat)*
Cast: Fredric March starred, with same cast as April 18 production.

Music: Bernard Herrmann.

June 6—*Sandburg*
Cast: Featured Charles Laughton, with Hans Conreid, Wally Maher, Mercedes McCambridge, Dick Ryan, Joan Lorring, Will Wright, Joe Granby, Lurene Tuttle, Bob Bruce, Norman Field, Earl Ross, Horace Willard, Peter Chong, Franklin Parker, Harry Bartel, Edward Marr, and Earl Robinson.

Music: Bernard Herrmann.

June 13—*Wolfe*
Cast: Charles Laughton starred, with Elliott Lewis, Hans Conreid, Janet Scott, Franklin Parker, Alfred Ryder, Joseph Forte, and Peter Leeds.

Music: Bernard Herrmann.

June 20—*Whitman*
Cast: Starred Charles Laughton, with John Dehner, Wally Maher, and Peggy Miller.

Music: Bernard Herrmann.

July 4—*Home for the 4th*
Cast: Dane Clark, Wally Maher, Betsy Kelly, Regina Wallace, Byron Kane, Paul McVey, Joan Lorring, and Billy Roy.

Music: Bernard Herrmann.

July 18—*The Moat Farm Murder*
Cast: Charles Laughton and Elsa Lanchester, with Raymond Lawrence.

Music: Bernard Herrmann.

July 25—*El Capitan and the Corporal*
Cast: Joseph Julian and Katherine Locke, with Kermit Murdock, Burl Ives, Minerva Pious, Robert Dryden, Paul Mann, Cecil Roy, and Sam Raskyn.

Music: Alexander Semmler.

August 8—*A Very Fine Type Girl*
Cast: Starred Minerva Pious, with Robert Dryden, Joseph Julian, Paul Mann, Kermit Murdock, Hester Sondergaard, Larry Haines, Adelaide Klein, Eleanor Sherman, and Kathleen Carnes.

Music: Alexander Semmler.

August 15—*There Will Be Time Later*
Cast: House Jameson was featured; with Hester Sondergaard, Robert Dryden, Paul Mann, and Shannon Day.

Music: Bernard Herrmann.

ELECTION EVE SPECIAL
November 3—*The Roosevelt Special*
Cast: From Hollywood: Joan Bennett, Mr. and Mrs. Irving Berlin, Humphrey

---

*Due to heavy listener response to first production, Corwin chose to repeat this program in the same series.

Bogart, Virginia Bruce, Jimmy Cagney, Harry Carey, Claudette Colbert, Joseph Cotten, Linda Darnell, John Garfield, Judy Garland, James Gleason, Paulette Goddard, Susan Hayward, Rita Hayworth, Walter Huston, Rex Ingram, George Jessel, Danny Kaye, Gene Kelly, Evelyn Keyes, Groucho Marx, Paul Muni, George Raft, Edward G. Robinson, Gale Sondergaard, Lana Turner, Richard Whorf, Monty Woolley, Jane Wyman, and Keenan Wynn. Guests included the youngest and oldest voters, 19-year-old Betty Hall (of Decatur, Georgia) and 94-year-old Julius Oscar.

From New York: Constance Bennett, Gertrude Berg, Milton Berle, Charles Boyer, Marc Connelly, Bennett Cerf, John Dewey, Eddie Dowling, Olin Downes, Edna Ferber, John Gunther, Fannie Hurst, the Ink Spots, Dorothy Maynor, Vilhjalmur Stefansson, Alonzo Myers, Dorothy Parker, Waldo Pierce, Elmer Rice, Barney Ross, Vincent Sheean, Frank Sinatra, Paul Strand, Franchot Tone, Louis Untermeyer, Benay Venuta, and Fay Wray. From Washington: President Franklin Delano Roosevelt.

Music: E. Y. Harburg and Earl Robinson.

1945

U.N. SAN FRANCISCO CONFERENCE SPECIAL

April 25—*Word from the People*

Cast: Thomas Hart Benton, Madeleine Carroll, Bette Davis, Dr. Alexander Fleming, Virginia Gildersleeve, Thomas Mann, Jan Masaryk, Paul Robeson, Elmo Roper, Carl Sandburg, Secretary of State Edward Stettinius, Carl Van Doren, and Bruno Walter. Also, personalities picked up live from various parts of the country and the world, including a Red Army soldier from the Soviet Union, a Chinese pilot from Chungking, a member of the Free French from Paris, a Filipino from Manila, a Czech refugee, a U.S. Army chaplain from Iwo Jima, and others.

Music: E. Y. Harburg and Earl Robinson.

VE-DAY SPECIAL

May 8—*On a Note of Triumph*

Cast: Martin Gabel narrated, with Ludwig Donath, Peggy Rae, Joan Lorring, Elliott Lewis, Merton Koplin, Lucille Meredith, Raymond Lawrence, Alex Hartford, George Sorel, Dick Nelson, Bob Bruce, Joe Worthy, Lurene Tuttle, Regina Wallace, June Foray, Pat McGeehan, Harry Bartell, Jim Nusser, Peter Witt, Fred Essler, Norbert Muller, Ramsey Hill, Irene Tedrow, Eula Beal, and Johnny Bond.

Music: Bernard Herrmann; conducted by Lud Gluskin.

COLUMBIA PRESENTS CORWIN

July 3—*Unity Fair*

Cast: Alfred Drake, Groucho Marx, Keenan Wynn, June Richmond, William Spier, Harry Lang, Joe Worthy, Bill Shaw, and Elmore Vincent.

Music: Earl Robinson, E. Y. Harburg, Burton Lane.

July 10—*Daybreak*
Cast: Starred Ronald Colman, with Corrinha Murra and others.
Music: Lyn Murray; conducted by Lud Gluskin.
July 17—*The Undecided Molecule*
Cast: Elliott Lewis, Groucho Marx, Robert Benchley, Vincent Price, Norman
   Lloyd, Sylvia Sidney, and Keenan Wynn (performing four roles).
Music: Carmen Dragon; conducted by Lud Gluskin.
July 24—*New York: A Tapestry for Radio*
Cast: Orson Welles narrated, with Olive Deering, Bill Shaw, Eddie Marr,
   Norman Field, Joe Worthy, Merton Koplin, Paul McVey, Charles Seel,
   Gerald Kean, Eddie Harburg, and Maxine Marx.
Music: Frederick Steiner; conducted by Lud Gluskin.
July 31—*A Walk with Nick*
Cast: John Hodiak, Joan Lorring, Elliott Lewis; others.
Music: Wilbur Hatch; conducted by Lud Gluskin.
August 7—*Savage Encounter*
Cast: Glenn Ford and others.
Music: Harry Simeon; conducted by Lud Gluskin.

VJ-DAY SPECIAL
August 14—*14 August*
Cast: Orson Welles.
Music: Lud Gluskin.

DAY OF PRAYER SPECIAL
August 19—*God and Uranium*
Cast: Orson Welles and Olivia de Havilland.
Music: Lud Gluskin.
NOTE: This program was an extended version of *14 August* and was aired in
   the regular time slot of *Columbia Presents Corwin*. The series resumed the
   following week.

COLUMBIA PRESENTS CORWIN (Continuation)
August 21—*L'Affaire Gumpert*
Cast: Charles Laughton and Elsa Lanchester, with Emil Corwin and others,
   including violinist David Frisina.
Music: Carmen Dragon; conducted by Lud Gluskin.

CBS PROMOTION SPECIAL
September 16—*Stars in the Afternoon*
Cast: Personalities from the CBS fall schedule, including House Jameson,
   Katherine Raht, Raymond Ives, and Jackie Kelk of *The Aldrich Family;* Pa-
   trice Munsel, Earl Wrightson, Jack Smith, Al Goodman and orchestra of
   The Prudential Family Hour; Milo Boulton, Oscar Bradley orchestra of *We the
   People;* Paul McGrath of *Inner Sanctum;* Bob Hawk of *Thanks to the Yanks;*
   James Melton of *The Texaco Star Theatre;* Helen Hayes read excerpts from
   Corwin's *On a Note of Triumph;* Jan Peerce, Jean Tennyson of *Great Moments*

in Music; Phil Baker of *Take It or Leave It;* Dr. Artur Rodzinsky of the *New York Philharmonic;* Tom Howard, George Shelton, Lulu McConnell, Harry McNaughton of *It Pays to Be Ignorant;* Les Tremayne and Claudia Morgan of *The Thin Man;* John Charles Daly, Edward R. Murrow of *Report to the Nation;* also, Bess Myerson as Miss America and Danny Kaye, with announcers Harry Marble, Stewart Young, Kermit Murdock, and Art Gentry.
Music: Bernard Herrmann; with Al Goodman, Archie Blyer, André Kostelanetz.

SPECIAL: RADIO'S 25th ANNIVERSARY
November 6—*Seems Radio Is Here to Stay*
Cast: This repeat was performed by the original cast of the first production, April 14, 1939.
Music: Bernard Herrmann.

1946

NOTE: Officially announced February 18, Norman Corwin became the first recipient of the One World Award, as granted by the Wendell Willkie Memorial. With CBS associate Lee Bland, he departed June 15 for a four-month global mission to thirty-seven countries. He recorded, on magnetic wire, interviews and impressions of a postwar world. Upon his return, he wrote a series of thirteen actuality documentaries about the trip.

1947

ONE WORLD FLIGHT
January 14—*Introduction*
Cast: Author narrated, with selected excerpts from the programs to follow. Production was assisted by Guy Della Cioppa.
Music: Lyn Murray.
January 21—*England*
Cast: Author narrated; with Prime Minister Clement Attlee, Dr. Alexander Fleming, Lord Van Sittart, Minister of State Philip Noel-Baker, Czech Ambassador to the U.S. Vladimir Hurban (interviewed en route), writer J. B. Priestley, and others.
Music: Lyn Murray.
January 28—*France, Denmark, Norway, Sweden*
Cast: Author narrated; with (in Paris) MRP party spokesman Maurice Schumann, Nobel Prize winner Frederick Joliot-Curie, architect Paul Nelson, poet Louis Aragon; (in Copenhagen) Finance Minister Thorkild Kristensen, Foreign Minister Gustav Rasmussen; (in Oslo) Foreign Minister Halvard Lange and Sigurd Evensmo (sole survivor of aborted plan to escape Nazis); (in Stockholm) Prince Bertil, newspaperwoman Baroness Eren Krona, and the first woman member of Swedish parliament: 70-year-old Kersten Hesselgren; others.

Music: Lyn Murray.

February 4—*Poland*

Cast: Author narrated, with interviews featuring President Bierut, Polish workers, and Madame Rabecwisz, noted musician; others.

Music: Lyn Murray.

February 11—*Soviet Union*

Cast: Author narrated, with Sergei Eisenstein, composer Aram Katchaturian, scientist Peter Kapitza, *Pravda* editor David Zaslavsky, Michael Borodin, Sergei Prokofieff; others.

Music: Lyn Murray.

February 18—*Czechoslovakia*

Cast: Author narrated, with students, lawyers, doctors, Minister Plenipotentiary Jan Papanek, President Beneš; Lidice massacre remembrance, miners underground at Kladno; others.

Music: Lyn Murray.

February 25—*Italy*

Cast: Author narrated, with MP Ugo LaMalfa, *Open City* film writer Sergio Amidei and producer Roberto Rossellini, communist leader Palmiro Togliatti, Prime Minister Alcide De Gasperi, Italian resistance fighters; others.

Music: Lyn Murray.

March 4—*Egypt, India*

Cast: Author narrated; in Cairo, no high officials—house servants, workers, a pasha, street urchins, a man going blind; in New Delhi, Viceroy Lord Wavell, Jawaharlal Nehru; others.

Music: Lyn Murray.

March 11—*China*

Cast: Author narrated, with Shanghai Mayor K. C. Wu, Chinese film personnel, Chou En-lai, Minister of Information Pung She Pay, U.S. Commissioner Walter Robertson, three Chinese Commissioners of Executive Headquarters.

Music: Lyn Murray.

March 18—*Philippines*

Cast: Author narrated, with President Manuel Roxas, U.S. Ambassador Paul V. McNutt, students, clerk, wife of American businessman, and a scientist.

Music: Lyn Murray.

March 25—*Australia*

Cast: Author narrated, with governmental officials, including the Premier of New South Wales, J. B. McKell; soldiers, dockmen, laborers; and others.

Music: Lyn Murray.

April 1—*New Zealand*

Cast: Author narrated, with administrators of governmental agencies and some socialized programs, Prime Minister Peter Fraser, cross-section of citizenry.

Music: Lyn Murray.

SPECIAL: COMMITTEE FOR THE FIRST AMENDMENT
October 26—*Hollywood Fights Back*
Cast: From Hollywood: Humphrey Bogart, Charles Boyer, Eddie Cantor, Richard Conte, Joseph Cotten, Florence Eldridge, Ava Gardner, Judy Garland, James Gleason, Paul Henreid, Marsha Hunt, John Huston, Danny Kaye, Gene Kelly, Evelyn Keyes, Burt Lancaster, Peter Lorre, Vincent Price, Margaret Sullavan, Walter Wanger, Jane Wyatt, and Robert Young.
From New York: John Garfield, Artie Shaw, Frank Sinatra, Deems Taylor, Dr. Harlow Shapley of the Harvard Observatory, Senators Elbert Thomas of Utah, Wayne Morse of Oregon, and Glen Taylor of Idaho.
NOTE: This program, broadcast over ABC, protested the House Un-American Activities Committee investigation of the film industry and was partly written by Norman Corwin. It originated from Hollywood under the direction of Corwin, and also from New York under the direction of William N. Robson.

1949

CBS DOCUMENTARY UNIT
July 10—*Citizen of the World*
Cast: Lee J. Cobb, narrator; with Paul Bouchon, Butch Cavell, Robert Dryden, Steven Hill, Gerald Kean, Paul Mann, Bryna Rayburn, Joseph DeSantis, Ann Shepherd, Hans van Stuwe, Karl Swenson, Charles Irving, Oscar Brand.

UN RADIO
September 11–*Could Be*
Cast: Ben Grauer, Robert Trout, Martin Gabel, Charles Irving, and others.
Music: Alexander Semmler.

1950
THE PURSUIT OF PEACE
March 26—*Document A/777*
Cast: Richard Basehart, Charles Boyer, Lee J. Cobb, Ronald Colman, Joan Crawford, Maurice Evans, Lena Horne, Marsha Hunt, Alexander Knox, Charles Laughton, Laurence Olivier, Vincent Price, Edward G. Robinson, Robert Ryan, Hilda Vaughn, and Emlyn Williams.
Music: Lyn Murray.
NOTE: Corwin, as UN Radio Chief of Special Projects, produced a six-program series for broadcast over the Mutual network, and *Document A/777* was the premiere show. He was also actively involved with development of the third program, *Fear Itself,* by Allen Sloane.
May 7—*Fear Itself*
Cast: Martin Gabel, narrator; Frank Waldecker, announcer; with the recorded voices of Winston Churchill, Harry Truman, Douglas MacArthur,

Joseph Stalin, King George, Bernard Baruch, Fiorello LaGuardia, Trygve Lie, and others.

1951

UNITED NATIONS RADIO
November 4—*Windows on the World*
Cast: Douglas Fairbanks Jr., narrator, with personnel of the UN Secretariat Building; Gerald Kean, director.

1955

UNITED NATIONS RADIO
October 4—*A Charter in the Saucer*
Cast: Sir Laurence Olivier as UN investigator, with Allen MacClelland as Vuz; others.
NOTE: This UN program was produced by the British Broadcasting Corporation and featured an all-English cast.

Notes

Chapter 1

1. Charles Beaumont, "Requiem for Radio," *Playboy* (May 1960), p. 84.

2. Milton Allen Kaplan, *Radio and Poetry* (New York: Columbia University Press, 1949), p. 5.

3. Robert J. Landry, "One Who Loved Radio for Its Own Sake," *Variety*, January 5, 1955, p. 102.

4. At a very early age, Orson Welles had been acknowledged a leading theatrical producer. At twenty-two, he had experienced Broadway success and was pictured on the cover of *Time* magazine. He was only twenty-three when he produced for CBS the electrifying adaptation of H. G. Wells' *The War of the Worlds*.

5. Albert N. Williams, "The Radio Artistry of Norman Corwin," *Saturday Review of Literature*, February 14, 1942, p. 6.

6. Max Wylie, *Radio and Television Writing* (New York: Rinehart, 1950), p. 131.

7. "Corkscrew in the Sky," *Time*, February 27, 1942, p. 55.

8. Erik Barnouw, *The Golden Web* (New York: Oxford University Press, 1968), p. 55.

9. At the Annual Advertising Awards dinner in New York (February 1942), Norman Corwin was the recipient of the Edward Bok Memorial Medal for being "the individual who by contemporary service has added to the knowledge of technique of radio advertising."

10. Barnouw, *The Golden Web*, p. 163.

11. *Variety*, July 18, 1945, p. 47.

12. Clifton Fadiman, "Introduction," in *More by Corwin* (New York: Holt, 1944), p. ix.

13. Cameron Shipp, "Corwin of the Airwaves," *Coronet* (December 1945), pp. 37–38.

14. José Rodriguez, "Our Cover Couch," *Script*, August 25, 1945, p. 6.

15. William Matthews, "Radio Plays as Literature," *Hollywood Quarterly* (October 1945), pp. 41–42.

16. Wylie, *Radio and Television Writing*, pp. 128–31.

17. Gilbert Seldes, *The Great Audience* (New York: Viking, 1951), p. 121.

18. "This Is War!" *Time*, February 23, 1942, p. 60.

19. Personal interview, Norman Corwin, April 15, 1968.

20. Williams, "The Radio Artistry of Norman Corwin," p. 6.

21. Fadiman, "Introduction," p. xi.

22. Shipp, "Corwin of the Airwaves," p. 33.

23. Personal interview, Norman Corwin, January 22, 1974.

24. Shipp, "Corwin of the Airwaves," p. 36.

25. Barnouw, *The Golden Web*, p. 241.

26. Will Tusher, "Corwin Asks Radio Revival," *Hollywood Reporter*, November 18, 1974, p. 6.

27. Letter to author from Erik Barnouw, November 28, 1972.

28. Seldes, *The Great Audience*, p. 120.

29. Including Fletcher Markle, outstanding radio writer-producer and former Canadian Broadcasting Corporation executive; Perry Lafferty, senior vice president of the National Broadcasting Company; Charles Lewin, advertising executive; and Byron Kane, actor; as well as prominent leaders in world broadcasting.

30. Carolyne Malloy, "An Empirical Analysis of Selected Radio Dramas of Norman Corwin" (unpublished master's thesis, University of California, Los Angeles, 1968), p. 119.

Chapter 2

1. Unless otherwise noted, details and incidents concerning Norman Corwin's youth and family history, as recorded in this chapter, were derived from personal interviews with Samuel Corwin, father (September 14–15, 1972); Emil Corwin, brother (April 27, 1972); Alfred Corwin, brother (March 30, 1973); Beulah Belkowitz, sister (September 14, 1972); Mildred Cohen, aunt (September 13, 1972); Harry Ober, uncle (September 15, 1972); Lucy Drew Stuetzel, former teacher (September 12, 1972); and Norman Corwin himself (March 2–9, 1972; January 21–25, 1974; and June 1–4, 1976).

2. "Drummer Boy," *American Magazine* (June 1942), p. 88.

3. Norman Corwin, "Corwin on Media: Boston," *Westways* (February 1976), p. 73.

4. Norman Corwin, unpublished memoirs.

5. From private papers of Norman Corwin.

6. Norman Corwin, "Corwin Tells His Story as $15 'Recorder' Scribe," *Greenfield Recorder-Gazette*, February 1, 1958, p. 7.

7. Norman Corwin, unpublished memoirs.

8. Ibid.

9. Norman Corwin, *Untitled and Other Radio Dramas* (New York: Holt, 1945), p. 486.

10. From private papers of Norman Corwin.

11. *Variety,* September 4, 1935, p. 34.

12. Considered in their historical context, ACLU knowledge of the incriminating memos must have been a matter of substantial concern to WLW's management. In the early 1930s, the Federal Radio Commission was perturbed about continued licensing of so-called "propaganda" stations: stations which tended to subordinate the public interest to their private interests as licensees and corporations. In 1931 and 1932, with the Brinkley (*KFKB Broadcasting Association, Inc.* vs. *Federal Radio Commission,* 47 F.2nd 670, D.C. Cir.) cases, the courts clarified that stations could lose their broadcast licenses for such activities. WLW, while not a "propaganda" station, might have been troubled by the implication that business interests had been placed ahead of news service to the public.

Chapter 3

1. Abel Green and Joe Laurie Jr., *Show Biz* (Garden City, N.Y.: Doubleday, 1951), p. 380.

2. Norman Corwin, unpublished memoirs.

3. Ibid.

4. Personal interview, Sarita Corwin, March 30, 1973.

5. Elliott M. Sanger, *Rebel in Radio* (New York: Hastings House, 1973), pp. 14ff.

6. Personal interview, Elliott Sanger, March 29, 1973.

7. Norman Corwin, unpublished memoirs.

8. Personal interview, Norman Corwin, January 23, 1974.

9. Ibid.

10. "Radio Review: Poetic License," *Variety,* January 26, 1938, p. 33.

11. Albert N. Williams, "The Radio Artistry of Norman Corwin," *Saturday Review of Literature,* February 14, 1942, p. 5.

12. Personal interview, Norman Corwin, January 23, 1974.

13. Ibid.

14. Ibid.

15. Robert J. Landry, "One Who Loved Radio for Its Own Sake," *Variety,* January 5, 1955, p. 102.

16. Irving Reis left for Hollywood to produce, within the next fifteen years, a number of commercially successful films. He died of cancer in 1953 at the age of forty-six.

17. It was considered poor practice to "double spot"—to present more than one commercial announcement at a given break. A network series was normally supported by a single sponsorship, so that clients became associated with individual programs or stars—such as Pepsodent and *Amos 'n' Andy,* Jello and *Jack Benny,* DuPont and *Cavalcade of America.*

18. Sam J. Slate and Joe Cook, *It Sounds Impossible* (New York: Macmillan, 1963), p. xxiv.

19. Norman Corwin, "Corwin on Media: Counting Losses," *Westways* (June 1975), p. 71.

20. "Hitler Comes Home," *Time*, March 21, 1938, p. 19.

21. *New York Post*, December 3, 1938.

22. *New York Journal-American*, December 8, 1938.

23. *Springfield Sunday Union and Republican*, February 5, 1939.

24. Personal interview, William N. Robson, April 29, 1972.

25. Personal interview, Norman Corwin, January 24, 1974.

26. Norman Corwin, *Thirteen by Corwin* (New York: Holt, 1942), pp. 89–90, 103.

27. William S. Paley, *As It Happened* (Garden City, N.Y.: Doubleday, 1979), p. 113.

Chapter 4

1. Personal interview, William N. Robson, April 29, 1972.

2. Llewellyn White, "Rags to Riches," in *Mass Communications*, ed. Wilbur Schramm (Urbana: University of Illinois Press, 1949), p. 69.

3. Corwin, "Corwin on Media: Counting Losses," p. 71.

4. Personal interview, William B. Lewis, March 28, 1973.

5. Corwin, *Thirteen by Corwin*, p. 78.

6. Ibid., p. 55.

7. Ibid., p. 79.

8. Ibid., pp. 57–75.

9. Letter from House Jameson to Carolyne Malloy, reproduced in her unpublished master's thesis, "An Empirical Analysis of Selected Radio Dramas of Norman Corwin" (University of California, Los Angeles, 1968).

10. Erik Barnouw, ed., *Radio Drama in Action* (New York: Rinehart, 1945), p. 205.

11. Corwin, *Thirteen by Corwin*, p. 79.

12. *Detroit Free Press*, September 17, 1939.

13. Corwin, *Thirteen by Corwin*, pp. 215–16.

14. Ibid., p. 240.

15. *New York Journal-American*, April 26, 1939.

16. Corwin, *Thirteen by Corwin*, p. 240.

17. *Variety*, July 26, 1939, p. 36.

18. CBS program information, October 1939.

19. *Variety*, October 25, 1939, p. 36.

20. Irving Reis premiered his *Columbia Workshop* on July 18, 1936, with a two-part presentation (*A Comedy of Danger* by Richard Hughes and *The Finger of God* by Percival Wilde). Reis had his actors read from a chalked circle in one, and roam the studio and work the props in the other. It was said to have been "more embarrassment than triumph." See Landry, "One Who Loved Radio for Its Own Sake," *Variety*, January 5, 1955, p. 102.

21. *Broadcasting*, August 1, 1940, p. 137.

22. *Variety,* December 27, 1939, p. 28.

23. Personal interview, Norman Corwin, January 24, 1974.

24. From the private papers of Norman Corwin.

25. Personal interview, Norman Corwin, January 24, 1974.

26. Because of ASCAP's dispute with the networks and the resulting ban of ASCAP tunes, "My Bonnie Lies over the Ocean" was substituted for "Yes Sir, That's My Baby" when the show was repeated a year later on *Campbell Playhouse.*

27. From the private papers of Norman Corwin.

28. *New York World-Telegram,* March 8, 1940.

29. *Variety,* March 13, 1940, p. 30.

30. Max Wylie, *Best Broadcasts of 1939–40* (New York: Whittlesey House, 1940), pp. 3–22.

31. Paley, *As It Happened,* p. 112.

Chapter 5

1. Corwin, *Thirteen by Corwin,* p. 260.

2. Edith J. R. Isaacs, "Radio Poet," *Theatre Arts* (May 1942), p. 347.

3. The film was never produced.

4. From the private papers of Norman Corwin.

5. Ibid.

6. Personal interview, Norman Corwin, June 2, 1976.

7. From the private papers of Norman Corwin.

8. Ibid.

9. Ibid.

10. Herbert Mitgang, *The Letters of Carl Sandburg* (New York: Harcourt, Brace & World, 1968), p. 395.

11. Corwin, *Thirteen by Corwin,* p. 50.

12. "Pixie Primer," *Time,* May 12, 1941, p. 70.

13. *New York Post,* May 5, 1941.

14. Personal interview, Norman Corwin, June 2, 1976.

15. From the private papers of Norman Corwin.

16. *Variety,* May 7, 1941, p. 59.

17. Corwin, *Thirteen by Corwin,* p. 23.

18. Ibid., p. 169.

19. Personal interview, Norman Corwin, June 2, 1976.

20. Norman Corwin, "Corwin on Media: Confessions of a Map Addict," *Westways* (November 1973), p. 58.

21. Norman Corwin, *More by Corwin* (New York: Holt, 1944), p. 58.

22. The AFRA agreement regarding sustaining half-hour radio programs required the minimum guarantee of $23 per show for actors in New York: $12 basic fee, $3 for the first hour of rehearsal, and $2 for each succeeding hour of rehearsal.

23. Personal interview, Norman Corwin, June 2, 1976.

24. Corwin, *More by Corwin*, pp. 203–25.
25. Ibid., p. 249.
26. Personal interview, Norman Corwin, June 3, 1976.
27. From the private papers of Norman Corwin.
28. Corwin, *More by Corwin*, p. 177.
29. Ibid., p. xiii.
30. The OFF was established October 7, 1941. On June 13, 1942, the OFF was absorbed by the OWI (Office of War Information), which continued the function of coordinating government messages and wartime informational activity.
31. At this juncture in his career, Norman Corwin was earning $25,000 annually.

Chapter 6

1. Corwin, *More by Corwin*, p. 57.
2. Crossley estimated an audience of 60 million. See Barnouw, *The Golden Web*, p. 153.
3. Corwin, *More by Corwin*, p. 88.
4. Personal interview, Norman Corwin, January 23, 1974.
5. *Variety*, December 17, 1941, p. 44.
6. Letter to Norman Corwin by William B. Lewis, August 24, 1950.
7. *New York Times*, December 14, 1941.
8. From the private papers of Norman Corwin.
9. Norman Corwin, unpublished memoirs.
10. From the private papers of Norman Corwin.
11. Ibid.
12. Corwin, *More by Corwin*, pp. 85–87.
13. Personal interview, Norman Corwin, January 23, 1974.
14. Ibid.
15. Corwin, *More by Corwin*, p. 73.
16. From the private papers of Norman Corwin.
17. *Washington Post*, December 15, 1941.
18. Wylie, *Best Broadcasts of 1940–41*, pp. 19–20.
19. Corwin, *More by Corwin*, p. 59.
20. Ibid., pp. 86–87.
21. *New York Times*, December 16, 1941.
22. Corwin, *More by Corwin*, p. 93.
23. Ibid.
24. Letter to Norman Corwin by William B. Lewis, August 24, 1950.
25. Personal interview, Norman Corwin, January 23, 1974.
26. From the private papers of Norman Corwin.
27. Ibid.
28. Ibid.

29. Ibid.

30. *New York Times*, December 16, 1941.

31. *Variety*, December 17, 1941, p. 44.

32. Robert J. Landry, *This Fascinating Radio Business* (Indianapolis: Bobbs-Merrill, 1946), p. 250.

Chapter 7

1. Sherman H. Dryer, *Radio in Wartime* (New York: Greenberg, 1942), p. 5.

2. Ibid., p. 31.

3. Personal interview, William B. Lewis, March 28, 1973.

4. Dryer, *Radio in Wartime*, p. 246.

5. FDR obviously appreciated Woollcott's candid appraisal of matters. Woollcott had publicly and boldly reproved Nazism as early as 1935 on the CBS program *The Town Crier*, an act which promptly brought dismissal and cancellation by his sponsor.

6. Dryer, *Radio in Wartime*, pp. 300–301.

7. Ibid., p. 245.

8. Ibid.

9. *Variety*, February 25, 1942, p. 26.

10. Story accredited to Clarence Jordan of N. W. Ayer Agency in a letter to H. L. McClinton, as reported in *Variety* (March 11, 1942, p. 37).

11. *Variety*, February 25, 1942, p. 26.

12. Ibid., March 4, 1942, p. 36.

13. Ibid., March 11, 1942, p. 38.

14. Ibid., April 1, 1942, p. 34.

15. Erik Barnouw, ed., *Radio Drama in Action* (New York: Dodd, Mead, 1942), p. 163.

16. From private papers of Norman Corwin.

17. "Hate?" *Time*, May 18, 1942, p. 32.

18. *Variety*, May 13, 1942, p. 32.

19. Dryer, *Radio in Wartime*, p. 249.

20. *New York Times*, June 7, 1942, p. 19.

21. Dryer, *Radio in Wartime*, p. 302.

22. Corwin, *More by Corwin*, p. 299.

23. A "Cooperative Analysis of Broadcasting Survey" (Crossley) of *This Is War!*, programs 2 and 4, estimated an audience share of 20.7, slightly below the OFF assessment, and deemed "not too good" in view of the virtual monopoly of four-network exposure. See *Variety*, March 18, 1942, p. 32.

24. Corwin, *More by Corwin*, p. 299.

25. Corwin, *Untitled and Other Radio Dramas*, p. 157.

26. In June 1942, the Office of Information was established under Elmer Davis, superseding the Office of Facts and Figures. In July, the Lewis unit became the radio bureau of the OWI domestic branch and the main governmental voice at home.

27. *Variety*, May 13, 1942, p. 18.

28. Personal interview, Norman Corwin, January 23, 1974.

29. From private papers of Norman Corwin.

30. Alexander Kendrick, *Prime Time* (New York: Little, Brown, 1969), p. 252.

31. Corwin, *Untitled*, p. 163.

32. Ibid., p. 154.

33. Ibid., p. 165.

34. Joseph Julian, *This Was Radio* (New York: Viking, 1975), p. 80.

35. *Variety*, August 5, 1942, p. 44.

36. Bridson, a poet and producer, was assistant to Gilliam, founder and director of BBC Features; Gielgud headed the BBC Department of Drama.

37. John K. Hutchens, "That Realm, That England," *New York Times*, August 6, 1942, pt. 8, p. 8.

38. William S. Paley, in uniform, later joined Eisenhower in Algiers to head the radio branch of psychological warfare.

39. Corwin, *Untitled*, pp. 217–18.

40. Corwin, *More by Corwin*, p. 29.

41. John K. Hutchens, "Several Matters," *New York Times*, December 5, 1942, pt. 8, p. 12.

Chapter 8

1. *United States Treasury Report of the Secretary, 1947–48* (Washington: U.S. Government Printing Office, 1949), p. 520.

2. Ronald H. Bailey, *The Home Front: USA* (Alexandria, Va.: Time-Life Books, 1977), p. 180.

3. Congress, in an attempt to curb war profits, enacted tax rates up to 90 percent, which were deductible if devoted to advertising—which was declared a necessary business expense.

4. *Broadcasting*, January 5, 1942, p. 8.

5. From the private papers of Norman Corwin.

6. Corwin, *More by Corwin*, p. 401.

7. Ibid., pp. 395–99.

8. *Variety*, January 20, 1943, p. 38.

9. Robert Lasch, "Not So Fantastic," *Chicago Sun*, January 18, 1943, p. 8.

10. *Variety*, February 3, 1943, p. 32.

11. Ibid., February 17, 1943, p. 28.

12. D. G. Bridson, *Prospero and Ariel* (London: Gollancz, 1971), p. 97.

13. *Variety*, February 17, 1943, p. 28.

14. From the private papers of Norman Corwin.

15. CBS divested itself of its "artist bureau" in 1941 due to pressure from the FCC, which charged that, as principal employers, networks were not fit

agents for talent. Prior to this action, Columbia Artists, the CBS subsidiary, collected a 20 percent fee from each contract writer, director, and performer.

16. From the private papers of Norman Corwin.

17. Corwin, *More by Corwin*, pp. 127–34.

18. Ibid., p. 135.

19. Abel Green and Joe Laurie, *Show Biz* (New York: Holt, 1951), pp. 485–86.

20. Ibid., p. 500.

21. Corwin, *Untitled and Other Radio Dramas*, p. 366.

22. Ibid., pp. 367–68.

23. From the private papers of Norman Corwin.

24. Corwin's concern·was shared by other writers, notably Arch Oboler, who wrote in *Variety* (January 5, 1944, p. 113): "What is frightening about radio's prospects in the near future? Simply this—the business of radio has become so successful in these war days that the painful struggle over the years to give to radio writing maturity and meaningfulness has largely been forgotten. So much money is being made by the business, so much time has been sold, that the opportunities in which the mature writer can speak of the world he lives in as he sees it exist in radio with less and less frequency."

25. Continuation of letter annotated in footnote 5.

26. From the private papers of Norman Corwin.

27. Ibid.

28. Norman Corwin, "Radio and Morale," *Saturday Review of Literature*, July 4, 1942, p. 6.

29. From the private papers of Norman Corwin.

30. Ibid.

Chapter 9

1. *Variety*, March 15, 1944, p. 48.

2. *New York Post*, March 8, 1944, p. 36.

3. "Hollywood Heckled," *Time*, March 20, 1944, p. 58.

4. *Variety*, March 15, 1944, p. 48. NBC's *The Bob Hope Show*, radio's top-rated program of the era, twice opposed Corwin (the present series and, previously, *An American in England*). After the second program of Corwin's current series, *Billboard* asked, insinuatingly, "Wonder how *The Bob Hope Show* is doing?" Wryly, Corwin replied, "Well, Bob Hope never had to worry."

5. *Newsweek*, March 20, 1944, p. 94.

6. Corwin, *Untitled and Other Radio Dramas*, p. 428.

7. *Billboard*, March 25, 1944, pp. 10, 20.

8. Personal interview, Norman Corwin, January 24, 1974.

9. Bernard Asbell, *When F.D.R. Died* (New York: Rinehart and Winston, 1961), p. 161.

10. Erik Barnouw, *Radio Drama in Action* (New York: Rinehart, 1945), p. 250.

11. From the private papers of Norman Corwin.

12. A leading Broadway and radio actor, Johnson was best known perhaps as "Raymond," the host of *Inner Sanctum.*

13. Corwin, *Untitled,* p. 127.

14. Ibid., p. 270.

15. Ibid., pp. 273–74.

16. Ibid., pp. 47–63.

17. *Brooklyn Daily Eagle,* June 1, 1944, p. 8.

18. *Variety,* May 30, 1945, p. 32.

19. Unpublished memoirs, Norman Corwin.

20. Ibid.

21. Telecast May 25, 1972, *Untitled* was staged as a radio drama on TV, with actors reading scripts before a microphone—similar to the successful presentation of Corwin's *The Plot to Overthrow Christmas* by PBS, December 23, 1970 (*Homewood* series by KCET).

22. Corwin, *Untitled,* p. 312.

23. *Variety,* May 17, 1944, p. 32.

24. Corwin, *Untitled,* pp. 279–99.

25. Ibid., p. 106.

26. Ibid., p. 96.

27. Ibid., p. 311.

28. Ibid., p. 115.

29. Award-winning playwrights who, teamed since 1942, became prominent writers for radio and films, later television, and created such Broadway hits as *Inherit the Wind* (1955) and *Auntie Mame* (1956). Part founders of the Armed Forces Radio Service, they wrote the Corwin production while stationed at AFRS headquarters in Los Angeles.

30. Corwin, *Untitled,* p. 435.

31. Ibid., pp. 409–27.

32. FDR's reelection seemed to rest in the action of some 10 million independent voters, whom Dewey hoped to keep from the polls by not stirring up criticism of existing war and domestic policies.

33. Personal interview, Norman Corwin, January 25, 1974.

34. Barnouw, *The Golden Web,* 1968, p. 208.

35. Ibid., p. 209.

36. From the private papers of Norman Corwin.

Chapter 10

1. Corwin, *Untitled and Other Radio Dramas,* p. 483. See also Norman Corwin, *On a Note of Triumph* (New York: Simon & Schuster, 1945).

2. From Norman Corwin's "San Francisco Program Journal," an unpublished assembly of documents and description of the Conference broadcast.

3. Ibid., Sandburg correspondence.

4. Ibid., Mann correspondence.

5. *Variety,* May 2, 1945, p. 50.

6. Corwin, "Journal."

7. Corwin, *Untitled,* p. 491.

8. Personal interview, Norman Corwin, January 25, 1974.

9. Corwin, *Untitled,* p. 498.

10. Personal interview, Martin Gabel, March 28, 1973.

11. Corwin, *Untitled,* p. 441.

12. Ibid., p. 443. Song copyright 1943, Bob Miller, Inc.

13. Ibid., pp. 452–56.

14. *Newsweek,* May 28, 1945, p. 110.

15. From the private papers of Norman Corwin.

16. Corwin, *Untitled,* p. 460.

17. Ibid., pp. 463–64.

18. From the private papers of Norman Corwin.

19. Personal interview, Martin Gabel, March 28, 1973.

20. Corwin, *Untitled,* pp. 468–69.

21. Personal interview, Martin Gabel, March 28, 1973.

22. Corwin, *Untitled,* p. 471.

23. Ibid., pp. 477, 479–80.

24. Ibid., p. 492.

25. Eric Sevareid used the phrase "not so wild a dream" as the title of his memoirs.

26. Corwin, *Untitled,* p. 484.

27. *Billboard,* May 19, 1945, p. 4.

28. *Variety,* May 16, 1945, p. 24.

29. Following newspaper excerpts from "Critical Reception," an appendix to Corwin's *Untitled,* pp. 541–42.

30. Corwin, *Untitled,* p. 492.

31. An LP recording, from a rare air check of the first broadcast, was issued in 1975 by Mark 56 Records, Anaheim, California.

32. From the private papers of Norman Corwin.

33. Ibid.

34. Jack Gould, "A Minority Report," *New York Times,* May 20, 1945, pt. 2, p. 1.

35. Bernard De Voto, "Easy Chair: Corwin's 'On a Note of Triumph,'" *Harper's Magazine* (July 1945), pp. 33–36.

36. "Critical Reception," in Corwin's *Untitled,* p. 541.

37. John Mason Brown, "On a Note of Triumph," *Saturday Review of Literature,* May 26, 1945, pp. 22–26.

38. Personal interview, Norman Corwin, January 25, 1974.
39. "Critical Reception," in Corwin's *Untitled*, pp. 544–45.
40. From the private papers of Norman Corwin.

Chapter 11

1. Corwin, *Untitled and Other Radio Dramas*, pp. 3–34.
2. Ibid., p. 333.
3. Ibid., pp. 499–504.
4. *Variety*, August 22, 1945, p. 42.
5. *Broadcasting*, February 10, 1969, p. 53.
6. From the private papers of Norman Corwin.
7. "Seabee" is an acronym, a phonetic reference to a member of a construction battalion, a naval unit in World War II. Excerpt from Norman Corwin's personal production script.
8. *Variety*, September 19, 1945, p. 29.
9. Ibid.
10. Norman Corwin, unpublished memoirs.
11. Corwin, *Untitled*, pp. 511–15.
12. Ibid., p. 502.
13. Personal interview, Norman Corwin, June 1, 1976. Unless otherwise indicated, data concerning Corwin's One World journey were derived from Mr. Corwin's personal diary.
14. Transcript, CBS (Western Network) special broadcast, March 31, 1946.
15. Norman Corwin, "One World Revisited," reprint from *Common Ground* (Winter 1947), p. 3.
16. Personal interview, Norman Corwin, June 1, 1976.
17. Corwin, "One World Revisited," p. 5.
18. Details from manuscript excerpt by Norman Corwin, Lilly Library, Indiana University, Bloomington.
19. Corwin, "One World Revisited," p. 7.
20. A year later, Polk was murdered in Salonika harbor after attempting to arrange an interview with the Greek Communist guerrilla leader, General Markos.
21. Corwin, "One World Revisited," p. 9.
22. Ibid., p. 10. The Chinese philosopher, centuries before, had advocated "under heaven, one family."
23. Jerome Lawrence, "A New Radio Form," *Hollywood Quarterly* (April 1947), p. 280.

Chapter 12

1. *Variety*, January 8, 1947, p. 107.
2. Barnouw, *The Golden Web*, pp. 231–32.

3. *Statistical History of the United States: From Colonial Times to Present* (New York: Basic Books, 1976), p. 796.

4. *Variety,* November 13, 1946, p. 24. Also, Corwin, "One World Revisited" (reprint from *Common Ground*), pp. 15–16.

5. Personal interview, Norman Corwin, June 3, 1976.

6. *Variety,* January 15, 1947, p. 34.

7. *Musical Courier,* February 1, 1947.

8. In his convention speech, Paley called for "the application of new and sparkling ideas in the presentation of educational, documentary and controversial issues." See *Variety,* November 13, 1946, p. 24.

9. Personal interview, Norman Corwin, June 3, 1976.

10. *New York Daily News,* February 21, 1937.

11. Personal interview, Katherine Locke Corwin, June 4, 1976.

12. From the private papers of Norman Corwin.

13. A Dore Schary production (1947), suggested by the book *The Brick Foxhole* by Richard Brooks; released by RKO Radio Pictures and featuring Robert Young, Robert Mitchum, Gloria Grahame, and Paul Kelly.

14. An allusion to testimony by Adolph Menjou, who, when asked if a Communist actor could inject propaganda into a scene, answered, "Under the proper circumstances, by a look, by an inflection, by a change in the voice, I think it could easily be done."

15. From the private papers of Norman Corwin.

16. *Variety,* October 29, 1947, p. 4.

17. From the private papers of Norman Corwin.

18. *Variety,* December 24, 1947, p. 23.

19. From the private papers of Norman Corwin.

20. Barnouw, *The Golden Web,* p. 241.

21. Benny's "defection" to CBS, officially announced in January 1949, highlighted the big-network talent raids, which also saw *Amos 'n' Andy* leave NBC to join Columbia.

22. From the private papers of Norman Corwin.

Chapter 13

1. The first contingent of the One World Commission had departed the day before, aboard the *Queen Mary,* and a third group followed by plane four days after the second group sailed on the *Batory.* See *New York Times,* August 13, 1948, p. 9.

2. When Edward R. Murrow became CBS vice president of news and public affairs, he authorized the organization of the CBS Documentary Unit (September 1946), an autonomous group of radio writers, researchers, directors, and producers. Its function was to create investigatory programs, one a month, about vital issues of the day.

3. From the private papers of Norman Corwin.

4. *Variety,* January 26, 1949, p. 29.

5. From the private papers of Norman Corwin.

6. *New York Times,* June 9, 1949, pp. 1ff.

7. Ibid.

8. Ibid.

9. Ibid.

10. From the private papers of Norman Corwin.

11. *New York Times,* July 17, 1949, pt. 2, p. 7.

12. *London Daily Express,* September 14, 1949.

13. *New York Times,* August 9, 1949, p. 12.

14. Ibid.

15. Norman Corwin, *Overkill and Megalove* (Cleveland: World, 1963), pp. 87–114.

16. From the private papers of Norman Corwin.

17. *Variety,* September 14, 1949, p. 30.

18. *Radio Times,* October 21, 1949.

19. Dr. Serge Koussevitzky, in fact, conducted his final concert in Boston on May 1, 1949, which marked his retirement after twenty-five years on the podium.

20. Norman Corwin, unpublished memoirs.

21. *Variety,* March 8, 1950, p. 28.

22. Ibid., March 15, 1950, p. 29.

23. Dr. Herbert V. Evatt, Australian Minister for External Affairs, was president of the Third General Assembly of the United Nations.

24. The United Nations building at Lake Success had been constructed near a former World War II Sperry bombsight factory.

25. Script excerpts from the recorded transcription by United Nations Radio of the actual broadcast.

26. *Variety,* March 29, 1950, p. 36.

27. *New York Times,* April 2, 1950, pt. 2, p. 9.

28. *Billboard,* April 8, 1950, p. 10.

29. *New York World-Telegram and Sun,* March 28, 1950, p. 29.

30. *London Evening Express,* January 30, 1951.

31. *Glasgow Herald,* February 2, 1951.

32. *Variety,* March 29, 1950, p. 36.

33. *Variety,* July 13, 1949, p. 25.

34. Barnouw, *The Golden Web,* p. 266n.

Chapter 14

1. From the private papers of Norman Corwin.

2. Personal interview, William N. Robson, April 29, 1972.

3. Norman Corwin, "Radio Writing, USA," *Writer* (February 1951), pp. 35–37.

4. "Cut Rate Radio," *Time*, April 23, 1951, p. 101.

5. The FCC "freeze" on TV allocations was lifted in 1952.

6. Personal interview, Norman Corwin, March 4, 1972.

7. Alexander Kendrick, *Prime Time* (Boston: Little, Brown, 1969), p. 45.

8. Personal interview, Norman Corwin, June 4, 1976.

9. *New Yorker*, February 21, 1959, p. 88.

10. Personal interview, Norman Corwin, June 4, 1976.

11. Norman Corwin, "Don't Write This Man," *Modern Maturity* (April–May 1976), p. 56.

12. Of twenty-six teleplays presented, Corwin wrote thirteen and, with Joel Katz as producer, supervised development of the series in Toronto for Group W stations and syndication. The project was to afford quality programming for possible local-station use in meeting the proposed prime-time access regulation (an FCC edict to encourage local programming by limiting network control of nighttime TV).

13. The film, *The Naked Maja*, was directed by Henry Koster. Corwin shared writing credits with Giorgio Prosperi, Albert Lewin, and Oscar Saul.

14. Norman Corwin, *Holes in a Stained Glass Window* (Secaucus, N.J.: Lyle Stuart, 1978), pp. 265–72. Also, Norman Corwin, *Jerusalem Printout* (Bloomington, Ind.: Raintree Press, 1978) (limited edition), pp. 1–27.

15. Norman Corwin, "The Fourth of July, 1976," *Los Angeles Times*, July 4, 1976, pt. 5, p. 5.

16. Peter Fornatale and Joshua E. Mills, *Radio in the Television Age* (Woodstock, N.Y.: Overlook Press, 1980), p. 23.

17. From the private papers of Norman Corwin.

18. Personal interview, Norman Corwin, January 14, 1976.

Bibliography

Books

Asbell, Bernard. *When F.D.R. Died.* New York: Holt, Rinehart & Winston, 1961.

Bailey, Ronald H. *The Home Front: USA.* Alexandria, Va.: Time-Life Books, 1977.

Barnouw, Erik. *The Golden Web.* New York: Oxford University Press, 1968.

――――, ed. *Radio Drama in Action.* New York: Rinehart, 1945.

Bridson, D. G. *Prospero and Ariel: The Rise and Fall of Radio.* London: Gollancz, 1971.

Corwin, Norman. *Holes in a Stained Glass Window.* Secaucus, N.J.: Lyle Stuart, 1978.

――――. *Jerusalem Printout.* Bloomington, Ind.: Raintree Press, 1978.

――――. *More by Corwin.* New York: Holt, 1944.

――――. *On a Note of Triumph.* New York: Simon & Schuster, 1945.

――――. *Overkill and Megalove.* Cleveland: World, 1963.

――――. *Prayer for the 70s.* Garden City, N.Y.: Doubleday, 1969.

――――. *Thirteen by Corwin.* New York: Holt, 1942.

――――. Unpublished memoirs.

――――. *Untitled and Other Radio Dramas.* New York: Holt, 1945.

――――. Unpublished journal of the San Francisco Conference.

Coulter, Douglas. *Columbia Workshop Plays.* New York: Whittlesey House, 1939.

Dryer, Sherman H. *Radio in Wartime.* New York: Greenberg, 1942.

Fornatale, Peter, and Joshua E. Mills. *Radio in the Television Age.* Woodstock, N.Y.: Overlook Press, 1980.

Green, Abel, and Joe Laurie Jr. *Show Biz.* Doubleday, 1951.

Julian, Joseph. *This Was Radio.* New York: Viking, 1975.

Kaplan, Milton Allen. *Radio and Poetry.* New York: Columbia University Press, 1949.

Kendrick, Alexander. *Prime Time: The Life of Edward R. Murrow.* Boston: Little, Brown, 1969.

Kronenberger, Louis, ed. *The Best Plays of 1958–1959.* New York: Dodd, Mead, 1959.

———, ed. *The Best Plays of 1960–1961*. New York: Dodd, Mead, 1961.

Landry, Robert J. *This Fascinating Radio Business*. Indianapolis: Bobbs-Merrill, 1946.

Malloy, Carolyne. "An Empirical Analysis of Selected Radio Dramas of Norman Corwin." Unpublished master's thesis, University of California, Los Angeles, 1968.

Metz, Robert. *CBS: Reflections in a Bloodshot Eye*. New York: Playboy Press, 1975.

Miller, Francis Trevelyan. *History of World War II*. Philadelphia: Universal Book & Bible House, 1945.

Mitgang, Herbert. *The Letters of Carl Sandburg*. New York: Harcourt, Brace & World, 1968.

Paley, William S. *As It Happened*. Garden City, N.Y.: Doubleday, 1979.

Sanger, Elliott M. *Rebel in Radio: The Story of WQXR*. New York: Hastings House, 1973.

Schramm, Wilbur, ed. *Mass Communications*. Urbana: University of Illinois Press, 1949.

Seldes, Gilbert. *The Great Audience*. New York: Viking, 1951.

Slate, Sam J., and Joe Cook. *It Sounds Impossible*. New York: Macmillan, 1963.

Statistical History of the United States: From Colonial Times to Present. New York: Basic Books, 1976.

This Is War! New York: Dodd, Mead, 1942.

United States Treasury Report of the Secretary, 1947–48. Washington: U.S. Government Printing Office, 1949.

Wylie, Max. *Best Broadcasts of 1939–40*. New York: Whittlesey House, 1940.

———. *Radio and Television Writing*. New York: Rinehart, 1950.

Periodicals, Articles, and Newspapers

Beaumont, Charles. "Requiem for Radio," *Playboy*, May 1960.

"Best Busts," *Time*, August 27, 1945.

Billboard, 1940–57.

Broadcasting, 1940–50.

Brooklyn Daily Eagle, June 1, 1944.

Brown, John Mason. "On a Note of Triumph," *Saturday Review of Literature*, May 26, 1945.

Carson, Saul. "Whose World Flight?" *New Republic*, April 7, 1947.

"Corkscrew in the Sky," *Time*, February 27, 1939.

"Corwin—1949," *Newsweek*, September 26, 1949.

Corwin, Norman. "Careers in Screen and Radio," *Theatre Arts*, July 1941.

———. "Coast to Coast with a Dramatized Debate," *Theatre Arts*, February 1959.

———. "Corwin on Media: Boston," *Westways*, February 1976.

———. "Corwin on Media: Confessions of a Map Addict," *Westways*, November 1973.

_____. "Corwin on Media: Counting Losses," *Westways,* June 1975.

_____. "Corwin Tells His Story as $15 'Recorder' Scribe," *Greenfield* (Mass.) *Recorder-Gazette,* February 1, 1958.

_____. "Don't Write This Man," *Modern Maturity,* April–May 1976.

_____. "I Can Be Had," *Theatre Arts,* June 1948.

_____. "Looking for Art, Bub?" *Theatre Arts,* May 1947.

_____. "One World or None?" *New Zealand Listener,* October 25, 1946.

_____. "One World Revisited," *Common Ground* (reprint by Common Council for American Unity), Winter 1947.

_____. "Radio and Morale," *Saturday Review of Literature,* July 1942.

_____. "Radio Writing, USA," *Writer,* February 1951.

_____. "Samson," *Theatre Arts,* September 1942.

_____. "The Plot to Overthrow Christmas," *Scholastic,* December 13, 1943.

_____. "The Sovereign Word," *Theatre Arts,* February 1940.

_____. "The Unseen Theatre," *Action,* November–December 1969.

_____. "Untitled," *Scholastic,* December 13, 1944.

"Corwin without Props," *Newsweek,* May 28, 1945.

"Cruising with Corwin," *Newsweek,* March 4, 1946.

Detroit Free Press, September 17, 1939.

DeVoto, Bernard, "Easy Chair: 'On a Note of Triumph,'" *Harper's,* July 1945.

"Drummer Boy," *American Magazine,* June 1942.

Glasgow Herald, February 2, 1951.

Gould, Jack. "A Minority Report," *New York Times,* May 20, 1945.

Hamburger, Philip. "Profiles: The Odyssey of the Oblong Blur," *New Yorker,* April 5, 1947.

"Hate?" *Time,* May 18, 1942.

"Hollywood Heckled," *Time,* March 20, 1944.

Hooker, Helene Maxwell. "Radio Growing Up," *Hollywood Quarterly,* Fall 1947.

Hutchens, John K. "That Realm, That England," *New York Times,* August 16, 1942.

_____. "Several Matters," *New York Times,* December 6, 1942.

Isaacs, Edith J. R. "Radio Poet," *Theatre Arts,* May 1942.

"It's a Living," *Time,* January 29, 1951.

Lasch, Robert. "Not So Fantastic," *Chicago Sun,* January 18, 1943.

Lawrence, Jerome. "A New Radio Form," *Hollywood Quarterly,* April 1947.

London Daily Express, September 14, 1948.

London Evening Express, January 30, 1951.

London Sunday Times, November 6, 1949.

Los Angeles Times, July 4, 1976.

Marshall, Allen. "Radio," *Socialist Leader,* November 12, 1949.

Matthews, William. "Radio Plays as Literature," *Hollywood Quarterly,* October 1945.

"More by Corwin," *Time,* May 28, 1945.

Musical Courier, February 1, 1947.

"New Trends in Radio Programming," *Scholastic,* September 24, 1945.

New York Journal-American, December 8, 1938; April 26, 1939.

New York Post, December 3, 1938; May 5, 1941; March 8, 1944.

New York Times, March 1939–August 1949.

New York World-Telegram and Sun, March 28, 1950.

"Pixie Primer," *Time,* May 12, 1941.

"Prizes for Corwin," *Time,* March 4, 1946.

Radio Times, October 21, 1949.

Rodriguez, José. "Our Cover Couch," *Script,* August 25, 1945.

Shipp, Cameron. "Corwin of the Airwaves," *Coronet,* December 1945.

Springfield (Mass.) *Sunday Union and Republican,* February 5, 1939.

"13 by Corwin," *Newsweek,* August 11, 1941.

"This Is War!" *Time,* February 23, 1942.

Van Horne, Harriet. "The Bard of Radio Row," *Saturday Review of Literature,* April 22, 1944.

Weisberg, Maggie. "A Board Member Profile: Norman Corwin," *WGAW News,* April 1974.

Williams, A. N. "Radio Artistry of Norman Corwin," *Saturday Review of Literature,* February 14, 1942.

Woolf, S. J. "Corwin Presents—Britain at War," *New York Times Magazine,* August 2, 1942.

"The World and Norman Corwin," *Time,* January 27, 1947.

"The World and the Theatre: 'On a Note of Triumph,'" *Theatre Arts,* July 1945.

Index

Acheson, George, 184
Adler, Larry, 61
Adler, Luther, 228
Air Raid, 34
Albert, Eddie, 229
Aldrich Family, The, 174–75
All the King's Men, 198–99
Allen, Andrew, 209
Allen, Fred, 6, 60, 135
Allison, Bob, 148
America at War, 95–96, 237
American in England, An, 102–10, 114, 134, 203, 238
American in Russia, An, 113
Americans at Work, 32
Anderson, Maxwell, 6, 52, 95, 96
Anglo-American Angle, An, 108, 109, 238, 239
Ann Rutledge, 57–58, 65, 234, 235
Appointment, 9, 60, 61, 62, 235
Arnold, Edward, 78, 80, **91**
Arthur, Jean, 211
Ashworth, Lou, 149, 174, 175
Astor, Lady Nancy, 106–07
Attlee, Clement, 179
Austin, Sally, 50
Aylen, Peter, 203, 204, 211

Baker, Harry, 130–31
Ball, Lucille, 141
Ballad for Americans, 48–49, 128, 177
Bankhead, Tallulah, 141
Barlow, Howard, 53
Barnouw, Erik, 47, 60
Barrymore, Lionel, 80, 82–83, **91**
Basehart, Richard, 213
Baxter, Frank, 225

Becker, I. S., 201
Benchley, Robert, 49, 170–71
Beneš, Eduard, 118, 182
Benét, Stephen Vincent, 6, 53, 59, 88, 135, 208
Bennett, Joan, 141
Benny, Jack, 200
Benton, Thomas Hart, 149–50
Berger, Sylvia, 113
Berlin, Irving, 142
Bernstein, Leonard, 211–12, 217
Bessie, Alvah, 205
Best, Edna, 78, 85
Between Americans, 65, 78, 235
Bierly, Kenneth M., 216
Bland, Lee, **165**, 178–85
Blankford, Michael, 205
Blitzstein, Marc, 52
Blue Veil, The, 221
Blyer, Archie, 176
Bogart, Humphrey, 142, 196
Bond, Johnny, 153
Bond, Ward, 219, 220
Boone, Richard, 225
Boyer, Charles, 196, 213
Brand, Millen, 205–06
Brennan, Walter, 80, **91**
Bridson, D. Geoffrey, 106, 114–15
Britten, Benjamin, 104, 108
Brown, John Mason, 161
Burns, Bob, 80, 82, **91**
Burroughs, Eric, 133
Bushman, Francis X., 225

Cagney, James, 99, 142
Capra, Frank, 87
Carradine, John, 98

Carey, Harry, 142
Carmer, Carl, 49, 116
Carpenter, Clifford, 71
Cavalcade of America, 58, 234
Cervantes, 228
Charter in the Saucer, A, 223–24, 248
Christians, Mady, 66
Church, T. Wells, 28–31, 32, 60
Churchill, Winston, 145–46, 215
Citizen of the World, 206–07, 247
Clark, Dane, 121, 178
Clark, John L., 24
Cliché Expert, The, 134, 241
Clipper Home, 110, 239
Cobb, Irving S., 87
Cobb, Lee J., 206, 217
Cohen, Philip, 75
Colbert, Claudette, 142
Collingwood, Charles, 105, 107
Collins, Ray, 37
Colman, Ronald, 115, 116, 169, 213
Columbia Presents Corwin, 123–24, 125–
  39, 169–74, 240, 243, 244
Columbia Workshop, 3, 31, 32, 34, 40, 48,
  52, 59, 63, 66, 69, 231, 233, 234
Comden, Betty, 53, 134
Committee for the First Amendment, 195
Concerning Propaganda, 99
Cooper, Wyllis, 3
Copland, Aaron, 211–12, 217
Corwin, Alfred, 14, 17, 18, 20, **89**; joins
  Fox publicity, 24–27; supports Nor-
  man, 36, 46, 64, 70, 86; joins army,
  108; notifies Norman of opera prize,
  191
Corwin, Anthony, 222
Corwin, Beulah, 14
Corwin, Diane, 222
Corwin, Emil, 14, 17, 18, 21, **89**; makes
  Fox appointment, 24; joined by Nor-
  man, 25; supports Norman, 28–29,
  30, 31, 36, 46, 109; consulted about
  Triumph script, 145
Corwin, Freda. *See* Feder, Freda
Corwin, Norman, **91**, **92**, **164**, **168**; birth
  and boyhood, 13–17, **89**; reporter,
  Greenfield Recorder, 17–18; as film crit-
  ic, 18; reporter, *Springfield Republican*,
  19–21, 23; as radio editor, 3, 20; ash

can rolling incident, 20; European
  trip, 21–23; as film publicist, 26–27;
  WQXR, 27–30; joins CBS, 30–31;
  network apprenticeship, 31–32; on
  Lewis and artistic credit, 34; on radio
  and writing, 4, 7–9, 220, 232; on radio production, 7, 8, 80; on music, 9,
  105, 137–38; on sound, 137; on Hollywood and movie-making, 8, 55, 88,
  120, 121–22, 125, 198; on Communist
  investigations, 194, 198, 205, 208,
  212, 217, 219; Coulter dismissal, 71–
  72; career talk with Paley, 199–201;
  contractual concerns, 113–14, 117–
  18, 203–04; on art and propaganda,
  126; compares Gabel and Welles, 171–
  72; One World flight as working trip,
  165, **166**, 177; on the wire recorder,
  180; One World conclusions, 189–90;
  marriage, **167**, 193–94
Corwin, Rose, 14, 63, **89**, 226–27
Corwin, Samuel, 13–14, 63, **89**, 226–27
Corwin, Sarita (also Consuelo de Cordova), 26–27, 64
Cotten, Joseph, 142, 196
Could Be, 114, 209–211, 247
Coulter, Douglas, 30, 32, 49; urges Cor-
  win to adapt *My Client Curley*, 52, 62;
  dismisses Corwin, 71–72, 81, 112;
  names Corwin series, 124; asks Cor-
  win to develop VE show, 138; pro-
  poses star-studded promotion
  program, 174–75
*Counterattack: The Newsletter of Facts on
  Communism*, 216–17
Court Martial of the Tiger of Malaya, The,
  227–28
Crane, Katherine, 29, 103
Crawford, Broderick, 199
Crawford, Joan, 213
Cresta Blanca Carnival, The, 113, 239
Crisp, Donald, 99
Cromer, 109, 134, 239, 241
Cronkite, Walter, 231
Crosby, Bing, 114, 120
Crouse, Russel, 145

Darnell, Linda, 142
Davidson, Jo, 202, 205

Davis, Bette, 149
Daybreak, 7, 64, 169, 235, 244
de Corsia, Ted, 71
De Gasperi, Alcide, 182
de Havilland, Olivia, 174
Della Cioppa, Guy, 113, 190
Descent of the Gods, 66–69, 235, 237
Deutsch, Armand, 226
De Voto, Bernard, 160–61
Dewey, Thomas E., 98, 140
Document A/777, 213–16, 219, 247
Donald, Peter, 66
Dorie Got a Medal, 133, 241
Dorsey, Tommy, 120
Double Concerto, 66, 235
Douglas, Kirk, 224
Drake, Alfred, 149, 169, 178, 217
Drew, Lucy, 16–17
Dryer, Sherman, 95
Durante, Jimmy, 53, 142
Durr, Clifford J., 202, 217

Eisenstein, Sergei, 181–82
El Capitan and the Corporal, 136–37, 242
Eldridge, Florence, 196, 205
Elmer, John, 212
Enemy, The, 98, 237
Esther, 67, 68, 236
Evans, Maurice, 213
Evensmo, Sigurd, 180

Fadiman, Clifton, 6, 8, 53, 87, 98
Fairbanks, Douglas, Jr., 222
Fall of the City, The, 162
Faulkner, George, 47, 95, 97
FDR, 227
Fear Itself, 215, 247
Feder, Freda, 24, 25, 36, 46, 188
Fennelly, Parker, 71
Ferrand, Jacques, 177
Ferrer, José, 213, 217
Fickett, Homer, 58
Fineshriber, William, 150–51, 172, 174,
   198
Fleming, Sir Alexander, 150
Fletcher, Lucille, 52, 102
Foot, R. W., 107
Ford, Glenn, 172, 225
Ford, John, 123

Forecast, 54, 56, 234
Forrest, Helen, 120
14 August, **164**, 173, 177, 244
Fragments of a Lost Cause, 68
Franciosa, Anthony, 228
Francis, Arlene, 70, 71
Franklin, Sidney, 121, 123
Free Company, 58
Friendly, Fred W., 223

Gabel, Martin: in *Plot*, 37, 61; as Sam-
   son, 66, 71; in *Long Name*, 126; nar-
   rator of *Triumph*, 145, 151, 153, 156–
   57, **163**; in rebroadcast, 159, 171–72,
   178, 215, 217, 224–25
Gardner, Ava, 196, 228
Gardner, Reginald, 213
Garfield, John, 97, 142, 197, 217
Garland, Judy, 142, 195
Garson, Greer, 222
Gaynor, Leonard, 24, 26
Geer, Will, 37, 217
Gibson-Parker, W., 203, 209
Gielgud, Val, 106
Gilliam, Lawrence, 106, 108
Gluskin, Lud, **91**, 151, 157, 173
God and Uranium, 173, 244
Goddard, Paulette, 142
Golden Door, The, 228
Goldman, Maurice, 228
Good Heavens, 69, 236
Goodman, Al, 176
Goodman, Benny, 120
Goodman, Jack, 145
Gordon, Ruth, 68, 69, 217
Gould, Jack, 160
Grant, Arnold, 198
Green, Adolph, 53, 134
Guthrie, Woody, 153

Halffter, Cristobal, 228
Harburg, E. Y.: songs for *Word from the
   People*, 149; hosts Corwin, 150; *Unity
   Fair*, 169; cited Communist, 217
Hardwicke, Sir Cedric, 58
Harrell, Mack, 192
Havoc, June, 65
Hayes, Helen, 82, 174, 176, 178
Hayworth, Rita, 142

Heflin, Van, 213–14
Heller, Robert, 100, 147
Hellman, Lillian, 97, 217
Herrmann, Bernard, 46, 52; scores *Samson*, 66–67; music for Truths, 76, 79, 82, 86; President's birthday program, 114; *Moat Farm Murder*, 135; *El Capitan*, 136; scores *Triumph*, 150–51, 157; coordinates music for CBS special, 176; criticizes Rogers's operatic score, 191
Hersholt, Jean, 213
Hitchcock, Alfred, 58
Hitch Hiker, The, 52
Hitler, Adolf, 34, 60, 85, 93, 137, 128, 154, 161
Hodiak, John, 172
Hogan, John, 27
Hollywood Fights Back, 195–97, 247
Home Is Where You Hang Your Helmet, 109, 239
Hope, Bob, 126
Horne, Lena, 213, 217
House Committee on Un-American Activities, 194–95, 196–98
Houseman, John, 224
Hulick, Budd, 70
Hull, Henry, 98
Human Angle, The, 69, 236
Hunt, Marsha, 194, 196
Hurban, Vladimir S., 127
Huston, John, 194, 196
Huston, Walter, 52, 80, 82, **91**

Ingram, Rex, 142
Inside the Movie Kingdom, 227
Institute for Education by Radio, 99
It's in the Works, 97, 237
Ives, Burl, 61, 71, 128, 217

Jackson, Charles, 33
James, Harry, 120
Jameson, House, 43, 44, 45, 139
Jerusalem Printout, 229
Jimmy Smith against the Axis, 99
Job, 65, 67, 68, 236
Johnson, Raymond Edward, 129
Joshua, 228
Julian, Joseph, 99, 105–06, 136–37

Kalman, Benjamin, 20
Kaltenborn, H. V., 169
Kaufman, George S., 145
Kaye, Beatrice, 53, 71
Kaye, Danny, 53, 196, 197
Kaye, Sammy, 114
Kean, Gerald, 209
Keenan, John G., 216
Kelly, Gene, 196, 198
Kelly, Nancy, 225
Kern, Jerome, 87
Kesten, Paul, 112, 160
Keyes, Evelyn, 196
Kiley, Richard, 228
Kirkpatrick, Theodore C., 216
Klauber, Ed, 40
Knox, Alexander, 214
Kobak, Edgar, 160
Koch, Howard, 203, 217
Kollek, Teddy, 229
Kostelanetz, André, 174, 176
Koussevitzky, Serge, 211
Krasna, Norman, 221
Kreymborg, Alfred, 40
Kroeger, Berry, 119

L'Affaire Gumpert, 172, 174, 244
Lafferty, Perry, 61, 69, 71
LaGuardia, Fiorello H., 178, 199, 202, 215
Lampell, Millard, 128, 153, 209
Lancaster, Burt, 225
Lanchester, Elsa: and Charles Laughton, 55–56, 68, 135, 174
Landry, Robert J., 94
Lane, Burton, 169
Lange, Halvard, 180
Latouche, John, 48
Laughton, Charles: working with Corwin, 53–54; Corwin's visit, 55–56; as Job, 68, 86; in *Moat Farm Murder*, 135; in *L'Affaire Gumpert*, 172, 174, 178; in *Document A/777*, 213; *Blue Veil*, 221
Lawrence, Jerome, 129, 138, 185, 209
Lee, Robert E., 129, 138, 209
Lemmon, Jack, 225
Lesueur, Larry, 113
Lewin, Charles, 147, 151, 175
Lewis, Elliott, 83, 170, 172

Lewis, William B.: hires Corwin, 29–30; approves *Words Without Music*, 33–34; as CBS executive 39–40; acclaims *Seems Radio*, 46; starts *Pursuit of Happiness*, 47, 48; suggests Robeson for *Ballad*, 49; receives Corwin's *Pursuit* memo, 50; informed of Corwin's *26* idea, 57, 58–59; criticizes *Radio Primer*, 61, 62; as head of radio, OFF, 71; instigates Bill of Rights show, 74–75, 76–77; relays FDR's approval, 78–79, 80; sends congratulations, 86; inaugurates *This Is War!*, 94; arranges *American in England*, 101, 123

Lie, Trygve, 215, 222

Lighthouse Keepers, The, 32

Lindsay, Howard, 145

Lip Service, 61, 235

Liss, Joe, 75

Living History, 32

Lloyd, Norman, 170

Locke, Katherine: in Corwin plays, 97, 136–37, 148–49, 179, 188, 190; theatrical career and marriage, **167**, 193–94, 199, 202–03, 218; children, 221–22

Log of the R-77, 61, 69, 234

Lomax, Alan, 75

London by Clipper, 105–06, 238

London to Dover, 107, 238

Lonesome Train, The, 127–29, 149

Long Name None Could Spell, The, 118–19, 126–27, 240

Lorring, Joan, 172, 178

Losey, Joseph, 118–19

Lovejoy, Frank, 61, 71

Lust for Life, 224

Lycke, Paul, 180

MacArthur, Douglas, 184, 215

McCarran, Pat, 207–08, 218

McCarthy, Joseph, 217, 218, 222–23

McClinton, Harold L., 94–95, 98

McDonnel, Commander R. P., 104

MacDougall, Ranald, 95, 98, 99

McGill, Earle, 3, 33, 56

Mack, Nila, 31

McKenney, Ruth, 205

MacLeish, Archibald: as author of *Air Raid*, 34; as liaison for Bill of Rights show, 76, 78, 86; as head of OFF, 94; on "hatred," 99–100, 122; as writer of classic *Fall of the City*, 162, 204

McNutt, Paul V., 184

Magic Key of RCA, The, 28

Main, Marjorie, 78, 80, **91**

Maltz, Alfred, 205

Mann, Thomas, 148

Man with a Platform, A, 70, 237

Marble, Harry, 130

March, Fredric, 131, 196–97, 205, 206

Marsh, Daniel L., 206

Marx, Groucho, 142, 169, 170

Mary and the Fairy, 7, 68, 69, 236; stage adaptation, 204, 211, 224

Massey, Raymond, 48, 99, 128, 129, 225

Masters, Edgar Lee, 30, 44

Mayehoff, Eddie, 69, 70, 71

Mearns, David, 75

Menjou, Adolphe, 219

Meredith, Burgess: as narrator of *Pursuit*, 47, 48, 50, 51–52; involved in Communist witch-hunt, 194, 217

Meredith, Lucille, 71

Merservey, Douglas, 76, 86

Michel, Werner, 203

Miller, Glenn, 120

Miner, Worthington, 132

Minnelli, Vincent, 224

Mitchell, Thomas, 97

Mishkin, Leo, 174

Moat Farm Murder, 135, 242

Moment of the Nation's Time, A, 114, 239

Monroe, D. H., 105

Montgomery, Robert, 96

Moorehead, **Agnes**, 225

Morgan, Henry, 66, 69, 71

Moss, Arnold, 71

Moss, Jack, 80

Muni, Paul, 96, 142

Munson, Ona, 178

Murder in Studio One, 69, 236

Murray, Lyn: as composer for *26* programs, 60, 64, 65, 67, 68; attends cast party, 71; scores stateside English series, 110; conducts score for *Long Name*, 119; scores *One World Flight*, 190; scores *Document A/777*, 214

Murrow, Edward R.: commends Corwin for *Plot*, 37–38; as London's influential American, 102; assists Corwin's English series, 104, 105, 107; releases Trout to narrate *Transatlantic Call*, 114, 122; philosophizes about radio, 176; McCarthy exposé, 222–23, 225
Mussolini, Vittorio, 41
My Client Curley, 102, 120, 234
Myerson, Bess, 176

National Association of Broadcasters, 44, 46, 234
Nehru, Pandit, 183
Nelson, Paul, 130
Network at Fifty, 231
New York: A Tapestry for Radio, 134–35, 137, 171, 241, 244
Nimitz, Admiral Chester W., 204, 210–11
Norman Corwin Presents, 227
Nussbaum, Howard, 97

Oboler, Arch: produces *Lights Out*, 3; as NBC's asset, 40; credited on Corwin 26 present, 71; advocates hate, 99; 117, 257 (n. 24)
O'Brien, Joel, 62, 71, 98
Odyssey of Runyon Jones, The, 7, 61–62, 63, 130, 235, 241; musical adaptation, 228
O'Keefe, Winston, 71
Old Salt, 64–65, 235
Olivier, Laurence, 211, 213, 223
On a Note of Triumph, 5, 7, 118, 144–45, 150–62, 172, 173, 176, 214, 243
One World Flight, **165**, **166**, 190, 192, 194, 199, 245–46
Oracle of Philadelphi, The, 52, 234

Paley, William S., 38, 39, 54; in England, 107, 112, 160; One World Award, 178; on programming, 192; meets Corwin on train, 9–10, 199–201
Papanek, Jan, 118, 182
Parker, Dorothy, 205, 206
Parnell, Thomas J., 195
Passport for Adams, 120–21, 122, 134, 240

Peck, Gregory, 194
People, Yes, The: from Carl Sandburg work, 59–60, 61, 128, 235
Peterson, Len, 209
Pidgeon, Walter, 222
Pious, Minerva, 69, 71, 138
Pitch to Reluctant Buyers, A, 138
Plot to Overthrow Christmas, The, 36–37, 41, 58, 94, 133, 170, 233
Poetic License, 28–29, 30; CBS pilot, 34
Pommer, Eric, 54
Porter, Paul, 140
Power, Tyrone, 97
Prayer for the 70s, 229
Price, Vincent, 170, 213
Priestley, J. B., 106
Program to Be Opened in a Hundred Years, A, 113, 114, 239
Prokofiev, Sergei, 181–82
Polk, George, 182
Pope Pius XII, 182
Psalm for a Dark Year, 71, 237
Public service programming, 187–88
Pursuit of Happiness, 47–52, 53, 54, 122, 212–15, 234

Quinn, Anthony, 224, 225

Radio Primer, 60–61, 65, 126, 234
Rains, Claude, 97
Rajchman, Ludwig, 207
Rankin, John, 195, 196, 198
Ration Island, 107, 238
Red Badge of Courage, The, 32
Red Channels: The Report of Communist Influence in Radio and Television, 217, 219
Reid, Mrs. Ogden, 176
Reis, Irving, 31, 122, 251 (n. 16), 252 (n. 20)
Resnik, Regina, 192
Rhymes and Cadences, 20, 28
Rivalry, The, 224–25
Robeson, Paul: *Ballad for Americans*, 48–49, 50; in *Word from the People*, 149; in *Set Your Clock*, 176–77; tribute to Corwin, 178; cited, 205
Robinson, Earl: introduces *Ballad*, 48; collaborates on *People, Yes*, 59–60;

(Robinson, Earl, continued)
  Lonesome Train, 128; *Word from the People,* 149
Robinson, Edward G., 80, 82, **91**, 178, 205, 213
Robinson, Larry, 65, 71
Robson, William N., 3, 31; *Workshop,* 33; produces *Air Raid,* 34; recalls CBS, 39; *This Is War!,* 96; lauded by Corwin, 122; directs Hollywood portion of *Stars in Afternoon,* 174; meets Corwin's global return, 185; directs New York *Hollywood Fights Back,* 195; cited in *Red Channels,* 217; before vigilantes, 220
Rogers, Bernard, 190–92
Roosevelt, Eleanor, 127, 132, 204, 216
Roosevelt, Franklin D.: on Bill of Rights show, 74–76, 78, 81–82, 84–85, 86, 87; invites Willkie, 107; parallels *Lonesome Train,* 128, 129, 149; on election program, 140–42; Crimean conference, 145; death of, 148–49
Roper, Elmer, 150
Rossellini, Roberto, 182
Rossen, Robert, 198–99
Roxas, Manuel, 184
Rubin, Renée, 56, 68
Ryan, Robert, 214

Saint, Eva Marie, 225
Samson, 66–67, 236; *See also Warrior, The*
Sandburg, Carl: commends Corwin, 6; on *People, Yes,* 59, 60; compared to *Truths* idealism, 88; on *Transatlantic Call,* 115–16; participation on *World from the People,* 147–48 149; applauds *Triumph,* 161–62; honored in Los Angeles, 225–26
Sanger, Elliott, 27–28
Savage Encounter, 129, 138, 172, 241, 244
Scandal for Scourie, 221
Schary, Dore, 69, 88, 219
Schirmer, Mabel, 194, 201, 202
Scott, Raymond, 50
See It Now, 222–23
Seeger, Pete, 153, 217
Seems Radio Is Here to Stay, 45–46, 233, 245

Seldes, Gilbert, 7, 32, 132
Selznick, David O., 98, 103
Selznick, Irene, 204
Semmler, Alexander, 69–71, 130
Set Your Clock at U235, 176
Seven Seas, 227
Shaw, Artie, 114, 197, 217
Shaw, George Bernard, 106
Shepherd, Ann, 71
Sherwood, Robert, 88
Shirer, William L., 154, 199–200, 217
Sidney, Sylvia, 170, 196
Sinatra, Frank, 120, 197
Sloane, Allen, 209, 215
Sloane, Everett, 46, 53, 65, 71
Smith, Howard K., 107, 217
Smith, Kate, 119, 174
Sokolsky, George, 219
Soliloquy to Balance the Budget, A, 63, 64, 235
Sondergaard, Gale, 52, 68, 71, 217
Sondergaard, Hester, 217
Sorry, Wrong Number, 52
So This Is Radio, 46–47, 233
Stalin, Joseph, 146, 181, 215
Stanton, Frank, 112, 158, 192, 200, 221
Stars in the Afternoon, 175, 178, 244
Stevens, George, 194, 225
Stewart, James, 77–78, 80–84, 86, **90, 91**, 98
Stewart, Paul, 66
Stokowski, Leopold, 82, 85
Stone, Ezra, 60
Story of Ruth, The, 227
Stuart, Donald Ogden, 205
Sullavan, Margaret, 56, 196
Surrey, Berne, 151
Sweets, William, 216

Taberna, Giuliana, 67, 193
Taggart, Genevieve, 30
Taylor, Davidson: supervises *Pursuit,* 47, 49; suggests budget soliloquy, 63; checks transatlantic sound effects, 104; on Corwin contract, 117; hears of Corwin's Hollywood interest, 121–22; on *Columbia Presents,* 124; approves One World Award, 178
Taylor, Deems, 60, 67, 68, 197

Taylor, Glenhall, 98
Tazewell, Charles, 33
Tel Aviv, 134, 240, 241
There Will Be Time Later, 138–39
They Fly Through the Air, 4, 34, 41–44, 60, 140, 233
They Were Expendable, 121, 123
This Is War!, 5, 94–101, 102, 140, 153, 193, 237
To the Young, 99, 238
To Tim at Twenty, 56, 234
Together Tonight! Jefferson, Hamilton, and Burr, 228
Tracy, Sterling, 79
Tranghese, Carlo, 20
Transatlantic Call: People to People, 114–16
Trout, Robert, 33, 101, 103, 107
Truman, Harry, 174, 180, 215
Trumbo, Dalton, 205
Turner, Lana, 142
Tuthill, Betsy, 31–32
26 by Corwin, 59–71, 97, 125, 129, 169, 171
Two on an Island, 54, 55, 57
Tyler, Keith, 99

Undecided Molecule, The, 170–71, 244
United Nations, The, 97
Unity Fair, 169, 243
Untitled, 7, 131–33, 135, 173, 241, 242

Vallee, Rudy, 80, **91**
Van Doren, Carl, 49, 50, 65, 67, 149
Van Rooten, Luis, 71
Vaughn, Hilda, 213

Wald, Jerry, 221
Walk with Nick, A, 62, 172, 244
Walsh, William H., 19, 23
Walter, Bruno, 150
War of the Worlds, The, 3, 34
Warnow, Mark, 47
Warren, Robert Penn, 198
Warrior, The, 190–92. See also *Samson*
Wavell, Archibald, 183
Waxman, Franz, 228
We Hold These Truths, 5, 73–88, 94, 98, 214, 237; Corwin and Stewart in rehearsal, **90**; cast, **91**

Weill, Kurt, 52
Welles, Orson: produced Martian show, 3, 34; *Citizen Kane*, 59, 60; on Bill of Rights show, 48, 80–81, **91**, 117, 122; *14 August*, **164**; in *New York: A Tapestry*, 171–74, 211; cited in *Red Channels*, 217
White House, The, 96
Whitman, Walt, 135, 144, 208, 242
Wiesner, Jerome, 75
Williams, Emlyn, 213
Willkie, Wendell, 107–08, 116, 177–78, 186, 189–99
Winchell, Walter, 196, 218
Windows on the World, 222, 248
Winters, Shelley, 127
Witt, Peter, 156
Wiseman, Joseph, 228
Wolff, Nat: with Corwin Pearl Harbor Day, 78; witness Bill of Rights show, 85; confers with Dore Schary, 88; on film rights to *My Client Curley*, 102; suggests Colman's ranch, 116; on contract negotiation, 117–18
Wolfe, Thomas, 69, 135, 242
Wolfeiana, 69
Women of Britain, 107, 238
Woollcott, Alexander, 95
Word from the People, 146–50, 151, 243
Words Without Music, 33, 35, 36, 40, 41, 44, 46, 233
World of Carl Sandburg, The, 226
Wyatt, Jane, 196
Wyler, William, 194
Wylie, Max, 3, 4; describes Corwin's style, 7, 59
Wyman, Jane, 142, 221
Wynn, Keenan, 169, 170, 178

Yanks Are Here, The, 107, 238
Yes Speak Out Yes, 228
You Can Dream, Inc., 130, 241
Young, Robert, 121, 178, 196
Your Air Force, 98
Your Army, 97
Your Navy, 96
You're On Your Own, 97
Yours Received and Contents Noted, 99, 238

About the Author

R. LeRoy Bannerman is Professor Emeritus of Telecommunications, Indiana University. He has been recognized nationally and internationally for his work on drama and documentary programming for radio.